W9-BWN-523

450 MORE
STORY
S-T-R-E-T-C-H-E-R-S
FOR THE
PRIMARY GRADES

450 MORE Story S-t-r-e-t-c-h-e-r-s

for the

Primary Grades

Activities to Expand
Children's Favorite Books

Shirley C. Raines

gryphon house
Mt. Rainier, Maryland

ACKNOWLEDGMENTS

CHAPTER 1

From **AMAZING GRACE** by Mary Hoffman, illustrated by Caroline Binch. Copyright © 1991 by Mary Hoffman, text. Copyright © 1991 by Caroline Binch, illustrations. Used by permission of Dial Books for Young Readers, a division of Penguin Books USA Inc.

Cover illustration by Kevin Henkes from **CHRYSANTHEMUM**. Copyright © 1991 by Kevin Henkes. By permission of Greenwillow Books, a division of William Morrow and Company, Inc.

Jacket illustration from **JEREMY'S DECISION** by Ardyth Brott, illustrated by Michael Martchenko. Text copyright © 1990 by Ardyth Brott. Illustrations copyright © 1990 by Michael Martchenko. Reprinted by permission of Kane/Miller Book Publishers.

Cover illustration from **MOLLY'S PILGRIM** by Barbara Cohen, illustrated by Michael Deraney. Illustrations copyright © 1983 by Michael Deraney. By permission of Lothrop, Lee and Shepard Books, a division of William Morrow and Company, Inc.

Jacket illustration from **OH, THE PLACES YOU'LL GO!** by Dr. Seuss. Copyright © 1990 by Theodor Geisel and Audrey Geisel. Reprinted by permission of Random House, Inc.

CHAPTER 2

Jacket illustration from **CLEVERSTICKS**, by Bernard Ashley, illustrated by Derek Brazell. Text copyright © 1991 by Bernard Ashely. Illustrations copyright © 1991 by Derek Brazell. Reprinted by permission of Crown Publishers, a division of Random House, Inc.

Cover illustration from **GALIMOTO** by Karen Lynn Williams, illustrated by Catherine Stock. Illustrations copyright © 1990 by Catherine Stock. By permission of Lothrop, Lee and Shepard Books, a division of William Morrow and Company.

Cover illustration by Judith Caseley from **HARRY AND WILLY AND CARROTHEAD**. Copyright © 1991 by Judith Caseley. By permission of Greenwillow Books, a division of William Morrow and Company.

Jacket illustration by Emily Arnold McCully from **MIRETTE ON THE HIGH WIRE** by Emily Arnold McCully, copyright © 1992 by Emily Arnold McCully. Reprinted by permission of G. P. Putnam's Sons.

Jacket illustration from **RUBY MAE HAS SOMETHING TO SAY** by David Small. Copyright © 1992 by David Small. Reprinted by permission of Crown Publishers, a divison of Random House, Inc.

CHAPTER 3

Jacket illustrations from **ANGEL CHILD, DRAGON CHILD** by Michele Maria Surat, illustrated by Vo-Dinh Mai. Text copyright © 1983 by Carnival Press, Inc. Illustrations copyright © 1983 by Vo-Dinh Mai. Reprinted by permission of Raintree-Steck Vaughn Company.

Jacket illustrations by Patricia Polacco from **CHICKEN SUNDAY** by Patricia Polacco, copyright © 1992 by Patricia Polacco. Reprinted by permission of G. P. Putnam's Sons.

Jacket illustrations from **FROG AND TOAD ARE FRIENDS** by Arnold Lobel. Copyright © 1970 by Arnold Lobel. Reprinted by permission of HarperCollins Publishers.

From **THE LION AND THE LITTLE RED BIRD** by Elisa Kleven. Copyright © 1992 by Elisa Kleven. Used by permission of Dutton Children's Books, a division of Penguin Books USA Inc.

Jacket illustrations from **SAM, BANGS, AND MOONSHINE** by Evaline Ness. Copyright © 1966 by Evaline Ness. Reprinted by permission of Henry Holt and Company, Inc.

CHAPTER 4

Cover illustration by Vera Williams from **A CHAIR FOR MY MOTHER**. Copyright © 1992 by Vera Williams. By permission of Greenwillow Books, a division of William Morrow and Company, Inc.

From the book **MAMA, DO YOU LOVE ME?** by Barbara Joosse and Barbara Lavallee. Copyright 1991. Published by Chronicle Books, San Francisco.

Jacket illustrations from **MY MOTHER'S HOUSE MY FATHER'S HOUSE** by C. B. Christiansen, illustrated by Irene Trivas. Text copyright © 1989 by C. B. Christiansen. Illustrations copyright © 1989 by Irene Trivas. Reprinted by permission of Atheneum, a division of Macmillan Publishing Company.

Jacket illustration from **OUR BROTHER HAS DOWN'S SYNDROME** by Shelley Cairo, photographs by Irene McNeil. Copyright © 1985 by Shelley Cairo. Reprinted by permission of Annick Press Ltd.

Jacket illustration from **THE WEDNESDAY SURPRISE** by Eve Bunting, illustrated by Donald Carrick. Text copyright © 1989 by Eve Bunting. Illustrations copyright © 1989 by Donald Carrick. Reprinted by permission of Clarion Books, a division of Houghton Mifflin Company.

Library of Congress Cataloging-in-Publication Data

Raines, Shirley C.

    450 more story stretchers for the primary grades : activities to expand children's favorite books / Shirley C. Raines.

        p.   cm.

    Continues: Story stretchers for the primary grades.

    Includes bibliographical references and index.

    ISBN 0-87659-167-5

    1. Children's literature—Study and teaching (Primary)—United States. 2. Education, Primary—Activity programs — Handbooks, manuals, etc. 3. Teaching—Aids and devices—Handbooks, manuals, etc. I. Raines, Shirley C. Story stretchers for the primary grades. II. Title. III. Title: Four hundred fifty more story stretchers for the primary grades.

LB1527.R35 1994   94-9450

372.64—dc20   CIP

v

To my son
Brian Scott Smith

—Shirley Raines

CONTENTS

---
16 • Author Study—Eloise Greenfield

---
17 • Author Study—Bill Peet
---

18 • Famous Characters In A Series

PREFACE

Many people helped me over the course of planning, selecting books, writing and revising the manuscript for 450 MORE STORY S-T-R-E-T-C-H-E-R-S FOR THE PRIMARY GRADES. Thank you, friends and colleagues for your encouragement.

To the authors and illustrators who recognize the value of the Story S-t-r-e-t-c-h-e-r-s series, thank you for letting me include your books. We selected your works for this teacher resource book because of their quality as stories and as pictorial art, and because of the respect you demonstrate for the child as a learner.

To my husband, Robert J. Canady, who was instrumental in the writing of the first three books, thanks for believing in me. Bob has now retired from university teaching and from writing to devote his time to his work as an accomplished stained-glass artist. He can also be found flying his small airplane around Florida in pursuit of beautiful sunrises and sunsets.

To Leah Curry-Rood, Vice-President of Gryphon House, and to Kathy Charner, Editor, thanks for tracking down hundreds of books recommended by teachers, librarians, bookstore owners and children. Leah's knowledge of children's books and of the entire field of children's literature continues to astonish me. Kathy, thank you for your sensitive editing and for the belief we share in the importance of good literature in children's lives.

Others at Gryphon House who made 450 MORE STORY S-T-R-E-T-C-H-E-R-S FOR THE PRIMARY GRADES a reality include Sarabeth Goodwin, Mary Rein, Lorin Kilby and Larry Rood. Sarabeth produced and formatted the book to make it user-friendly. Mary located some of the additional references recommended for each unit. Lorin contacted publishers and secured permissions to use their books. And I would be remiss if I failed to thank Larry Rood, President of Gryphon House, who champions the cause of providing teachers

with resource books of the highest quality at a reasonable cost. Larry and Leah also run a company of the highest quality, whose employees are all treated with dignity and valued for their contributions. I am pleased to have my name associated with Gryphon House. Thank you for your assistance.

And the children—every teacher and teacher-educator must thank the children. I have come to count on you for the honesty, the joy and the seriousness with which you tackle the world that we adults share with you. Thank you for the time we have spent together in your classrooms and libraries, searching for books whose titles you could not remember, but whose covers you knew you would recognize. You are the reason that we always include illustrations of the book covers of our selections for the Story S t-r-c-t-c-h-e-r-s series.

I am especially grateful to the teachers and librarians who have shared many valuable insights with me. Thank you for communicating that you value the Story S-t-r-e-t-c-h-e-r-s series as a tool for selecting books as well as a curriculum resource. I celebrate your successes and cherish our lifelong friendships.

INTRODUCTION

Teachers, thank you for welcoming the Story S-t-r-e-t-c-h-e-r series into your classrooms and for asking me to write more books. Our hope is that the Story S-t-r-e-t-c-h-e-r books offer a friendly accompaniment to your own creative teaching.

450 MORE STORY S-T-R-E-T-C-H-E-R-S FOR THE PRIMARY GRADES is the fourth book in the Story S-t-r-e-t-c-h-e-r series. We wrote the first and second books, STORY S-T-R-E-T-C-H-E-R-S and MORE STORY S-T-R-E-T-C-H-E-R-S, for preschool and kindergarten teachers. Bookstore owners soon told us, however, that first and second grade teachers were also purchasing the book.

Because of the teachers' interest in our first two books, we decided to write a Story S-t-r-e-t-c-h-e-r book just for first, second and third grade teachers. We wrote STORY S-T-R-E-T-C-H-E-R-S FOR THE PRIMARY GRADES and were thrilled with the response from teachers. However, soon after the release of that book, teachers began to ask us for more resources for science, the environment, multicultural curriculum and literature studies.

Organization By Social Studies, Science And Literature Units

450 MORE STORY S-T-R-E-T-C-H-E-R-S FOR THE PRIMARY GRADES is the book that these teachers requested, for the first, second and third grades. You will find more children's books that focus on science, environmental issues, ecosystems and endangered species; more books suitable for multicultural and social studies; and more books related to literature studies.

Social Studies Units

Self-Esteem—Chapter 1

Abilities and Talents—Chapter 2

Friends—Chapter 3

Families—Chapter 4

Family Stories from the Past—Chapter 5

Neighborhoods—Chapter 6

Science Units

Endangered Animals—Chapter 7

Oceans—Chapter 8

Ponds, Lakes, Rivers and Swamps—Chapter 9

Rainforests and Trees—Chapter 10

Deserts—Chapter 11

Literature Units

Native American Stories—Chapter 12

Folktales from Around the World—Chapter 13

Fantasy and Fantastic Tales—Chapter 14

Poetry—Chapter 15

Author Study—Eloise Greenfield—Chapter 16

Author Study—Bill Peet—Chapter 17

Famous Characters in a Series—Chapter 18

Multicultural books are found in every unit. We have also included more books that have received such honors as the Caldecott Medal, Coretta Scott King, Redbook, Parent's and Reading Rainbow book awards.

Children's Books And How They Were Selected

With more than 70,000 children's and juvenile books currently in print, one of the best services that we provide teachers is to match good books with the curriculum. Ninety different children's books form the basis for 450 MORE STORY S-T-R-E-T-C-H-E-R-S FOR THE PRIMARY GRADES. From among thousands of children's books, we chose hundreds of potential Story S-t-r-e-t-c-h-e-r selections that would fit the eighteen curriculum topics required by many school districts and included by teachers in their annual instructional plans. To become a Story S-t-r-e-t-c-h-e-r selection, however, each book must have met an additional test: children must like it.

Children are our best critics. Each book was read to classrooms of children for a thumbs up or a thumbs down. Some of the books recommended by teachers did not become final selections because they failed this test. We take our subtitle, "Activities to Expand Children's Favorite Books," very seriously.

About one-third of the books we selected are well-known, award winners and classics. Another third, written by famous authors, are readily available in libraries and bookstores. The remaining selections are recently published—within the last three years—providing teachers with a convenient reference to new books for the curriculum.

The Format Of The Book

450 MORE STORY S-T-R-E-T-C-H-E-R-S FOR THE PRIMARY GRADES contains eighteen unit topics. Each unit features five children's books, ninety different books in all. Each book is introduced by an illustration of the book cover and a synopsis of the storyline. Suggestions for presenting the book during a "read-aloud" time are also offered.

Each book is then "stretched" at least five different ways. The story s-t-r-e-t-c-h-e-r-s are teaching ideas based on the stories and the illustrations in the featured children's books. Each story s-t-r-e-t-c-h-e-r is organized with the components of a good lesson plan in mind: what the children will learn, materials you will need, what to do and something to think about.

Most of the materials needed are readily available in primary classrooms. We sometimes suggest asking parents, grandparents and community volunteers for materials. All these materials, however, are inexpensive and easily found in homes and the community.

The "something to think about" section contains pointers for varying the story s-t-r-e-t-c-h-e-r: to make it more complex for older students or simpler for younger ones, related topics to explore, cautions about materials, or ways to guide children's behavior.

Most story s-t-r-e-t-c-h-e-r-s are designed for small groups or for individual children. None should be required of every child in a class. Rather they should be made available, and children allowed to choose to participate. The "what to do" and "something to think about" sections often suggest an appropriate group size.

Story S-t-r-e-t-c-h-e-r-s And Process Learning

Literacy Processes

The story s-t-r-e-t-c-h-e-r classroom offers a rich literature, language and literacy environment that nourishes children's growth and development as learners. In each of the four Story S-t-r-e-t-c-h-e-r books, we emphasize the reading process by suggesting more effective ways to read with children, to engage children as thinkers and to model the processes of studying a text. The suggested "read-aloud" presentations are designed to link children's prior knowledge and experiences to the book's main ideas and concepts.

Primary grade children enjoy listening to these books read aloud. They can easily read many of the books themselves, but the books were selected to be read aloud by the teacher.

Classroom libraries and writing centers are physical arrangements integrated into the story s-t-r-e-t-c-h-e-r approach. By providing space and arranging books for a classroom library, teachers show children that choice is an important aspect of reading. The classroom library should contain the featured story s-t-r-e-t-c-h-e-r books, additional titles on the unit topic and books that the children simply enjoy reading for pleasure.

The writing process is emphasized in 450 MORE STORY S-T-R-E-T-C-H-E-R-S FOR THE PRIMARY GRADES. Every unit offers writing center suggestions, including character sketches, learning logs, literature-response journals and writing inspired by the featured topic or book. However, writing story s-t-r-e-t-c-h-e-r-s are always suggested activities, not required. Children are often inspired by the content of the literature and by the quality of the author's writing. The proof that we have selected good books is in the excitement of children inspired to write by a wonderful book that was read to them.

Some reviewers describe the Story S-t-r-e-t-c-h-e-r books as "whole language curriculum." Our definition of a whole language curriculum is one that respects children as constructors of knowledge, as readers and writers learning to use literacy processes and as thinkers connecting the concepts in books to their own lives. Whole language means using the whole text: connecting the main ideas of the featured books to the unit topic, encouraging children to read additional books and to respond to literature in numerous ways. A whole language curriculum provides many opportunities for children to become listeners, speakers, readers and writers.

Problem-Solving Processes In Mathematics, Science And Social Science Studies

In a story s-t-r-e-t-c-h-e-r classroom, one observes children engaged in problem solving. Problem solving is the domain of children as thinkers and organizers, whether they are creating a dramatic set or a recycling project for the neighborhood. The teacher provides the opportunities for children to solve problems.

Science, social studies and mathematics are often interrelated. Concern about an endangered animal incorporates both the scientific study of that animal and the social study of the ways people try to save the species. Hands-on science activities that include natural specimens and displays invite questioning and problem solving, linking the story and the basic goals of the curriculum.

Mathematics is a vocabulary or a tool kit for organizing and describing data acquired from scientific investigations. Mathematics processes, like literacy

processes, require much practice. Story s-t-r-e-t-c-h-e-r-s make practice fun and interesting, whether children are counting fascinating objects, graphing solutions to problems, or exploring activities that encourage relational thinking—like predicting, logical guessing and patterning.

Story S-t-r-e-t-c-h-e-r-s And The Expressive Arts

Art, music, movement, drama and sociodramatic play are central to the integration of good children's literature across the curriculum. All four of the Story S-t-r-e-t-c-h-e-r books are brimming with ways for children to respond to literature through the expressive arts.

Award-winning artists have illustrated the children's books selected for the Story S-t-r-e-t-c-h-e-r series, and each storyline synopsis identifies the media used by the illustrator. Art story s-t-r-e-t-c-h-e-r-s are provided for most of the featured books. Like the writing story s-t-r-e-t-c-h-e-r-s, art activities should be the child's to choose, or not. We recommend neither end-products nor patterned approaches, but rather exploration of a medium's possibilities and experimentation that enables each child to create an individual response, uniquely his or hers.

Music and movement and primary children cannot be separated. The music story s-t-r-e-t-c-h-e-r-s use familiar melodies, chants, fingerplays and rhythms. Musical instruments are introduced to the children by visiting child-musicians, teachers and volunteers during concerts staged in the classroom. Children move in response to music, learning to control their bodies and to use them to express feelings. Movement also includes noncompetitive games. The music and movement story s-t-r-e-t-c-h-e-r-s also help to create a sense of community, as children enjoy singing, dancing and moving together for the sheer pleasure it provides.

Cooking, Special Projects And Special Events As Story S-t-r-e-t-c-h-e-r-s

Cooking is a valuable activity for primary children. Cooking involves science, mathematics and culture, and it is simply fun to work and eat together. Numerous special projects and special events are also described, including serious activities such as cleaning up our physical environment, and the not-so-serious fun and folly of costume making. We suggest field trips, visits to local businesses and invitations to storytellers, craftspeople, artists and leaders to visit the classroom. The young child's ever-widening interest in the social and physical world is expanded by food, projects and special events that make the classroom an invigorating learning environment and a place children want to be.

The Story S-t-r-e-t-c-h-e-r Triangle

The triangle illustrates the relationship between good children's books, the curriculum and the story s-t-r-e-t-c-h-e-r-s. The foundation line of the triangle is "selection." We select good books to fit the child.

The left line of the triangle represents the "curriculum." We select books to fit curriculum units that are designed to help children develop the knowledge, concepts, skills, attitudes and beliefs suitable for their stage of development as learners.

The right line of the triangle represents the story s-t-r-e-t-c-h-e-r-s, activities that encourage concept development and create open-ended learning environments in which children are playful meaning-makers. Story s-t-r-e-t-c-h-e-r-s suggest and open up possibilities: they do not provide one right answer or approach.

The apex of the triangle points to the child. Story s-t-r-e-t-c-h-e-r-s are developmentally appropriate because they respect learners as individuals, as members of families and cultures, and as members of a classroom community of learners.

As a postscript, I want to add that fundamental to the Story S-t-r-e-t-c-h-e-r-s series is my belief in teachers as creative, caring, resourceful and sensitive professionals.

Respectfully,

Shirley Raines

SELF-ESTEEM

Chrysanthemum

Molly's Pilgrim

Jeremy's Decision

Amazing Grace

Oh, The Places You'll Go!

SELF-ESTEEM

CHRYSANTHEMUM

By Kevin Henkes

Chrysanthemum was a wonderfully happy child who loved her name, until she started to school. There the children made fun of her name, and she longed for a shorter name of only a few letters. Plagued by insults, Chrysanthemum dreamed that her name was Jane. It was only after meeting the music teacher, Delphinium Twinkle, that Chrysanthemum grew to love her name again. On every page, the line drawings with water color washes by Henkes wonderfully express the personalities of the characters. The details of the illustrations show life at school and home as a celebratory frenzy of activity and emotion. Even though Henkes draws the characters as mouse children, he gives them human qualities.

Read-Aloud Presentation

Ask the children to think of people's names that are also the names of flowers, like "Daisy," "Rose," and "Iris." Show the cover of CHRYSANTHEMUM and talk about the significance of the little girl mouse holding onto the stem of the large golden flower. Discuss with the children some of the problems a child named Chrysanthemum might have. Read the book and discuss whether the problems the children mentioned are those that Chrysanthemum encountered. End the read-aloud session by announcing some of the story s-t-r-e-t-c-h-e-r-s for the day.

STORY STRETCHER

For Art: Decorative Name Plaques

What the children will learn
To create their own interpretations of their names

Materials you will need
Large index cards, markers

What to do
1.   Show the illustrations of Chrysanthemum's name written in icing on a cake, and in her own handwriting, decorated with hearts.

2.   Fold a large index card in half. Instruct the children to write their names expressively on one fold, and then decorate the card with symbols they like, such as butterflies, rainbows, baseballs, etc.

3.   Ask the children to place the personal name plaques they have made at their work stations, as they move from center to center during the day.

Something to think about
Laminate the name cards for extended use. So they can be folded after laminating, cut a straight line through the plastic at the fold.

STORY STRETCHER

For Creative Dramatics: Mrs. Twinkle's Play

What the children will learn
To take the seed of an idea and develop it into a script

Materials you will need
Writing supplies, pencils, paper

What to do
1.   Read CHRYSANTHEMUM again and discuss the play Mrs. Twinkle might have organized.

2.   Let the children who are interested create a script for the play.

3.   After the children have written the script, ask them to draw story boards to help them decide how to stage the play.

4.   After the script writers and the story board artists have finished, encourage other children to help with props and staging.

5.   Choose the actors for the play from among the script writers.

6.   Continue the play by rotating roles. On different days, other children can act in the play.

Something to think about
With younger children, dramatize the book CHRYSANTHEMUM itself. Assign the roles, making sure to include some of the less popular children. Let the children improvise the actions as you read the book aloud.

STORY STRETCHER

For Mathematics: Ordering From Flower And Seed Catalogues

What the children will learn
To read catalogues, select flowers and calculate costs

Materials you will need

Flower and seed catalogues, scrap paper, photocopies of the order blanks, pretend money, calculators

What to do

1. Place the catalogues in the mathematics area along with the calculators and the photocopied order blanks.

2. Begin by looking through the catalogues for flowers named after people.

3. Compare the pictures of chrysanthemums to Kevin Henkes' illustration of a chrysanthemum on the book cover.

4. Ask the children to find flowers they would like to have named after them.

5. Give each child ten dollars of pretend money with which to order seeds.

6. Work with the children as they read and complete the order forms, helping them understand that they must save money for shipping and handling costs.

7. Help them become good consumers by finding ways to make their dollars go further, by placing orders together, for example.

Something to think about

If your budget allows, let the children order packages of seeds. Vary the activity according to the mathematical abilities of the students. With first graders, use the catalogues to count different varieties of flowers. With second graders, add the dollar amounts. With third graders, add the actual costs.

For Special Project: Field Trip To A Florist

What the children will learn

To identify different greenhouse flowers and plants and appreciate the florist's artistry and services

Materials you will need

None

What to do

1. Determine if any parents or grandparents of the children are in the floral business. Contact either these relatives or a local florist and plan a field trip to see real chrysanthemums and other flowers.

2. Visit the florist ahead of time and explain that the inspiration for this story s-t-r-e-t-c-h-e-r field trip was the book CHRYSANTHEMUM. Discuss the age of the children who will be coming, and plan as active and educational a field trip as possible.

3. Arrange for parent volunteers to assist with the field trip.

4. Tour the florist shop and the delivery van to see how flowers are transported.

5. Watch the florist make a beautiful arrangement. Encourage the floral designer to include a chrysanthemum in the arrangement.

Something to think about

This special project story s-t-r-e-t-c-h-e-r is both a science and a social studies activity. Learning about caring for flowers and plants involves science, and learning about running a florist shop is social studies.

For Writing Center: Acrostic Of Names

What the children will learn

To write descriptive words and phrases

Materials you will need

Heavy typing paper or construction paper, markers, crayons

What to do

1. Ask the children to write the letters of their names vertically down the left margin of a sheet of paper.

2. Then ask them to write words or phrases, beginning with those letters, to describe themselves. Use the name Chrysanthemum to explain.

Chrysanthemum stands for:

C is for Coloring my name

H is for Happy

R is for Radiant

Y is for Young

S is for Starting school

T is for Teased

H is for Hungry for special dessert

E is for Envying people with short names

M is for Macaroni and cheese, favorite dinner

U is for Understanding

M is for Me,

CHRYSANTHEMUM!

3. Display the name acrostics on a bulletin board along with the dust jacket of the book CHRYSANTHEMUM.

Something to think about

As an extension of the story s-t-r-e-t-c-h-e-r, ask the children to do acrostics of their favorite book characters or of their last names.

MOLLY'S PILGRIM

By Barbara Cohen

Illustrated by Michael J. Deraney

The third grade girls make fun of Molly and her imperfect English. They tease her about how she looks and dresses. Molly tells her mother that she wants to go home to Russia, but they must stay in America. When Molly's teacher, Miss Stickley, has the children build a pilgrim village, Molly is assigned to make a doll. When Molly explains to her mother what a pilgrim is, Mama decides that she is a pilgrim and makes a clothespin doll dressed in Russian clothes. Molly is embarrassed to take the doll to school. When Miss Stickley hears that Molly's mother thinks of herself as a pilgrim, she calls the doll beautiful and places it in an honored place on her desk. Miss Stickley said that Molly and her mother are modern day pilgrims and that it takes all kinds of pilgrims to make a Thanksgiving. The charcoal drawings by Michael J. Deraney depict the school days of a generation ago, in the clothing, hairstyles, classrooms and schoolyard. The children's expressive faces, especially Molly's, convey the story's deep emotions.

Read-Aloud Presentation

Invite the students to recall how Chrysanthemum felt at school when the children teased her about her name. Show the cover of MOLLY'S PILGRIM and talk about how Molly is also teased at school, but not about her name. Molly is one of the new children at school, and she is learning English. Ask the children to imagine that they have had to travel to another country, that they do not know how to speak the language, but that as soon as they start to learn, they understand that the other students are making fun of them. Discuss how courageous Molly is. Read the story to find out why we describe Molly as courageous.

STORY STRETCHER

For Art: Modern Thanksgiving Dolls

What the children will learn
To make representations of themselves or their families celebrating Thanksgiving

Materials you will need
Wooden head clothespins, large tongue depressors, glue, water, margarine tubs, small glue brushes, newspaper, fabric, scissors, needles and thread, permanent markers

What to do
1.   Look again at the illustrations of Molly's pilgrim doll.

2.   Lead the children in a discussion of how Molly's mother might have constructed the doll.

3.   Ask the children to think of all the family members who will be at their family Thanksgiving table. Let each child decide whether to make a doll of himself or of a family member with whom he will celebrate Thanksgiving.

4.   Demonstrate three techniques for making dolls. Using watered-down glue and torn newspaper, layer wet paper on top of wet paper to form a body. While the newspaper is damp, shape it. Allow the paper to dry overnight or longer if needed. When the doll forms are dry, paint clothes onto them with permanent markers. When the marker has dried, paint another layer of glue on top for protection.

5.   The second technique for doll making is simpler. Let the children cut clothing shapes from fabric. Glue the pieces together or sew them with simple stitches, and fit them onto the clothespins.

6.   The third technique for doll making is the simplest. Let the children make clothing from scraps of construction paper and glue them onto the clothespins.

Something to think about
As an alternative project, make paper dolls by cutting human figures out of catalogs.

STORY STRETCHER

For Classroom Library: Yiddish Words And Phrases From Storytellers

What the children will learn
To enjoy a story from another culture and to pronounce some Yiddish words

Materials you will need
Chalkboard and chalk or chart paper and markers

What to do
1.   Invite a Jewish storyteller to come to class. Talk with the storyteller ahead of time about your class and its cultural diversity. Explain that your

invitation was inspired by the book MOLLY'S PILGRIM.

2. After the storyteller has told a Yiddish story, ask him or her to write the Yiddish phrases used in the story on the chalkboard and teach the children how to pronounce them.

3. Let the children decide what the phrases mean, based on how they are used in the story.

4. On the chalkboard or chart paper, print the Yiddish words and phrases from MOLLY'S PILGRIM. Ask the storyteller to help with their pronunciation.

Something to think about
Invite storytellers from different cultures to come to class and share stories. Stories and storytelling are excellent ways to build connections between cultures.

For Music And Movement: "We're Coming To America" Song

What the children will learn
To interpret the story of immigrating to America through song

Materials you will need
Tape cassette, record, or compact disc of Neil Diamond's song "We're Coming to America" (written to celebrate the restoration of the Statue of Liberty), chart paper and markers or overhead projector and transparency

What to do
1. Read again the passage in MOLLY'S PILGRIM where Molly's mother explains to Molly why they cannot return to Russia.

2. Explain that many people from all over the world want to come to America because we have religious freedom.

3. Play the song "We're Coming to America" by Neil Diamond.

4. Display the lyrics of the song on a chart tablet or overhead transparency.

5. Sing the song together. Practice the song and sing it at different group times throughout the week.

Something to think about
Teach younger children the chorus. Add the recording and copies of the lyrics to the listening station in the library area.

For Social Studies: Geography—Charting Molly's Family's Journey

What the children will learn
To use a world map to find the places where Molly and her family lived

Materials you will need
World map, push pins, string or yarn, construction paper, scissors

What to do
1. While we are not told in which state Winter Hill is located, we do know that Molly and her family lived in New York City for a while.

2. Ask if any of the children have relatives in New York City.

3. Find New York on the world map and place a push pin there.

4. Locate Russia on the map and mark it with a push pin.

5. Tie a string to the push pins so that it extends from Russia to New York City.

6. Locate your town and state on a world map, marking it with a push pin to which a small construction paper flag is attached.

Something to think about
Helping children understand how long it takes to go from one part of the world to another is one step toward understanding distances.

For Writing Center: Our Triumphs Over Adversity

What the children will learn
To relate personal feelings to those in the story

Materials you will need
Diaries or stapled pages with construction paper covers, markers, crayons, stapler

What to do
1. Discuss with the writers in the writing center the emotions Molly felt in the story. She was embarrassed and fearful at the beginning. Later, when taunted by the other girls, she felt angry. In the end, she triumphed, feeling understood and appreciated for her uniqueness. She also found a new friend, Emma.

2. Allow the children to share similar experiences.

3. Talk about how writing helps us understand our feelings, and explain that many people keep diaries or journals to record their feelings.

4. Invite the children to make their own diaries and encourage them to write about situations where they felt they were treated unfairly but, in the end, triumphed.

5. Allow the children to decide whether they want to read what they have written to the class, or that it feels too personal and should be kept private or reserved for a special friend or the teacher.

Something to think about
First graders may prefer drawing pictures to express their triumphs.

JEREMY'S DECISION

By Ardyth Brott

Illustrated by

Michael Martchenko

Jeremy's father is a famous conductor. Jeremy doesn't like going to concerts because everyone always asks, "Are you going to grow up to be a conductor like your father?" Embarrassed, Jeremy replies, "I don't know." On one particular evening, four different people ask Jeremy "the question." Jeremy retreats to his dinosaur book and will not talk to anyone until Gordon, a newspaper reporter interviewing Jeremy's father, reads the title of Jeremy's book and begins talking with him about dinosaurs. It is during this conversation that Jeremy decides he wants to be a paleontologist and dig up dinosaur bones. Years later, we see Jeremy on a dig. While he works, he listens to music on his headphones. Allegra, Jeremy's sister, has become a famous conductor. Michael Martchenko's comic full-color illustrations hilariously render the musical life and its patrons in the city.

Read-Aloud Presentation

Talk with the children about careers you considered before you decided to become a teacher. Ask the children what they want to be when they grow up. Many will not know. Discuss whether grownups—grandparents, uncles and aunts—ask them what they want to be when they grow up. Show the cover of JEREMY'S DECISION and point out who the people are. Be sure to mention that Jeremy's father is a famous orchestra conductor. Tell the children that Jeremy is often embarrassed when he talks with adults, because he is asked at least three times a day if he is going to be a famous conductor like his father. He is very tired of the question, especially since he does not know the answer. Read the story and find out how Jeremy makes his big decision and who becomes a famous conductor.

S T O R Y   S T R E T C H E R

For Art: Concert Posters

What the children will learn
To read posters and create posters for special events

Materials you will need
Concert series poster, scrap paper, pencils, markers, posterboard, poster paints, brushes

What to do
1. Call or visit a local musical organization to request a poster announcing one of their future performances.

2. Examine the design of the poster. Note the important information about time, place, cost, performers.

3. Plan a poster for a musical event at the school or in your classroom. Invite the students to sketch out their design ideas on scrap paper and select colors by using markers.

4. Consider the information on the announcement you obtained, and decide what information must be added to turn their posters into announcements—who, what, when, where and cost.

5. Let the poster artists complete their posters, using poster paints and markers.

6. Display the posters throughout the school, office, cafeteria and hallways.

Something to think about
With older students, design the posters using computer graphics. If no concerts are performed in your area, check with the Chamber of Commerce for free promotional posters.

S T O R Y   S T R E T C H E R

For Music and Movement: Concert

What the children will learn
To know how to act at a concert

Materials you will need
Free tickets to a concert

What to do
1. If possible, take a field trip to a concert. If this is not possible, plan to have your students attend a concert performed by music students at the school.

2. Talk with parent volunteers who will accompany you about your expectations of the children and what you hope they will learn from the experience.

3. Depending on the type of music to be performed, discuss good manners and what behavior is expected.

4. Let each child handle his or her own ticket.

5. After the concert, if possible, visit the conductor or band leader and ask him or her to demonstrate how the baton is used in directing.

6. After the concert, write letters thanking the donors for the tickets.

Something to think about
Promote an appreciation of music from many different cultures by attending performances that feature music familiar to some children and new to others.

ANOTHER STORY STRETCHER

For Music and Movement: Conductors Pass The Baton

What the children will learn
To understand the role of the conductor

Materials you will need
Conductor's baton and classical music record, tape cassette or compact disc

What to do
1. Point out the illustrations in JEREMY'S DECISION that show Jeremy's father and Allegra conducting. Call attention to the batons that each holds.

2. Invite a conductor or music teacher to come to class and demonstrate how to use the baton for emphasis, for pausing, for shifting to different sections of the orchestra, band or chorus.

3. Play a classical music recording and wave the baton in the way that a conductor would.

4. Pass the baton to a child who is enjoying the music and ask her to pretend to lead the orchestra.

5. Encourage other children to pretend to play an instrument. Join in their imaginary orchestra and pretend along with the violinists, the pianists, the kettle drummers, the flutist.

Something to think about
Encourage the girls to be conductors by telling them to pretend that they are Allegra, Jeremy's sister.

STORY STRETCHER

For Social Studies: Musical Careers

What the children will learn
An interest in music can lead into many career paths

Materials you will need
Chalkboard and chalk or chart paper and markers

What to do
1. Have the children brainstorm as many people as they can think of who have something to do with music. Begin with musicians, using the names that indicate the instrument each plays: pianist, flutist, drummer, cellist, french horn player, trombonist, tuba player, percussionist, conductor.

2. Add to the list throughout the week. Include choir director, organist, high school band leader, disc jockey, newspaper reporter (like Gordon, who covers musical events), musical instrument store owner, recording engineer.

3. Survey the parents and other relatives of your students to find out whether any are professionals in music. Ask that person to come to class and, if possible, play a musical instrument and talk about how their career developed.

Something to think about
Ask a teenager who is a musician to come to class and play for your students. Invite the musician to discuss how to learn about music, and how she or he became interested in music and at what age.

STORY STRETCHER

For Writing Center: When I Grow Up

What the children will learn
To consider many different careers and jobs

Materials you will need
Writing paper, writing folders, pens, pencils

What to do
1. Remind the writers who choose this assignment that you considered other careers before you became a teacher.

2. Ask the children to fold a sheet of paper three times. The first will fold it into halves; the second makes four sections; the third creates eight sections.

3. Unfold the paper and ask the children to write at least eight different things they might like to become when they grow up, one on each section.

4. Younger children can draw pictures of themselves doing those jobs on each section. Older students can write what they would like about the jobs (the pros), and what they would not like about the jobs (the cons).

Something to think about
As an alternative to this writing assignment, ask a small group of children to rewrite the story of JEREMY'S DECISION and change the setting to a jazz band, a church choir or a country music group.

SELF-ESTEEM

AMAZING GRACE

By Mary Hoffman

Illustrated by Caroline Binch

Grace loves acting out stories. She dresses up in costumes, dramatizes fairy tales and imagines all the different things she might be when she grows up. One day, Grace's teacher announces that the class will put on a play. Grace volunteers to be Peter Pan, but some of the children say she cannot be Peter Pan, because Grace is a girl and Peter Pan was a boy. They also tell her she cannot be Peter Pan because she is black and Peter Pan was white. Upset, Grace tells her mother and grandmother. They tell her she can be anything she wants to be and encourage her to try out for the part. Grandmother also takes her to see Rosalie Wilkins, an African American ballerina, perform in "Romeo and Juliet." Grace tries and wins the part. She is a terrific Peter Pan and believes again in her abilities. Caroline Binch's illustrations are beautiful, full-color, many full-page. Grace and her family are painted in beautiful, realistic African-American skin tones.

Read-Aloud Presentation

Tell the children about an incident in your life when someone said you could not do something and you proved differently. For example, when you were a child your big brother said you were too little to ride a bicycle but you learned. Talk with the children about how it feels to be told you cannot do something when you know you are capable. Let some children share examples from their lives. Discuss how Grace, the little girl in the story, was told she could not do something and it was not because of ability. Read AMAZING GRACE and let the children talk about Grace's feelings and how she showed them that she was capable. Talk with the children about how skin color is not a reason to think one cannot do something that others do.

STORY STRETCHER

For Art: The Real Me And The Pretend Me

What the children will learn
To portray themselves realistically and imaginatively

Materials you will need
Tractor feed computer paper or drawing paper, stapler, crayons, markers, index cards

What to do
1.   Give each child two sheets of tractor feed computer paper or two sheets of drawing paper stapled together. On one side, ask the children to draw a self-portrait.

2.   Ask them to lift the sheet of paper and draw another picture on the second sheet, this time of themselves pretending to be a famous person they would like to be like, from stories, movies or sports.

3.   To create captions, ask the children to write on an index card a riddle describing the famous person he or she is pretending to be.

4.   Post the drawings and cards on a bulletin board. Bulletin board readers will read the riddles, try to guess who the student is pretending to be, then lift the outside page to see which student it is.

Something to think about
Older children can create a series of "pretend me" pictures.

STORY STRETCHER

For Classroom Library: Reading And Predicting Peter Pan

What the children will learn
To listen while a book is read, and predict the next events

Materials you will need
Copy of PETER PAN, chart tablet, marker, tape recorder, tape.

What to do
1.   Read the classic version of PETER PAN, one chapter at a time. The 1983 Random House version, adapted by Josette Frank, is a good one for primary grade children.

2.   At the end of each chapter, invite the children to predict what they think will happen next.

3.   At the beginning of the next reading session, review their predictions. Read on, contrasting the children's predictions with what actually happens.

4.   Alternate printing the children's predictions on chart paper with tape recording them.

Something to think about
Read about the other characters Grace enjoyed pretending to

ABILITIES AND TALENTS

Mirette on the High Wire
Harry and Willy and Carrothead
Cleversticks
Galimoto
Ruby Mae Has Something to Say

ABILITIES AND
TALENTS

MIRETTE ON THE
HIGH WIRE

By Emily Arnold McCully

Set in Paris, this beautifully illustrated 1993 Caldecott Medal winner tells the fascinating story of a child helping a great performer. Mirette, the daughter of a boardinghouse owner, is intrigued by the man attempting to walk a wire stretched across their backyard. The Great Bellini was a master wire walker until he lost his nerve. Mirette asks him to teach her how to walk the wire. When he refuses, she attempts on her own and often falls. Finally, he agrees to teach her. Creating an atmosphere of great anticipation, the book culminates with Mirette and the Great Bellini performing together, and the child rescuing the great performer. McCully's superb and evocative watercolors show depth of perspective and excellent composition, illustrating a city at the turn of the century alive with spirited human emotions and activity.

Read-Aloud Presentation

Looking at the cover of the book, discuss the meaning of the Caldecott Medal. This gold medal is given each year to the most distinguished illustrator of a picture book published in the United States. Ask the children what they know about the story by looking at the cover. Tell them that the setting is Paris, and let them figure out that the way Mirette is dressed suggests the story takes place at an earlier time. Read MIRETTE ON THE HIGH WIRE without pausing for discussion. The suspense and absorbing drama will hold the children's attention. At the end of the discussion afterwards, ask the children whether they felt nervous, and for whom.

STORY STRETCHER

For Art: Watercolors, Varying Perspectives

What the children will learn
About perspective

Materials you will need
Scrap paper, pencils, heavy construction paper or watercolor paper, watercolors, brushes, masking tape

What to do
1. Look through McCully's illustrations and call attention to the high wire scenes. Point out to the children that the wire appears at different angles. Discuss why the artist might paint the wire from different angles.

2. Let the children experiment with drawing the high wire straight across, slanting upward from left to right, and slanting downward from left to right.

3. Ask the children to draw a high wire on their papers at any angle they wish. Encourage them to experiment with the scratch paper. Explain to them that different perspectives are created by where we are in regard to the wire: for example, whether we stand to one side looking up at it, or directly below it.

4. Invite the children to paint a picture with watercolors and include themselves walking on a high wire, if they choose.

Something to think about
Some young children will not be able to vary their perspectives. Others in second and third grade may be able to understand and depict other views.

ANOTHER STORY
STRETCHER

For Art: Posters Announcing Performances

What the children will learn
To compose and paint an art poster

Materials you will need
Posterboard, poster paints or markers

What to do
1. With the children who want to make posters, look at the poster of Mirette and Bellini on the last page of MIRETTE ON THE HIGH WIRE.

2. Ask the children the purpose of the poster. Call attention to the design, fancy lettering, borders and exciting language such as "stupendous feats."

3. Let the children design posters for a real classroom event, such as a parents' night, or an imaginary event, such as a high wire performance.

Something to think about
Encourage children to work in teams on their posters. One could be the fancy printer and border maker, another the painter of pictures.

STORY STRETCHER

For Classroom Library: Story Retellings

What the children will learn
To retell a story in their own words

Materials you will need
Tape recorder, fork, glass

What to do
1.   Form pairs of children interested in this activity. One child is the speaker, the other, the recorder.

2.   The recorder announces at the beginning of the tape that this is the story of MIRETTE ON THE HIGH WIRE as told by _____.

3.   Suggest that the recorder explain the page-turning signal. For example, "When you hear this sound, (tap the fork on the glass), turn the page."

4.   Place the tape in the classroom library.

Something to think about
If you have a parent who speaks French, consider asking the parent to tape-record a few French phrases, then add them to the tape.

STORY STRETCHER

For Movement: Walking The Tightrope

What the children will learn
To balance

Materials you will need
Low balance beam or masking tape, small umbrella, book

What to do
1.   Let the children pretend to be walking a tightrope. Use low balance beams or place masking tape across the floor.

2.   Add to the challenge by having children walk with a small open umbrella, or with a book balanced on their head.

Something to think about
If you have a gymnastics coach in the school or neighborhood, arrange a demonstration of walking a real balance beam.

STORY STRETCHER

For Writing Center: Challenges And Fears

What the children will learn
To express their fears in writing

Materials you will need
Writing folders or journals, pencils

What to do
1.   With small groups of writers, discuss the high wire walker's fears.

2.   Express a fear that you had as a child, like climbing high in a tree and becoming too afraid to climb down, or going into a tunnel at an amusement park.

3.   Encourage the children to talk about physical challenges they feared that they successfully faced. What helped them face their fear?

4.   Discuss physical challenges they currently face. For example, some may be learning to swim, ride bikes, rollerblade, climb ropes or play a game.

5.   Ask the children to write about a fear they have faced or now face.

6.   Read their journals and write an encouraging response to each child.

Something to think about
After reading the journals, decide whether or not to invite any children to read what they have written to the class. Respect the privacy of these journals. It must be a child's decision whether or not to share a journal.

2
ABILITIES AND TALENTS

HARRY AND WILLY AND CARROTHEAD
By Judith Caseley

HARRY AND WILLY AND CAR-ROTHEAD is the story of three boys whose friendship grows over time. The story opens with Harry, who was born without a left hand. When Harry enters kindergarten, he meets Willy, a boy who teases and calls red-haired Oscar, "Car-rothead," which Oscar doesn't like. Harry and Oscar soon become friends and eventually learn to be Willy's friends, too. The story ends when the three boys are older, but still in elemen-tary school. In the closing scene, Oscar writes the story of their three-way friend-ship. Judith Caseley's story succeeds in helping children confront prejudice and stereotypes about appearance. The full-color watercolor and pencil art illustrations are large enough to share in reading aloud to the class.

Read-Aloud Presentation

Ask the children to guess why one boy is called "Carrothead." Discuss nicknames that they would like to be called and others they would not like. Call attention to Harry's left arm and hand in the cover illustrations. Read HARRY AND WILLY AND CARROTHEAD. Stop during the story to explain briefly that Harry's prosthesis is an artificial hand. After reading the story, let the children tell what they think the "problem" was in the story. (Adapted from a review by Rose Mary Culp.)

S T O R Y S T R E T C H E R
For Art: Handprint Fingerpaintings

What the children will learn
To use their hands as print makers

Materials you will need
Old shirts for painting smocks, flat plastic trays, fingerpaints, liquid soap, fingerpaint paper, sponges, paper toweling

What to do
1. Look at the illustration at the beginning of the book that shows Harry making a fingerpainting by stamping his handprint and his arm print.

2. Cover table surfaces with old newspaper.

3. Pour the fingerpaint into flat plastic trays or large bowls. Add a few drops of liquid soap to make the paint easier to clean off hands and surfaces.

4. Let the children make handprint fingerpaintings by pressing their hands into fingerpaint, then opening their fingers wide and pressing them onto fingerpaint paper.

5. Encourage the children to experiment with the handprints by overlapping them, turning the paper and their hands at different angles, and doing thumb, finger and knuckle prints.

Something to think about
If you have students who are reluctant to get messy, provide old shirts as painting smocks.

S T O R Y S T R E T C H E R
For Classroom Library: Who Is Jim Abbott?

What the children will learn
To associate real people with their exceptional abilities, rather than with their disabilities

Materials you will need
Newspaper clipping or reference material on Jim Abbott

What to do
1. Visit a neighborhood public library or the school library and find an article, book or newspaper clipping about Jim Abbott, a famous one-handed professional baseball player. As a New York Yankee pitcher in 1993, Abbott pitched a no-hitter, a perfect game.

2. Read the material to the children and lead a small group discussion about recognizing people's abilities, rather than focusing on their disabilities. Talk about how Harry and Willy and Carrothead were more alike than different.

3. Post the Jim Abbott article on the bulletin board in the classroom library.

Something to think about
If you have access to baseball cards or a baseball card shop, ask the card owner to show a Jim Abbott baseball card to the class.

For Cooking And Snack Time: Harry's Snack

What the children will learn
To think about simple tasks and how often they require two hands

Materials you will need
Bananas, raisins in a small cardboard box, chocolate chip cookies, milk in cartons, napkins

What to do
1. Show the children the picture of Harry and Willy and Carrothead at snack time. Read the description of Harry's snack: banana, raisins, chocolate chip cookies.

2. Talk with the children about how important it was for Harry to have his prosthesis to enable him to eat his snack.

3. Ask the children to place one hand behind their back and try opening a milk carton with one hand, opening a box of raisins with one hand, peeling a banana with one hand, and eating a chocolate chip cookie with one hand. The cookies will pose no problem, but all the other snack foods require two hands.

4. Read the end of the snack time conversation between the three friends, where Harry is described as "just like a regular kid."

Something to think about
For snack time all during the week, let the children try using only one hand.

For Movement: Playing Catch

What the children will learn
To throw and catch a ball

Materials you will need
Softballs or small rubber balls, cardboard boxes, baseball gloves (optional)

What to do
1. Pair the children.

2. Let them practice throwing and catching. Practice underhand and overhand throws.

3. Stand cardboard boxes along a wall or playground fence. Ask them to practice throwing into the boxes.

4. Show older children how to catch with baseball gloves.

Something to think about
Do not let the children choose with whom they will practice throwing and catching because some children will always be the last chosen. Instead, either count off, or write the names of famous baseball players on cards, two cards for each player, and let the children match up their cards: the two Babe Ruths play together and so forth.

For Writing Center: I Don't Like To Be Teased About...

What the children will learn
To express their feelings in writing

Materials you will need
Writing folders or journals

What to do
1. Let the children decide whether they want to write about the topic, "I don't like to be teased about...," or another topic. Some may prefer writing stories about friendships.

2. Write a reply to each child's journal. If you feel it is needed, talk privately with individual children who need to learn coping skills.

3. Invite a guidance counselor in to help the children think of ways to respond to teasing they do not like.

Something to think about
Be careful of young children's sensitivity about their appearance.

ABILITIES AND TALENTS

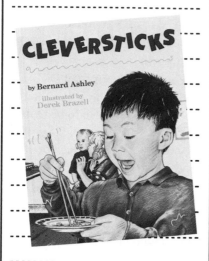

CLEVERSTICKS

By Bernard Ashley

Illustrated by Derek Brazell

Ling Sung wishes he were clever like the other children in his class. He does not tie his shoes well like Terry or paint like Munjit. When he accidently drops some cookies, which break into little pieces, he snaps up two paintbrushes, wooden ends down, and uses them like chopsticks. Everyone is amazed by Ling Sung's "cleversticks." The others try to use the paintbrushes like chopsticks, but have difficulty. Ling Sung shows the other children and even the teachers how to eat with chopsticks. Afterwards, Ling Sung gets the other children to teach him how to do the things that they do well. Brazell's brightly painted illustrations make the multicultural modern classroom and community an appealing and appropriate environment for this story.

Read-Aloud Presentation

Begin by complimenting several children on ordinary things that they do well, like cleaning up the classroom, organizing balls and games for outside play, arranging materials for the computer station. Compliment other children about good personal habits, like putting barrettes in their hair or lacing up high top sneakers. Show the cover of CLEVERSTICKS and introduce the children to Ling Sung, who doesn't feel that he does anything well. Read CLEVERSTICKS. Afterwards, announce that at snack time, they will have Ling Sung cookies.

STORY STRETCHER

For Art: Color-Patterned Names

What the children will learn
To write their names using a color pattern of their choice

Materials you will need
Index cards, crayons, heavy paper or posterboard, tempera paints, watercolor paints, liquid embroidery, acrylic paints, colored pencils, markers, pastel chalk, charcoal

What to do
1. Show the illustration of Manjit holding her painting of her name in large letters, each letter a different color.

2. Print each child's name on an index card and give it to that child.

3. Ask each child to write his or her name below your printing, using a different crayon for each letter.

4. Place all the art paper, paints, markers and chalk on a table in the art center.

5. Ask the children to each fill a sheet of posterboard or heavy paper by writing their names with different paints, markers and chalks.

6. First, they should write or print their names at the top of the sheet using crayons, just like they did on the index cards.

7. Next, they should choose another type of paint, marker or chalk, and write the name again, using a different pattern of colors for the letters.

8. Ask them to continue, varying the art materials and patterns of color they use.

Something to think about
Invite a calligrapher to the class and ask him or her to write each child's name on a separate index card or sheet of heavy paper.

STORY STRETCHER

For Cooking And Snack Time: Cookies And Chopsticks

What the children will learn
To manipulate chopsticks

Materials you will need
Cookies, plates, napkins, milk, chopsticks

What to do
1. Give each child at least two cookies on a plate.

2. Ask the children to break the cookies into large pieces, trying not to crumble them.

3. Show the children how to hold chopsticks and pick up the pieces of cookie.

4. Give the children the chopsticks to take home.

Something to think about
Keep a few sets of chopsticks in the classroom and let the children try using them to eat different snacks.

For Movement: Ling Sung's Somersaults

What the children will learn
To turn somersaults

Materials you will need
Tumbling mats

What to do
1. Show the illustration of Ling Sung at the park turning somersaults.

2. With the help of another teacher, demonstrate a somersault.

3. Repeat, this time in slow motion. Stand on the tumbling mat, bend over, putting hands to floor, bend knees, put head between legs and roll forward, flipping over.

4. Assist the children who are reluctant by gently pushing them over as they roll forward.

Something to think about
If you have students who can do somersaults, ask them to demonstrate as well.

STORY STRETCHER

For Writing Center: Specialty Lists

What the children will learn
To recognize their friends' specialties

Materials you will need
Chart tablet paper, markers, bulletin board

What to do
1. Write all the children's names down the left-hand side of the paper.

2. Invite each child to write beside his or her name a specialty: something they have done well.

3. Post the specialty list on the writing center bulletin board for use in the next writing story s-t-r-e-t-c-h-e-r.

Something to think about
Be sure to think of specialties ahead of time for those children who have low self-esteem and for the perfectionists who do not think they do anything well.

ANOTHER STORY STRETCHER

For Writing Center: What I Do Well/ What I'm Learning To Do

What the children will learn
To ask for help from others who can teach them

Materials you will need
Writing paper, pencils, bulletin board

What to do
1. Ask each child to fold a sheet of paper in half. On one side of the fold, tell them to write whatever they do well. On the other side, tell them to write about something they are trying to learn how to do, and why they think it is important to learn how to do it.

2. Suggest that the children look at the specialty list created during the writing story s-t-r-e-t-c-h-e-r above. Ask them to find someone to help them with what they are trying to learn.

3. Ask each child to write a request for help to another child, noted on the list as having that specialty, and place it in the child's classroom mailbox.

4. Tell the children who receive requests to write a reply to the child seeking help.

5. For some things that the children are trying to learn, there will be no match on the specialty list. Ask the children who do not find a match to post their requests on the bulletin board.

6. Find older children who can teach your students to do whatever it is they are trying to learn.

Something to think about
When we did this activity with first and second graders, we were surprised how many wanted to learn to play games and do magic tricks. Third graders requested help with sports, gymnastics, rollerblading, skateboarding, cheerleading, jump rope tricks and other physically demanding activities.

ABILITIES AND TALENTS

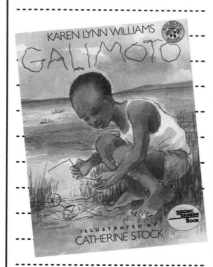

GALIMOTO

By Karen Lynn Williams

Illustrated by Catherine Stock

Selected as a Reading Rainbow Book, GALIMOTO tells the story of Kondi, a boy from Malawi, Africa. Kondi wanders through his village searching for the materials to make a galimoto, a toy constructed of wire. He trades materials with his friends, asks merchants for wires, disturbs the village corn grinder, shows some younger children a trick or two, goes through trash heaps, is accused of being a thief, and finally collects enough wire to build a galimoto. He works with the wires to fashion a pickup truck. The book ends as the children play with their galimotos, and Kondi thinks about reshaping the wires the next day into an ambulance or an airplane or a helicopter. Catherine Stock's watercolored pencil sketches perfectly complement the story of a child's creativity and persistence.

Read-Aloud Presentation

Teach the children to say galimoto. Draw their attention to the cover illustration and point out what Kondi does as he bends some wire. We can see the wheels he has already fashioned. Read the story without pausing, until the scene where the women wait in line for the miller to grind corn. Then ask a child or two to say what they think will happen to Kondi. Pause again when the police come, as the crowd calls "Stop thief!" Ask other children to predict what will happen to Kondi. At the end of the story, announce the story s-t-r-e-t-c-h-e-r-s. Call attention to the wire coat hangers in the art center that can be a source of wire for their own galimotos.

STORY STRETCHER

For Art: Galimotos, Wire Sculptures

What the children will learn
To bend and twist wire to shape toys

Materials you will need
Coat hangers, wire pliers, needle-nosed pliers, rocks, metal pipes, long wooden dowels or yardsticks

What to do
1. Let each child decide whether or not he or she wants to make a galimoto.
2. Have on hand a few untwisted wire coat hangers.
3. Let the children experiment with these, twisting them with pliers and bending them around rocks and metal pipes. Supervise closely.
4. Ask the children to collect pieces of wire from home to add to the collection.

5. Give the children several days to work on their galimotos.
6. Point out to the children the illustrations that show how to make steering wheels by placing a stick on the front axle of the pickup truck, then fixing a wire steering wheel at the end of the stick, enabling the child to stand and drive the truck.

Something to think about
Ask the children who are not interested in the galimotos to construct a toy out of some other material easily found; nothing can be purchased. Some might make cardboard doll houses, for example.

STORY STRETCHER

For Music and Movement: Chants To Come Out To Play

What the children will learn
To compose a chant or song

Materials you will need
Chart tablet paper, marker

What to do
1. Have the children recall or read the page where Kondi hears his friends singing,

*"Let the moon be bright
For us to play and sing tonight."*

2. Let the children think of ways to clap out this rhyme with their hands and sing it with their voices.
3. Compose a jump rope rhyme that includes an invitation to play, such as:

*"My name is An-na
I want to ju-mp rope tonight
Under the streetlight."*

4. Compose a bouncing ball chant, bouncing a basketball on each beat of the chant,

*"Hoops, hoops,
Shot some hoops,
Play some one-on-one
Dribble, dribble, shot,
Bounce, bounce, bounce."*

Something to think about

Children may think of chants for hopscotch, for hide and seek, for playing with favorite toys.

For Social Studies: Where Is Malawi?

What the children will learn

To think of Malawi as the place where Kondi lived

Materials you will need

Map of Africa

What to do

1. On a map of Africa, locate Malawi, a small country near Zambia and Mozambique. Help the children locate their state on the map and see how far away it is from Kondi's country.

2. Talk about things that Kondi does which are like what we do in the United States. For example, do older brothers often tease younger brothers?

3. Discuss what we admire about Kondi. He makes things, is creative, keeps on trying, has friends, knows how to trade, enjoys playing.

Something to think about

It is important to help children see similarities across cultures, as well as differences.

For Special Event: Classroom Toy Display

What the children will learn

To describe how their toys were made and appreciate the creativity of their friends

Materials you will need

Wire sculpture toys made by the students, other toys made of found materials, index cards, tape, tablecloths

What to do

1. Cover several tables with tablecloths or place runners across bookshelves.

2. Let the children arrange and group the toys.

3. On an index card, have the children write their names and describe what their galimoto is, what materials it is made of and where the materials were found.

4. Leave the toys on display for a few days and invite other classes to visit the display. During their visits, read GALIMOTO to them.

Something to think about

As an alternative, have a toy parade with the children's favorite toys, brought from home.

For Writing Center: My Galimoto

What the children will learn

To write a story about their finding the materials for their galimotos

Materials you will need

Writing paper, pencils, colored pens

What to do

1. Ask the children to tell about the difficulties they had finding materials to make their galimotos.

2. Ask them to write about their experience as a story, just like GALIMOTO. The story is written in four stages—how Kondi found his supplies, made his toy, played with his friends and dreamed of making other toys.

3. These four stages can also serve as the outline for the children's stories.

4. Allow the children several days to write and edit their stories, then have a galimoto-sharing day. Read the stories to the class and also to the classes who visit the toy display.

Something to think about

If some of the children work better with writing partners, let one child write what the other says about the adventure of making a galimoto.

2
ABILITIES AND TALENTS

RUBY MAE HAS SOMETHING TO SAY

By David Small

Ruby Mae Foote from tiny Nada, Texas, dreams of delivering a speech at the United Nations in New York. There is only one problem. Ruby Mae is tongue-tied, mixes up words, says what she doesn't mean. People in Nada think she is a goofball. Billy Bob, her young nephew, is an inventor and creates a hat from an old colander and kitchen utensils. This special hat gives Ruby Mae the ability to speak clearly. She is elected mayor, then governor of Texas. But everywhere she goes, she wears a huge hat to hide Billy Bob's invention. On the day of her big speech at the United Nations, she wears a hat covered with doves of peace, but a pigeon hawk flies down from a skyscraper and carries it away. Without her hat, Ruby Mae cannot speak. Billy Bob rushes down to the kitchen and creates a new one. Ruby Mae goes on to deliver her words of wisdom. Small's humor and poignant messages are clearly expressed in words and illustrations.

Read-Aloud Presentation

Ask the children if they remember IMOGENE'S ANTLERS, another of David Small's humorous books. Show the children the photograph of David Small wearing Billy Bob's colander hat. Read RUBY MAE HAS SOMETHING TO SAY. Encourage the children to talk about the importance of the hats and of Billy Bob's belief in his aunt. Discuss whether or not there are times that they feel misunderstood and just can't think how to say something important. Talk with the children about making Ruby Mae's hats as an art project.

STORY STRETCHER

For Art: Decorating Ruby Mae's Hats

What the children will learn
To create outrageous hats for Ruby Mae

Materials you will need
Colander, wire, small kitchen utensils, straw hats, newspaper, construction paper, crepe paper, glue, staplers, ribbons, scarves, scraps, collage materials

What to do
1.   Ask a small group of children to pretend to be Billy Bob and make the first hat for Ruby Mae.

2.   Look through the illustrations for the outrageous hats that Ruby Mae wore as her trademark.

3.   Let small groups of children work on a variety of creations. If needed, ask parents to contribute old straw hats and summer hats.

Something to think about
Plan a hat parade and make election posters for Ruby Mae.

STORY STRETCHER

For Classroom Library: Drama On Tape

What the children will learn
To read the roles of different characters

Materials you will need
Tape recorder, stapler, small kitchen utensils, box

What to do
1.   Select children to read the roles with dialogue in RUBY MAE HAS SOMETHING TO SAY. Also select a narrator and a sound person. You will need the narrator, Ruby Mae, Billy Bob, the woman in the country store, extras laughing in the background, a sound person who rattles kitchen utensils and a recorder who operates the tape recorder and clicks the stapler as the page-turning signal.

2.   Rehearse the lines and practice cuing the audience to laugh.

3.   Tell the recorder to announce the title of the book, its author and the page-turning signal.

4.   Place the recording of the book in the class library.

Something to think about
If necessary, read the narrator's part yourself. Of course, have Ruby Mae wear a hat from the art story s-t-r-e-t-c-h-e-r.

STORY STRETCHER

For Social Studies: A Message To The Leaders Of The World

What the children will learn
To express their feelings about universal peace and understanding

Materials you will need
Writing folders, chart tablet, stationery, envelopes, stamps

What to do

1. Talk with the children about Ruby Mae's message to the world encouraging people to speak plainly and simply.

2. Ask the children what message they would like to send to the world's leaders.

3. Ask the children to compose letters to the President. Help them make their messages plain and simple as Ruby Mae suggests.

4. Let the children print or type their letters to the President on the computer.

5. Mail the letters to The White House, 1600 Pennsylvania Avenue, Washington, DC. 20500

Something to think about
The President's office does reply to children, but it takes several weeks.

STORY STRETCHER

For Special Event And Project: Ruby Mae's Campaign

What the children will learn
To write slogans, make posters and give interviews for Ruby Mae's election

Materials you will need
Posterboards, paints, sign-maker software for computer, Ruby Mae's hats, camera, film

What to do

1. Have the class plan a Ruby Mae campaign. Talk about how politicians ask for votes.

2. Let the children decide Ruby Mae's political platform—what she stands for.

3. Write catchy slogans like "Ruby Mae Has Something to Say," "Vote for Ruby Mae, a Woman for Peace," "Ruby Mae Doesn't Have a Big Head, She Has a Big Hat."

4. Plan some posters and decorate the classroom.

5. Ask several children to pretend to be news reporters and several others to pretend to be Ruby Mae. Schedule interviews.

6. Have Billy Bob act as her campaign manager, scheduling all the events.

Something to think about
After the children have campaigned, ask them to determine whether or not they got Ruby Mae's message across.

STORY STRETCHER

For Writing Center: Ruby Mae's New Adventures

What the children will learn
To use events from one story to shape another

Materials you will need
Writing folders, pencils, colored pens, drawing paper

What to do

1. With a small group of interested writers, brainstorm things that might happen to Ruby Mae when she returns to Nada from her speech at the United Nations.

2. Once several ideas have been presented, ask the children to write another Ruby Mae adventure.

Something to think about
Some of the stories that children have written include, "Ruby Mae for President," "Ruby Mae Visits Russia," "Ruby Mae is Famous on MTV," "Ruby Mae and Billy Bob Strike Oil" and "Ruby Mae Returns to Nada."

References

Ashley, Bernard. (1992). **CLEVERSTICKS**. Illustrated by Derek Brazell. New York: Crown.

Caseley, Judith. (1991). **HARRY AND WILLY AND CARROTHEAD**. New York: Greenwillow.

McCully, Emily Arnold. (1992). **MIRETTE ON THE HIGH WIRE**. New York: G. P. Putnam's Sons.

Small, David. (1992). **RUBY MAE HAS SOMETHING TO SAY**. New York: Crown.

Williams, Karen Lynn. (1990). **GALIMOTO**. Illustrated by Catherine Stock. New York: Mulberry.

Additional References for Abilities and Talents

Booth, Barbara B. (1991). **MANDY**. Illustrated by Jim LaMarche. New York: Lothrop, Lee & Shepard. *The story of a deaf girl's search at night for her grandmother's lost silver pin.*

Brillhart, Julie. (1992). **STORY HOUR-STARRING MEGAN!** Morton Grove, IL: Albert Whitman. *When Megan's mother, the librarian, cannot read to the children at a story hour, beginning reader Megan takes over the job.*

Levine, Ellen. (1989). **I HATE ENGLISH!** Illustrated by Steve Bjokman. New York: Scholastic. *When her family moves to New York from Hong Kong, Mei Mei finds it difficult to adjust to school and to learn the alien sounds of English.*

MacLachlan, Patricia. (1980). **THROUGH GRANDPA'S EYES**. Illustrated by Deborah Kogan Ray. New York: Harper. *A young boy learns from his blind grandfather a different way to see the world.*

Williams, Vera B. (1986). **CHERRIES AND CHERRY PITS**. New York: Morrow (Mulberry). *Bidemmi draws pictures and tells stories in this tribute to a child's creativity.*

FRIENDS

Frog and Toad Are Friends

Angel Child, Dragon Child

Sam, Bangs & Moonshine

Chicken Sunday

The Lion and the Little Red Bird

3
FRIENDS

FROG AND TOAD
ARE FRIENDS
By Arnold Lobel

FROG AND TOAD ARE FRIENDS, a Caldecott Honor Book, contains five stories about these incomparable friends who enjoy each other's company even when faced with life's little inconveniences, such as awakening after hibernating, trying to think of a story to tell, losing a button, wearing a new bathing suit and waiting for a letter. First and second graders have adopted this wonderful pair of friends. Even though Frog must forgive Toad's depression and sometimes his lack of understanding, they endure, friends to the end. Arnold Lobel's famous friends are instantly recognizable.

Read-Aloud Presentation

Before announcing the read-aloud selection for the day, ask the children to talk about things they like to do with their friends. Then show the cover of FROG AND TOAD ARE FRIENDS. Undoubtedly some of your students will have read Frog and Toad stories. Ask them not to tell any of the secrets of the story, and you will have a special story s-t-r-e-t-c-h-e-r for them later in the library. Since there are five Frog and Toad stories, read one per day. Each is very different and should be savored on its own. Discuss with the children what very good friends Frog and Toad are. Look at the cover of the book. Tell the children that sometimes Toad likes to read stories to Frog, but they also love to tell stories. Then read, "The Story."

STORY STRETCHER
For Art: Lost Button Pictures

What the children will learn
To create a picture inspired by a book

Materials you will need
Thick construction paper, posterboard, buttons, glue, markers, crayons

What to do
1. Collect a lot of buttons.
2. Let the children select a button they like and glue it anywhere on their paper.
3. Then ask the children to imagine the place where this button is.
4. Pretend they are walking along and find Toad's lost button.
5. Encourage the children to draw a scene with themselves finding Toad's button.

6. Stimulate many alternatives among the artists. Someone might find Toad's button on a cloud as she parachutes to the ground. Another could discover Toad's button underwater while he snorkels.

Something to think about
Younger children enjoy the act of gluing buttons onto paper. They also like creating patterns with buttons. Consider taking an old jacket and letting each child sew a favorite button onto the jacket. Wear the jacket each time you read a Frog and Toad story.

STORY STRETCHER
For Classroom Library: Frog and Toad Tapes

What the children will learn
To read with expression

Materials you will need
Tape recorder, blank audiotapes, fork, glass

What to do
1. Ask the children who said they had already read Frog and Toad books to join you in the classroom library.
2. Have the children decide which Frog and Toad story they would like to read into the tape recorder.
3. Select four children to work together.
4. One child will read Frog's lines in each story, one will read Toad's lines, one will read the narrator's lines and one child will operate the tape recorder.
5. During the taping, the operator should also be responsible for creating a page-turning signal, such as tapping a glass gently with a fork.

50

6. Encourage the children to rehearse their reading and taping signals.

7. When the tapes are completed, label and store them at the classroom listening station, along with copies of the Frog and Toad books.

8. During the next read-aloud session, announce that the tapes are available and thank the readers for making tapes for the class.

Something to think about
Videotape children reading Frog and Toad stories. Scan the pages of the book while they read.

STORY STRETCHER

For Creative Dramatics: Dramatizing "A Lost Button"

What the children will learn
To extend a script and act out the parts

Materials you will need
Chalk board, chalk, posterboard, markers

What to do
1. Read the story "A Lost Button" again from FROG AND TOAD ARE FRIENDS.

2. Ask the children to recall other characters they have met in the Frog and Toad books. For example, the reader meets a snail, sparrow, raccoon, turtle, field mouse, lizards and dragonflies.

3. Ask the children to imagine that all of these characters have moved into the story of "A Lost Button."

4. Let the children imagine what Frog and Toad might say to each of these characters as they venture through the woods looking for the lost button.

5. Cut pieces of posterboard and print the name of a character on it. Punch holes in the posterboard and insert a length of string. Tie the

string so that the posterboard sign identifying the character can hang around a child's neck.

6. Distribute these name tags and begin the drama.

7. Encourage the children to act and sound like their characters. For example, the sparrow might chirp and say, "Chirp, chirp. Excuse me, did you lose a button?" The snake might say, "Hiss, hiss. Excuse me, did you lose a button?"

Something to think about
With younger students, read the story and let them act out the motions. Limit the characters to Frog, Toad, sparrow, and raccoon.

STORY STRETCHER

For Mathematics: Totaling Toad's Calendar

What the children will learn
To count months and days

Materials you will need
Five or more commercial calendars, pencils or markers

What to do
1. Gather small groups of children in the mathematics center.

2. Read "Spring" from FROG AND TOAD ARE FRIENDS.

3. Distribute the calendars and try to decide during which months Frog talks about the snow melting.

4. Encourage the children to listen for more clues in the story until they hear "April" mentioned.

5. Find out how long Toad has been asleep. (The story says he has been asleep since November.)

6. Ask the children to look at their calendars and count how many months Frog has slept.

7. Write down the number of days in each month and total them.

8. Later in the story, Toad says to wake him at "half past May." Let the children decide when half past May would be. Determine how many more days they should add to Toad's total.

Something to think about
Younger first graders can simply count the days and mark them off their calendars. Second graders can add the numbers of days, noting that different months have different numbers of days. Third graders can state the problems in multiplication terms by thinking how many months have 30 days, 29, 31. Consider making a board game which moves Frog and Toad through each season with different activities.

STORY STRETCHER

For Writing Center: Writing a Letter to Toad

What the children will learn
To communicate with a friend through a letter

Materials you will need
Writing paper, pens, pencils, mailboxes, stamps

What to do
1. Bring a letter from a friend to the classroom and discuss how pleased you were to receive the letter.

2. Read, or let a volunteer read, "The Letter" story from FROG AND TOAD ARE FRIENDS.

3. Ask the children to write letters to Toad.

4. Send these letters to reading and writing partners from other classrooms, who in turn will write back to the children.

Something to think about
Older children may prefer writing a letter to a friend or to a classmate who has moved away.

ANGEL CHILD, DRAGON CHILD

By Michele Maria Surat

Illustrated by Vo-Dinh Mai

Nguyen Hoa, affectionately called "Ut" at home, is a Vietnamese-American child who misses her mother, still in Vietnam. She does not understand the language nor how to act at school. To add to Hoa's problems, she is taunted by a red-haired boy named Raymond. When they get into a fight, the principal tells them to write together. Raymond must write Hoa's story, and Hoa must communicate it to him in English. Once the children learn about each other, they like each other. Raymond comes up with the idea of having a Vietnamese Fair to earn money to bring Hoa's mother to America. The entire school joins in, and the happy reunion takes place in the spring. Raymond is the first child to see Hoa's mother. Vo-Dinh Mai's illustrations are fragile and expressive, in colored pencils with much decorative shading.

Read-Aloud Presentation

Ask the children to talk about a special name or nickname that their families or friends call them. Tell the children that the child in the story has a special at-home name, as well as her formal name. The child in the story is called "Ut" at home. Read ANGEL CHILD, DRAGON CHILD. At the end, let any child speak who would like to reflect on the story's significance. Announce to the children that this story is the inspiration for many different Vietnamese projects and story s-t-r-e-t-c-h-e-r-s.

STORY STRETCHER

For Art: Flying Dragon For The Fair

What the children will learn
To work cooperatively on an art project

Materials you will need
Butcher paper, scissors, marker, tempera paints, brushes, tape, coat hangers, stapler, construction paper, fabric scraps, florescent paint, fishing wire or yarn, crepe paper

What to do
1. Spread a very long length of butcher paper from one end of the room to the other. Taper it at one end like the end of a tail.
2. Sketch a rough outline of a dragon on the paper.
3. Ask the children to fill in the outline by painting the dragon's scales onto the paper with the bright tempera paints.
4. After the tempera paint has dried, go back over the scales on top of the dragon, highlighting them with florescent paint.
5. Tape the body of the dragon along one wall of the classroom.
6. Assemble a head for the dragon by straightening two coat hangers and bending them into large circles.
7. Cover the circles with butcher paper and tape the paper onto the back.
8. Let the children paint the head of the dragon with florescent paints.
9. Make billowing flames of construction paper and tape them as if coming from the dragon's mouth.
10. Hang the head from fishing wire so that it floats at the end of the wall with the dragon's body.
11. Add streamers of colored fabric and crepe paper.

Something to think about
Children can make smaller versions of this dragon to take home as souvenirs of the Vietnamese Fair. (Adapted from Raines & Canady. (1992). STORY S-T-R-E-T-C-H-E-R-S FOR THE PRIMARY GRADES. Mt. Rainier, MD: Gryphon House. 181-82.)

STORY STRETCHER

For Cooking And Snack Time: Friendship Snacks—Rice Cakes And Sesame Seed Cookies

What the children will learn
To enjoy some Vietnamese snack foods

Materials you will need
Rice cakes, sesame seed cookies, cartons of milk

What to do
1. Shop in an Asian market for rice cakes and sesame seed cookies. If you do not have access to an Asian market, ask a Vietnamese-American parent to provide rice cakes or sesame seed cookies.

2. If possible, compare homemade to commercially prepared snacks, and ask the children to express their preferences.

3. Discuss with the children Hoa's sharing her sesame seed cookies with Raymond.

Something to think about
Invite a Vietnamese chef to prepare foods you know the children will enjoy. Serve them on Vietnamese dinnerware.

STORY STRETCHER

For Special Project: A Vietnamese Fair

What the children will learn
To recognize and appreciate various aspects of Vietnamese culture

Materials you will need
Vietnamese traditional clothing, music, food, household items, art, decorative items like Hoa's small box, children's toys and games

What to do
1. Invite Vietnamese-American adults to come to class and help you and the students plan the fair.

2. Ask the children what they want to know about Vietnamese culture and ask the Vietnamese-Americans what they think is important.

3. Organize the Vietnamese fair and invite children from other classes to participate.

4. Plan games so that the children can enjoy activities from another culture.

5. Use the dragon from the art story s-t-r-e-t-c-h-e-r as part of the decorations.

6. Invite the children to serve rice cakes and sesame cookies to the guests at the fair.

7. If possible, play Vietnamese music.

8. Ask Vietnamese-Americans from the community to dress in traditional clothing.

Something to think about
Involve the children in every stage of the planning, decorating, clean-up and evaluation of the event. It is better to have a smaller event in which the children are thoroughly involved, than to plan a big event which consumes a lot of the teacher's time.

STORY STRETCHER

For Writing Center: Our Names In Calligraphy

What the children will learn
To write their names decoratively

Materials you will need
Scrap pieces of paper, heavy typing paper, calligraphy pens, ink, crayons, colored pens

What to do
1. Show the children the illustrations on the title page of ANGEL CHILD, DRAGON CHILD, where Vo-Dinh Mai has decorated the title of the book with calligraphy and colored pencil markings.

2. Let the children practice writing their names with calligraphy pens on scrap pieces of paper.

3. For their final versions, use heavy typing paper.

4. Once the ink has dried, ask the children to decorate their names with colored pens to look like the title page of the book.

Something to think about
Show the children other examples of calligraphy which you may have at home or at school, like your name, a slogan or a poem.

ANOTHER STORY STRETCHER

For Writing Center: Writing To Get Acquainted

What the children will learn
To tell interesting stories about themselves and to help someone else write a composition well

Materials you will need
Writing paper, pencils, writing folders

What to do
1. Work with another class at the same or a higher grade level to form reading and writing partners.

2. As a way to get to know each other, ask your students to tell their partners the story of ANGEL CHILD, DRAGON CHILD and to explain how the two children become friends by writing Hoa's story.

3. Have the writing partners talk with each other and decide on interesting stories that they could write about to each other.

4. Let the children work on the compositions throughout the week and share their progress during a weekly writing partners session. The exercise may take two to three weeks to complete.

5. Encourage older students to work with younger students to refine their drafts to make the stories more interesting.

6. Share several stories each day until all have been shared. Do not schedule too many at once. Try to keep the presentations fresh and interesting.

Something to think about
If this unit is taught at the beginning of the year when many children do not know each other, pair the most popular children with new students.

SAM, BANGS & MOONSHINE

By Evaline Ness

Sam is short for Samantha, who is the daughter of a fisherman. Since Sam's mother died, she spends a lot of time with her cat Bangs, just pretending and making up stories—telling "moonshine," as Sam's father calls it. Sam's friend Thomas believes every word of Sam's moonshine. Each day Thomas comes to Sam's house asking to see her pet baby kangaroo. One day she sends him off to a distant rocky mound along the shore. Bangs, her cat, goes with Thomas. A violent storm comes in with the tide, cutting them off from the shore. Sam's father rescues Thomas but cannot find Bangs. Sam's moonshine almost costs Thomas his life and causes Bangs to be washed out to sea. That night, a water-logged Bangs scratches at Sam's window. Sam's father brings Sam a gerbil, which, to Sam, looks like a pet miniature kangaroo. Sam gives the gerbil to Thomas and promises no more moonshine. Evaline Ness' illustrations are line drawings upon which muted colors are pressed to intensify aspects of the sketches. SAM, BANGS & MOONSHINE was awarded the Caldecott Medal for 1966.

Read-Aloud Presentation

Talk with the children about how much fun it is to pretend. Recall some of the things you liked to play as a child. If you or a child you knew ever had an imaginary friend, describe how the child talked with the friend as though she or he were real. Talk about what a wonderful treasure a good imagination can be. We can entertain ourselves when we are lonely. Ask the children to discuss what they like to play and to pretend to be. Talk about how real what you are playing sometimes seems. Show the first page of SAM, BANGS & MOONSHINE, which shows Sam holding a starfish. Tell the children that Sam is excellent at pretending, but she believes a lot of what she pretends, and talks about it as if it were true. Mention that Sam's father calls this kind of pretending "moonshine." Because her friend Thomas believes anything she tells him, he believes the moonshine, even though it is imaginary. Read SAM, BANGS & MOONSHINE without pausing for discussion.

S T O R Y   S T R E T C H E R

For Art: Pet At The Window

What the children will learn
To associate size with distance

Materials you will need
Construction paper, scissors, crayons, colored pencils, chalks, tempera paint, brushes

What to do
1. Show the children working in the art center the illustration of Bangs returning to Sam's window. Call attention to the way the artist has portrayed Bangs outside the window, with the windowpanes in the foreground. Look at the size of Bangs, how large he appears.

Encourage the children to talk about how near he seems to be.
2. Ask the children to draw their pet, or a pet they would like to have, as if the pet were returning home and signalling its arrival by scratching at the bedroom window. Ask the artists to draw their pets very near the window.
3. Let each child select the color of construction paper he or she prefers for the windowpanes.
4. Show the children how to cut out windowpanes by folding paper and cutting in the right place. Fold the paper in halves, a second time to make fourths, and a third time to make eighths.
5. Cut a rectangle from the folded side of the paper, where no outside edges are exposed.
6. Open and flatten the paper.
7. Glue the windowpane onto the picture of their pet returning home, to create the appearance of a pet outside, looking through the windowpanes.

Something to think about
Give children as many choices as possible with media, materials and subjects. If the children are interested in illustrating another part of the story, or something the story reminds them of, certainly encourage them.

S T O R Y   S T R E T C H E R

For Classroom Library: Listening Station—Voices of Sam, Bangs And Moonshine

What the children will learn
To read in a dramatic voice

Materials you will need
A quiet area in which to tape-record, multiple copies of the book, tape recorder, cassette tapes, listening station with headphones and multiple jacks

What to do

1. Select children to read the roles of the narrator, Sam, Sam's father, Thomas and Bangs.

2. Read the story through, with each child reading his or her character's dialogue.

3. Talk with them about how the characters feel, and rehearse the dialogue a second time.

4. Record the entire story of SAM, BANGS & MOONSHINE.

Something to think about

Invite less proficient readers to play Bangs. Practice with the Bangs reader before the session so that she or he is more confident.

STORY STRETCHER

For Games: Searching For Baby Kangaroo

What the children will learn

To listen and follow directions

Materials you will need

Baby kangaroo picture or toy, classroom items

What to do

1. With the entire class seated in a semicircle, explain the game.

2. Select one child to be Thomas, who will go in search of the baby kangaroo. Ask the child to go outside the classroom or close her eyes. Hide the baby kangaroo.

3. When "Thomas" returns, she begins searching the room for the baby kangaroo.

4. While Thomas searches, the other children say "true" if Thomas is getting close, and "moonshine" if Thomas is moving farther from the baby kangaroo's hiding place.

Something to think about

With older students, hide the baby kangaroo, then ask the children to write clues about the hiding place. The child who is Thomas must follow the clues.

STORY STRETCHER

For Social Studies: Model Harbor Village

What the children will learn

To construct a village alongside a harbor

Materials you will need

Chalkboard, chalk, a sand or water table or a small plastic swimming pool, sand, water, toy boats, materials found around the classroom (toy fencing, interlocking building blocks, wooden popsicle sticks, toy people)

What to do

1. Look through the illustrations in SAM, BANGS & MOONSHINE and list the things that represent a harbor village.

2. Ask the children to think about how they might build a harbor village. What items would they need?

3. Select a small group of builders and let them work together constructing the harbor, the pier, the lighthouse and the blue rock from the story.

4. After they have the foundation, ask other children to add to the construction by bringing in toy boats, toy people for villagers, etc.

5. Leave the construction up for at least a week as an on-going project.

Something to think about

If space allows, have more than one group building harbor villages.

STORY STRETCHER

For Writing Center: Moonshine Story

What the children will learn

To write imaginatively

Materials you will need

Writing paper, pencils, art supplies for illustrations

What to do

1. Talk with the writers about moonshine stories and exaggeration. Ask them to recall Sam's moonshine stories. Talk about how entertaining and creative a good imagination is.

2. Invite them to write moonshine stories about what they would like to do, or something else very imaginative. One way to begin would be to think about the rag rug that Sam describes as a magic chariot which takes her to exciting places. Imagine where you might go if you were on Sam's magic chariot. What adventure would you have?

3. Some children might enjoy writing stories with just a "touch of moonshine." For example, the setting and the characters could be real, except for one magical part, like a magical car, a fish who talks or a celebrity who asks the child to perform on stage.

Something to think about

Some second and third graders tell stories with "just a touch of moonshine." Compare these stories to "fish tales," where the fisherman exaggerates just a bit in order to entertain.

3
FRIENDS

CHICKEN SUNDAY

By Patricia Polacco

*In this multicultural story, a Russian im-
migrant girl tells about her friendship
with two African-American children,
Stewart and Winston, and their grandmother, Miss Eula. The little girl often
eats Sunday dinner, which is usually
fried chicken, at Miss Eula's. The boys
and the girl love Miss Eula and want to
buy her the special Easter hat she has
admired in Mr. Kodinski's hat shop window. The three children contrive a plan
not only to purchase the hat, but also to
win over Mr. Kodinski's confidence and
friendship, by decorating Easter eggs in
the "Pysanky" style as they are done in
Russia. The children sell the eggs and
earn enough money to buy Miss Eula the
Easter hat, but Mr. Kodinski gives the hat
to them instead. Patricia Polacco's de-
lightfully whimsical and expressive color
illustrations are nevertheless so detailed
that they help tell the story.*

Read-Aloud Presentation

Ask the children which meals are
their favorites to share with
friends. Tell them the title of the
book, CHICKEN SUNDAY, and
let them predict what the favorite
meal of these three friends might
be. Show the cover of the book
and introduce the main characters.
Turn to a page showing Mr.
Kodinski and explain that he is
also a main character in the story.
Read CHICKEN SUNDAY, but
pause at the passage where the
friends are wrongly accused of
throwing eggs at Mr. Kodinski's
back door. Let the children think
up possible solutions. Continue
reading and find out what
happens. After reading, ask the
children what made this story
memorable.

STORY STRETCHER

For Art: Decorating "Pysanky" Eggs

What the children will learn
To follow directions and to create
patterns of their own

Materials you will need
Egg-dyeing kit, two boiled eggs
per child, crayons, basket

What to do
1. Look at the illustrations of the
decorated Pysanky eggs in
CHICKEN SUNDAY. Read again
about the process of decorating the
eggs.

2. Read the directions from the
egg-dyeing kit and follow them
closely.

3. Encourage the children to
decorate one of their eggs like the
Pysanky eggs and the other in a
pattern and colors of their own
design.

4. Display the decorated eggs in
a basket for all to admire.

Something to think about
If you have a craftsperson in your
community who decorates eggs,
either by dyeing them or by
painting and gluing on jewel-like
decorations, invite the person to
class to demonstrate how to make
decorative eggs.

ANOTHER STORY
STRETCHER

For Art: Decorating Hats And Caps

What the children will learn
To decorate a hat as a personal
expression

Materials you will need
Old caps, straw hats, men's hats,
women's hats, ribbons, badges,
logos from sports teams and
entertainment figures

What to do
1. Look at the hats that Mr.
Kodinski makes in CHICKEN
SUNDAY.

2. Display any fancy women's or
men's hats you can find.

3. Show the children a plain
straw hat or a cap and let them
think of how to make it fancy by
adding ribbons, buttons, badges,
stickers, pins.

Something to think about
Encourage both boys and girls to
participate. Talk about caps, visors
and hats. Show caps which have
commercial logos on them. Ask
the children to decorate hats so as
to say something personal about
themselves.

For Cooking And Snack Time: Friends' Poppy Seed Cake And Tea

What the children will learn
To brew tea and to slice loaf cake

Materials you will need
Non-caffeinated tea or tea bags, tea strainer, teapot, lemon, cream, sugar, honey, tea cups, plates, cake, knife, napkins

What to do
1.   Either make a poppy seed cake or buy a fruit loaf.

2.   Show the children how to cut slices of cake with a knife.

3.   Brew some tea following the directions on the package.

4.   Let the children try different flavorings for their tea, like sugar, honey, lemon or cream.

5.   Have a tea party. Invite the children to talk with each other about favorite books or what they like about Patricia Polacco's CHICKEN SUNDAY.

Something to think about
Use real cups and saucers to accustom the children to handling them. In our fast-food age, children are often more familiar with styrofoam packaging than with eating from china.

For Social Studies: Conflict Resolution

What the children will learn
To feel conflict and discover possible ways to resolve it

Materials you will need
Chart tablet paper, tape, marker

What to do
1.   During a large group circle time or a small group discussion, talk about conflict resolution. Begin by having the children state the problem in CHICKEN SUNDAY: the children were falsely accused of something they did not do.

2.   Ask the children to recall what Mr. Kodinski did by telling Miss Eula.

3.   Talk about what steps the children could have taken to resolve the problem, and evaluate the merit of each alternative. Tape three sheets of chart tablet paper up on the board. On the first sheet write possible solutions, on the second, the "pros," and on the third, the "cons."

4.   At the end of the discussion, write on the first sheet what the children actually did, and analyze what made it right: they told the truth, they talked it over with someone they trusted (Miss Eula), they devised a plan.

5.   Explain that sometimes conflicts are not so easily settled. Tell the children that they should go find an adult if they see a conflict becoming violent, with pushing and shoving or offensive language.

Something to think about
Young children often have difficulty expressing their feelings. In class, whenever conflicts arise, help the children take a few minutes to relax. Bring the children together and help them explain to each other how they interpreted the other person's actions. Listen attentively to each person.

For Writing Center: Being A Friend Means Understanding

What the children will learn
To express their feelings in writing

Materials you will need
Journals or writing folders, paper, pencils

What to do
1.   Ask the children who are interested in this activity to recall a time when they were misunderstood, and how the conflict was resolved or not resolved.

2.   Ask the children to write about friends who understood and sympathized with their problems.

3.   Read the children's writing, unless a child feels that it is too personal to be read by the teacher.

4.   Let those children who want to share their writings read to the class or to a small group assembled in the writing center.

Something to think about
Often when teachers ask children to write about conflicts, they write about personal problems at home. Plan special conferences with those children who seem to have little support at home, or who seem to need a special friend.

3
FRIENDS

THE LION AND THE LITTLE RED BIRD

By Elisa Kleven

An unlikely friendship forms between a lion and a little red bird who becomes fascinated with the way that the lion's tail changes color. While the two do not share a common language, they become very aware of each other and find a way to communicate. Mysteriously, each day the lion's tail is a different color. If the lion sees a beautiful blue lake one day, when he returns the next, his tail is blue. The mystery is solved when the bird goes into the cave where the lion lives, and discovers that he uses his tail to paint a mural of all he sees each day. The next day his tail remains that color, until he paints another beautiful scene he has happened upon. Elisa Kleven's joyous, sweet, magical, yet mysterious story is illustrated in multi-media of paint, chalk and collage.

Read-Aloud Presentation

Discuss unusual friendships. Recall a special friend you had and how there were times when you were together that you did not need to talk. Mention some friendships among the class members where the children like being near each other, working side-by-side, but not necessarily talking with each other. Show the cover of THE LION AND THE LITTLE RED BIRD and ask the children why these two, the Lion and the Little Red Bird, don't need to talk with each other. Point out Lion's tail and ask them to listen for the mystery of Lion's tail.

STORY STRETCHER
For Art: Mixing Lion's Paints

What the children will learn
To combine primary colors to make secondary and tertiary colors

Materials you will need
Plastic margarine tubs or meat trays, tempera paints (red, blue, yellow, black, white), coffee stirrers or popsicle sticks, brushes, newsprint

What to do
1. Encourage small groups of children to experiment with mixing primary colors to make secondary colors in margarine tub or meat tray palettes.

2. Mix a tiny bit of blue into yellow to make green.

3. Mix blue into red to make purple.

4. Mix red into yellow to make orange.

5. Experiment with creating tertiary colors by mixing primary and secondary together.

6. Experiment with darkening colors by adding a tiny bit of black. Mix in white to lighten colors.

7. Ask the students to compare their colors and shadings of color to those that the lion used to paint the mural in his cave.

Something to think about
Give the paints mixed by these students to the muralists doing the next story s-t-r-e-t-c-h-e-r.

ANOTHER STORY STRETCHER
For Art: A Multi-Media Mural

What the children will learn
To experiment and express themselves in a variety of art media

Materials you will need
Butcher paper, tape, watercolor paints and brushes, tempera paints and brushes, scraps of construction paper, fabric, yarn

What to do
1. Let the children look through the pictures in THE LION AND THE LITTLE RED BIRD and discuss all the kinds of art supplies and materials the artist used.

2. Talk with the children about the beautiful scenes that the lion painted.

3. Ask a small group of children to think about a beautiful scene they would like to paint. It could be a scene inspired by the book, THE LION AND THE LITTLE RED BIRD, or it could be a scene in their community.

4. When the muralists have decided upon their scene, help them organize their materials and art supplies.

5. Cut a sheet of butcher paper a bit longer than the longest table in your classroom. Tape down the edges so that the paper stays in place while the artists work.

6. When the mural is finished, title it and hang it in the classroom or on a bulletin board outside the room.

Something to think about
Younger children may have difficulty working with a large group. Consider sectioning the sheet of butcher paper into three sections and letting a pair of children illustrate each one.

STORY STRETCHER

For Classroom Library: Flannel Board Of THE LION AND THE LITTLE RED BIRD

What the children will learn
To retell the story using flannel board and felt pieces

Materials you will need
Flannel board, paper, pins, scissors, felt, zip-lock plastic bag, masking tape, permanent ink marker

What to do
1. With a small group of children, look through the book and identify the scenes that are essential to telling the story.

2. Considering these key scenes, decide which characters and scenery elements are needed, for example: Lion, Little Red Bird, different colors for Lion's tail, thorn, berries, paint pots, branch.

3. Let the children help you make the various felt shapes by drawing a pattern for the shape onto a sheet of paper, cutting out the pattern, pinning it to the felt and cutting out the felt.

4. After the flannel board pieces are constructed, let the children who helped you make them, use them to tell the story to the other children.

5. Store the flannel board pieces in a zip-lock plastic bag.

6. Make a label for the plastic bag by adding a strip of masking tape near the top of the closure. Write the title of the story on the label with permanent marker.

7. Store the flannel board and story bag in the classroom library for the children to borrow to retell the story on their own.

Something to think about
Using flannel board stories, even with third graders, enables the kinesthetic learners to manipulate a story, making associations between the story in the book and their retellings.

STORY STRETCHER

For Creative Dramatics: Communicating Without Language

What the children will learn
To interpret non-verbal communication

Materials you will need
Mirrors

What to do
1. Demonstrate a number of signals you use in the classroom to communicate without speaking, such as finger to lips to mean "quiet," a hand gesture to mean "come along," palm up and fingers together to mean "stop," moving head from side to side to mean "no" or up and down to mean "yes."

2. Demonstrate full-body communication, such as hands on hips to signal exasperation, jumping up and down with excitement, getting down on knees with hands clasped together to beg, throwing a kiss to mean "I love you."

3. Ask pairs of children to practice these signals in front of

mirrors and to think of other nonverbal communications.

4. At group time, let the pairs of children demonstrate their nonverbal communications and ask others to explain what the performers are "saying."

5. Read again the passages in THE LION AND THE LITTLE RED BIRD where the Little Red Bird takes the thorn from Lion's paw and where the Lion rescues Little Red Bird from the storm and brings him into his cave.

Something to think about
Cut pictures from magazines, newspapers and advertisements showing people with different expressions. Ask the children to say what these people are trying to communicate.

STORY STRETCHER

For Science And Nature: Absorption

What the children will learn
To experiment with various textures of paper and fabric and liquid

Materials you will need
Brown paper towels, white paper towels, paper napkins of various thicknesses, sponges, scraps of fabric of various fibers and thicknesses, scissors, plastic margarine tubs, paints, water, food coloring

What to do
1. At the science center, talk with the children who are interested about absorption. Look at the pictures of Lion's tail in THE LION AND THE LITTLE RED BIRD. Ask the children why lion's tail kept changing colors. Wait for a child to use the word, "absorption," or to say that the tail "absorbed" or "soaked up" the colors from the paints.

2. Point out that different materials absorb liquid in different amounts.

3. Set out a variety of colored liquids and ask the children to describe what they see. The colored water, and tempera paints differ in density or thickness.

4. Cut small squares from each of the papers, sponges and fabrics. Have the children experiment to see how much the different papers and fabrics will absorb of the various liquids.

5. Give the children extra margarine tubs in which to place the wet papers and fabrics.

6. At the end of the experience, ask the children to discuss what they observed about absorption.

Something to think about
Conduct these experiments over a number of days. Keep the groups small enough so that the experiments remain a "hands-on" experience for all the children.

References

Kleven, Elisa. (1992). **THE LION AND THE LITTLE RED BIRD**. New York: Dutton.

Lobel, Arnold. (1970). **FROG AND TOAD ARE FRIENDS**. New York: Harper.

Ness, Evaline. (1966). **SAM, BANGS & MOONSHINE**. New York: Henry Holt.

Polacco, Patricia. (1992). **CHICKEN SUNDAY**. New York: Philomel.

Surat, Michele Maria. (1983). **ANGEL CHILD, DRAGON CHILD**. Illustrated by Vo-Dinh Mai. New York: Scholastic.

Additional References for Friends

Clifton, Lucille. (1992). **THREE WISHES**. Illustrated by Michael Hays. *New York: Doubleday. When a young girl finds a good luck penny and makes three wishes on it, she learns that friendship is her most valued possession.*

Guy, Rosa. (1991). **BILLY THE GREAT**. Illustrated by Caroline Binch. *New York: Delacorte. Billy's parents try to plan his life for him, including his choice of friends, but he has ideas of his own.*

Lobel, Arnold. (1979). **DAYS WITH FROG AND TOAD**. New York: Harper Collins. *Frog and Toad spend their days together, but find sometimes it's nice to be alone.*

Polacco, Patricia. (1992). **MRS. KATZ AND TUSH**. New York: Bantam. *A long-lasting friendship develops between Larnel, a young African-American, and Mrs. Katz, a lonely Jewish widow, when Larnel presents Mrs. Katz with a scrawny kitten without a tail.*

Willner-Pardo, Gina. (1992). **NATALIE SPITZER'S TURTLES**. Illustrated by Molly Delaney. Morton Grove, IL: Albert Whitman. *When Jess thinks she is losing her friend Molly to the new girl in their second grade class, she gets interested in Natalie Spitzer and her pet turtles.*

4

FAMILIES

The Wednesday Surprise
Our Brother Has Down's Syndrome
My Mother's House, My Father's House
Mama, Do you Love Me?
A Chair for My Mother

THE WEDNESDAY SURPRISE

By Eve Bunting

Illustrated by Donald Carrick

Every Wednesday evening Anna's grandmother comes to take care of her while Dad drives a truck, Mother works late, and Sam practices basketball at the Y. Grandmother brings a big cloth bag of books to read. Anna and Grandmother are planning a surprise for Dad's birthday. The reader is left with the suspense of guessing what Anna's and Grandmother's surprise will be. Finally it is Dad's birthday. To entertain the family who have gathered to celebrate, Grandmother reads a book—and that is the surprise. Anna, who is only seven, has taught Grandmother to read. Donald Carrick's watercolor illustrations warmly and affectionately render family life in a modern household. The expressive faces of the characters, who even look like relatives, strengthen this story of family celebration.

Read-Aloud Presentation

Show the children the cover of THE WEDNESDAY SURPRISE. Introduce the children to Grandmother and Anna. Ask the children to describe what is happening in the cover illustration. They will probably say that Grandmother is reading to Anna. During your reading of the story, pause at the place where Anna and Grandmother have read together after supper. Pause again after the scene in which the family decorates Dad's cake, and ask why Grandmother and Anna are so excited. Continue reading the story without interruption. After the story is finished, let the children respond in a natural way. They will probably want to tell what surprised them, or someone may talk about how an older adult in their family learned to read. End with a discussion of how the family members in the story worked together.

STORY STRETCHER

For Classroom Library: Wednesday Is The Day For Family Reading Book Bags

What the children will learn
To select books that they think their family would enjoy

Materials you will need
Classroom library collection, cloth book bags

What to do
1.   To correspond to the title, THE WEDNESDAY SURPRISE, each Wednesday let a different child take home a bag of books to read to the family.

2.   Make two or three cloth book bags available so the child can choose which one to take home.

3.   Encourage the children to take home books that they are able to read as well as others that they would like parents or older brothers and sisters to read to them.

Something to think about
The next day, ask the child to read one of the books to the class.

STORY STRETCHER

For Cooking And Snack Time: Wednesday's Hot Dog Meals

What the children will learn
To take responsibility for simple food preparation and clean-up

Materials you will need
Toaster oven or saucepan, tongs, hot dots, buns, mustard, mayonnaise, ketchup, relish, spatula, plates, napkins, juice, cups, sponge, water for clean-up

What to do
1.   Look at the picture of Grandmother, Anna and Sam preparing their usual Wednesday night supper of hot dogs.

2.   Divide food preparation responsibilities among the small group of snack helpers for the class: select a short order cook, a dresser, a supplier, a cleaner.

3.   Prepare the hot dogs in a toaster oven or boil them in a saucepan with water.

4.   Demonstrate how to use the tongs.

5.   Ask the "dresser" to find out what the children want on their hot dogs.

6.   At snack time serve the hot dogs with juice at snack time.

7.   Tell the cleaner to wash the items used for the food, and to supervise other kitchen helpers.

Something to think about
As an alternative, consider baking a cake for the father's birthday. Celebrate by letting children take turns reading from their favorite books.

For Games: Favorite Family Card Games

What the children will learn
To play card games

Materials you will need
Decks of cards for playing games like UNO, Old Maid, Go Fish

What to do
1. Show the children the illustration in THE WEDNESDAY SURPRISE where Grandma, Anna and Sam play cards after Sam returns from basketball practice.

2. Ask the children what their favorite family card games are.

3. Ask them to bring the cards to school and teach each other how to play the games.

Something to think about
Playing cards motivates children to learn mathematics. Consider turning mathematics problems in the card games into word problems.

For Social Studies: Volunteering To Help

What the children will learn
To contribute time and effort to helping someone else

Materials you will need
Chart tablet, marker

What to do
1. Invite the principal, assistant principal, secretary, receptionist, librarian, cafeteria worker and cleaning staff to come to your classroom, one at a time.

2. Prepare them ahead of time for the discussion. Request that they come to class with a list of volunteer jobs that need to be done around the school, which members of your class could do.

3. Select one-half of your class to volunteer.

4. Declare Wednesday the day to volunteer to help someone else.

5. Continue volunteering for at least a month, so that the children feel the satisfaction of helping.

6. Talk with the children about how Anna volunteered to teach someone else, Grandmother, something Anna knew how to do—read.

7. After at least a month, have the volunteers teach the other half of the class how to do their volunteer assignments.

Something to think about
Ask second and third graders to volunteer to teach first graders to read.

For Special Project: Eighteen-Wheeler Comes To School

What the children will learn
To appreciate the job that truckers do and understand how difficult it is to drive a truck

Materials you will need
Eighteen-wheeler

What to do
1. Survey the parents and find out whether any are truck drivers. If not, ask whether they have relatives who are.

2. Invite a truck driver to bring a rig to school. Prepare the trucker for what will interest the children.

3. Park the truck on the edge of the playground or parking lot.

4. Organize the children into small groups to visit with the trucker, explore the truck and ask questions about how to drive the truck, where the trucker sleeps, routine maintenance, loading and unloading, talking on the CB, etc.

5. Be sure that the trucker talks about how she or he keeps in touch with the family while away from home as Anna's father did.

Something to think about
If possible, allow the children to ride around the parking lot in the truck.

FAMILIES

OUR BROTHER HAS DOWN'S SYNDROME: AN INTRODUCTION FOR CHILDREN

By Shelley Cairo

Photographs by Irene McNeil

Tara and Jasmine tell about their brother, Jai, who has Down's Syndrome. They explain how Jai is like other people's little brothers and sisters. Sometimes he is a pest, getting into their toys and clothes. He likes to do many of the things other children do, like playing monster with his father. Jai is also curious about the world, especially animals. The text is illustrated with family photographs in color.

Read-Aloud Presentation

Ask children with younger brothers or sisters to talk about what the young ones like to do. Ask whether little brothers and sisters are ever pests. Get the children talking about what they like to do with the young ones when they have to take care of them. Show the first two pages of OUR BROTHER HAS DOWN'S SYNDROME and introduce the children to Tara, Jasmine and Jai. Read to the end of the book. Discuss how Jai is different than other children, and how he is like any younger brother or sister. Also talk about how all of us have things we do well, and things that are harder for us to do than they are for others. Emphasize that we are all part of a family, and that, in a family, we accept each other as special people.

STORY STRETCHER

For Art: Talents And Takes A Little Longer Pictures

What the children will learn
To assess what they do well and what takes them a little longer

Materials you will need
Drawing paper, crayons, markers, colored pens, tempera paints, brushes

What to do
1. Read again the section of OUR BROTHER HAS DOWN'S SYNDROME where the two sisters explain that Jai takes longer to learn some things.

2. Talk about how each of us has things we do well and other things which take us a little longer. Use an example from your own life. For example, you may ride a bicycle well, but others in your family swim or play tennis better.

3. Let the children talk for a few minutes about what they do well and what takes them a little longer.

4. Ask the children to fold their drawing paper in half. On one side, they should draw or paint a picture of what they do well, and on the other, something that takes them a little longer.

5. Label one side of the picture, "What I Do Well," and the other, "What I Am Learning."

Something to think about
Start the activity with children in the classroom who do not always see themselves as successful. Comment on something each child does especially well at school. Recognize that students who appear quite capable sometimes do not see themselves that way.

ANOTHER STORY STRETCHER

For Art: Family Photo Gallery

What the children will learn
To select and display photographs in a pleasing manner

Materials you will need
Bulletin board, colorful paper, push pins, construction paper, marker

What to do
1. Ask children to bring to class three or four small photographs of family members.

2. With a small group, arrange the photographs on a bulletin board covered with brightly colored paper.

3. Let the children write captions for their family's pictures.

4. Print a title for the bulletin board, "Everyone in Our Family Is Special."

Something to think about
In some communities, children may not have family photographs. Arrange for instant print cameras or throwaway cameras with which to take pictures of families. Or, if there is a community photography class, arrange for class members to take pictures of families at a parent meeting night.

STORY STRETCHER

For Cooking And Snack Time: Preparing Snacks For Younger Children

What the children will learn
To prepare simple fruit snacks

Materials you will need
Oranges, apples, bananas, cutting board, knives, bowls, napkins

What to do
1. Have a few helpers go to a preschool class and prepare a fruit snack for the children.

2. Peel and section oranges, slice apples into quarters or sixths, cut bananas in half and make vertical slits in the peel.

3. Encourage your students to show the preschoolers how to peel the bananas down from the slit.

Something to think about
Ask the preschool teacher whether to serve the fruits as finger foods, or dice them small enough for a fruit salad.

STORY STRETCHER

For Social Studies: Helping Younger Children

What the children will learn
To assist with a preschooler

Materials you will need
None

What to do
1. Arrange with a preschool or Head Start teacher to visit a classroom and let your students interact with the younger ones.

2. Have a few children visit each day during play time and play whatever the preschoolers want.

3. Let the play partners come back another day and assist with snack or lunch.

Something to think about
Avoid having an entire class visit at once. It is too overwhelming to the preschoolers and to your students.

STORY STRETCHER

For Writing Center: Writing About My Family

What the children will learn
To appreciate their families and how they get along with each other

Materials you will need
Writing paper, pens, writing folders

What to do
1. Discuss with a small group of writers how Tara and Jasmine Cairo tell the story of their family by focusing on Jai.

2. Invite the children to write about their family members: what each likes to do, favorite foods, places they like to visit and special interests or hobbies.

3. Ask the children who want their writing to be public to place their writing folders under the class display of family photographs, so that others may read about their families.

Something to think about
If you know that one of your students has a family member with a disability, ask if the child would like to write about his or her relationship with that family member. Share the writing with the class only if the child wishes to do so.

MY MOTHER'S HOUSE, MY FATHER'S HOUSE

by C. B. Christiansen
illustrated by Irene Trivas

MY MOTHER'S HOUSE, MY FATHER'S HOUSE

By C. B. Christiansen

Illustrated by Irene Trivas

A girl splits her week between two parents. On Monday, Tuesday, Wednesday, and Thursday, she lives with her mother. On Friday, Saturday, and Sunday, she lives with her father. We see her pack and unpack her suitcase. The girl tells her story, describing what her mother likes to do (exercise) and what her father likes to do (visit the library). Her mother takes her to her father's house in the car, and her father takes her to her mother's house on the bus. The girl rides her bike to school. At the end, the girl describes the house she would like to have someday, when she has a family—there will be no suitcases. This warm and affectionate, yet realistic portrayal of family life, is told in detail, accompanied by the bright watercolor illustrations of Irene Trivas.

Read-Aloud Presentation

Talk with the children about families, how they come in all different shapes and sizes. Some children live with their mothers, some with their fathers, some with grandparents and some with foster parents. Some are only children and some have brothers and sisters. Show the cover of MY MOTHER'S HOUSE, MY FATHER'S HOUSE and ask a child sitting near you to describe what it shows: a girl with a teddy bear and a suitcase standing on the road between two houses. Tell the children that the girl has two homes. She lives with her mother and with her father, but in two different houses. If possible, before class speak with a child who lives in two different houses, perhaps going to one for summer vacation. Ask the child to tell the class about any differences between what each parent expects, and what it is like to live in two places.

STORY STRETCHER

For Art: My Future House

What the children will learn
To make a collage

Materials you will need
Construction paper, colored pens, home furnishing magazines, catalogs, scissors, glue, brushes

What to do
1. Let the children cut two identical house shapes from two sheets of construction paper.

2. On the top sheet, suggest they decorate the outside of the house using colored pencils.

3. Ask them to cut pictures of furniture and household items they would like to have from magazines and catalogs.

4. Let them glue these onto the second sheet in an overlapping collage fashion.

5. Staple the first sheet to the second sheet along the left margin to open like a book cover.

6. Open the house cover to see what is inside.

Something to think about
Include examples of many different kinds of houses, condos, apartments.

STORY STRETCHER

For Classroom Library: Visiting The Community Library

What the children will learn
The responsibilities of a library card

Materials you will need
None

What to do
1. Remind the children that in MY MOTHER'S HOUSE, MY FATHER'S HOUSE, one of the main character's favorite things to do on the weekend was to go to the library with her father.

2. Arrange with the librarian for a visit to the public library nearest your school.

3. Encourage parent volunteers to go with the class to the library.

4. Break the class into small groups and tour with a librarian.

5. Reconvene as a class for a special story.

6. Obtain library cards for the children.

7. Check out books in your name and in theirs.

Something to think about
Encourage parents who do not have library cards to go to the library . Ask the librarian to hold a special session with the parents about adult services provided by the library.

For Mathematics: Is There Enough Room?

What the children will learn
How to pack a suitcase

Materials you will need
Suitcase or backpack, toiletries, clothing, toys, books, games, posterboard, marker, note pad, pencils

What to do
1. On a table in the mathematics center, stack a huge amount of toiletries, clothing, toys, books and games.

2. Place a suitcase or backpack nearby.

3. Make a poster directing the children to pack for their weekend stay away from home. Tell them they must take fresh clothes, toiletries and something to play with. Direct them to make a list on the note pad of everything they want to take, then pack the items and see if they will all fit into the suitcase or backpack.

4. Let pairs of children work together.

5. Keep the note pad lists for comparison purposes.

Something to think about
Mathematics includes volume and capacity. Packing for a trip is an excellent hands-on activity that emphasizes both.

For Music and Movement: Exercising To A Videotape

What the children will learn
To follow directions for exercise

Materials you will need
Videotape of exercises which primary-aged children will enjoy

What to do
1. Videotape a television program with easy to follow exercises.

2. Plan warm-up and breathing exercises.

3. Encourage boys and girls to follow the routines.

4. Schedule daily exercise routines that the children seem to enjoy from the video.

Something to think about
Have the class make their own exercise video.

For Social Studies: Family And Community Transportation

What the children will learn
How to ride a city bus

Materials you will need
Directions from city bus service

What to do
1. Talk about how the girl in MY MOTHER'S HOUSE, MY FATHER'S HOUSE rode with her father on a city bus when she returned to her mother's home.

2. Invite a bus driver to class to talk about taking a bus, waiting at the bus stop, learning the bus route, knowing the fare, bus etiquette and safety precautions.

3. Take a bus ride from school to a neighborhood attraction and back again.

4. After the bus ride, observe that many families use buses as their major means of transportation. Explain that riding buses helps to save gasoline and reduce smog and pollution.

Something to think about
If you live in a community which does not have bus service, invite a school bus driver to come to class.

by Barbara M. Joosse   illustrated by Barbara Lavallee

MAMA, DO YOU LOVE ME?

By Barbara Joosse

Illustrated by Barbara Lavallee

An Inuit child asks her mother over and over, "Mama, do you love me?" As if testing her Mama's love, the child asks a series of questions: how much does Mama love her, would she still love her even if she did something bad, such as putting salmon in Mama's parka or lemmings in her mukluks. The story continues with the child's questions and Mama's reassurances. All the while the reader learns about Inuit culture, animals and dress. There is a helpful glossary of Inuit terms at the end of the book. Barbara Lavallee's illustrations are vibrantly colored stylized drawings, with wonderful patterns, masks and expressive movement. MAMA, DO YOU LOVE ME? won the Golden Kite Award given by the Society of Children's Book Writers.

Read-Aloud Presentation

Begin the session by observing that there is one question almost every child asks parents. Sometimes it is spoken aloud, and sometimes it is thought silently. Read the title of MAMA, DO YOU LOVE ME? Look at the cover of the book and ask the children what kind of family this is. Someone will probably say, "Eskimo." Tell the children that many native Arctic people call themselves "Inuit." Read MAMA, DO YOU LOVE ME? and announce the story s-t-r-e-t-c-h-e-r-s related to the book.

STORY STRETCHER

For Art: Ceremonial Family Masks

What the children will learn
To construct a mask with symbols for their family

Materials you will need
Wire coat hangers, pantyhose, yarn, needles, construction paper, stapler, glue, badges, fishing wire

What to do
1. Look at the ceremonial masks found throughout MAMA, DO YOU LOVE ME?

2. Read the back dust jacket, which describes how the Inuit people make ceremonial masks to represent themselves and things they want. For example, they make the shape of a fish to represent the salmon and the shape of a dog to represent the dogs that pull their sleds.

3. Look at the dust jacket illustrations of the ceremonial family masks which the author, Barbara Joosse, and the illustrator, Barbara Lavallee, designed for themselves. Let the children interpret what the masks might represent. For example, there are three people on Barbara Joosse's masks: perhaps they represent her family. The pad of paper and pencils signify that she is an author.

4. Straighten the wire coat hangers and reshape them into circles.

5. Stretch the pantyhose over the wire circles, cut off the excess and tie the hose in a knot in the back.

6. Ask the children to design their masks by adding symbols to represent their families.

7. Use fishing wire to hang the ceremonial masks in the classroom.

Something to think about
You can also make masks using clean cardboard pizza rounds. If possible, arrange for an art display of Inuit carvings.

STORY STRETCHER

For Cooking And Snack Time: Favorite Family Foods

What the children will learn
To taste a favorite family food from the Inuit

Materials you will need
Chalkboard, chalk, salmon, grill, oven, tray, knife, forks, napkins, lemon, crackers

What to do
1. Discuss with the children how we develop our food preferences from what our families enjoy. Have the children list favorite foods of their families.

2. Read in the glossary of MAMA, DO YOU LOVE ME? about salmon, a favorite food of the Inuit.

3. Grill a piece of salmon for the children to taste for their snack. Serve with crackers and slices of lemon.

4. Discuss with the children the popularity of salmon with many families.

Something to think about
If one of the parents is a chef, invite him or her to come to school to talk about the variety of ways to prepare salmon. Let a small group of junior chefs help with the food preparation.

For Science And Nature: Animals In Our Families' Lives

What the children will learn
Which animals are necessary for Inuit survival, pleasure and appreciation

Materials you will need
Chart paper, marker

What to do
1. Read or browse through MAMA, DO YOU LOVE ME? and list all the animals mentioned.

2. Classify the animals by whether or not they are needed for survival, for pleasure or simply appreciated because they belong to the natural environment where the Inuit live.

3. List animals that are part of the lives of the families of your students. Talk about whether these animals are needed for survival, for pleasure or simply appreciated as a part of the natural environment.

Something to think about
Talk about the difference between animals that are pets and animals that are needed for survival: contrast the dog that is a family pet and the dog that pulls a sled, for example.

For Social Studies: Finding Out More About Inuit Culture

What the children will learn
To use a reference book

Materials you will need
Note cards, pencils, Post-it notes

What to do
1. With a small group of children in the library center or book corner of the classroom, read MAMA, DO YOU LOVE ME? again, and suggest the children listen for any new words they do not understand.

2. Look at the glossary of Inuit terms at the end of the book.

3. Ask the children to become Inuit researchers who are going to find out more about the Inuit culture and teach their new findings to the rest of the class.

4. Ask the children to decide which term, phrase or animal they want to find out more about.

5. Help the children use encyclopedias and other reference materials.

6. Tell the children to write down a few key words to help them remember what they learn.

7. Place Post-it notes on the edges of the pages where they find their information, so that they can locate it again easily when they want to show the class their source.

Something to think about
Involve the school librarian in helping the children use reference materials. If older students are available, ask them to assist as well.

For Writing Center: Writing Questions To Answers

What the children will learn
To answer questions derived from new information in MAMA, DO YOU LOVE ME?

Materials you will need
Photocopies of the glossary pages of MAMA, DO YOU LOVE ME?, index cards, pencils, colored pens, scissors, glue

What to do
1. Read MAMA, DO YOU LOVE ME? again and have the children recall all the words and phrases they do not understand.

2. Show them the glossary at the back of the book that describes the animals and explains more about Inuit culture and some of the terms.

3. Distribute photocopies of the glossary pages of MAMA, DO YOU LOVE ME?

4. Divide the photocopied pages into sections so that each child has at least one paragraph.

5. Ask each child to read the paragraph and think of a good question that this paragraph answers. Each child then writes the question on one side of the index card and decorates it with colored pencils.

6. Cut the paragraph out that goes with each question and glue it to the opposite side of the card.

7. Display MAMA, DO YOU LOVE ME? and the question and answer cards in the writing center.

Something to think about
Write to a tourism office for the state of Alaska or British Columbia and request information about the Inuit who live there.

A CHAIR FOR MY MOTHER

By Vera B. Williams

A young girl tells the story of buying a new chair for her hard-working mother, a waitress at the Blue Tile Diner. Buying the chair is a big event, because she and her mother, grandmother, uncle and aunt have all been saving their money for the purchase. The chair is the first item of furniture to be bought after a fire destroyed their apartment. Kind relatives and neighbors provided all the other furnishings. The child earns money by helping her mother at the diner. The colorful illustrations by Vera B. Williams capture the lively spirit and warmth of a family and a community. A CHAIR FOR MY MOTHER was a Caldecott Honor Book for 1982.

Read-Aloud Presentation

Show the inside dust cover of A CHAIR FOR MY MOTHER, which features an illustration of the girl, her mother and grandmother. Point out that this is a picture of a family. Ask the children to recall a special item they saved up their money to purchase. List these items on the chalk board. Show the cover of the book and let the children guess what the girl is saving her money to buy. Read the book and pause after the scenes when the apartment burns, and ask the children what they think the family will do. Turn the page, but before beginning to read, let the children seated near you tell the group what is happening in that illustration, which shows everyone in the neighborhood bringing something to the family. After reading the book, ask a few children who want to respond to the book to tell how they felt, what they liked about the book or something memorable from their own family life.

STORY STRETCHER

For Art: Border Prints

What the children will learn
To adapt a style of painting to their own creative work

Materials you will need
Construction paper, scissors, glue, crayons, markers, watercolors, brushes, margarine tubs, water

What to do
1. Call attention to the illustrations in A CHAIR FOR MY MOTHER, noting their unique style. Vera B. Williams paints brightly colored borders on all her illustrations, and every page is completely covered in color, even the background.

2. Show the children the different border prints and how they relate to the illustrations. For example, the kitchen illustration is bordered with teapots and cups and saucers.

3. Ask the children to draw or paint a memorable event from the life of their family, perhaps a special purchase or a pet's arrival or a dear relative coming for a visit.

4. Demonstrate how to cut the paper to make border prints for their paintings or drawings. After the brief demonstration, let the children work on their own.

5. Trim borders of about one/half inch off several sheets of construction paper.

6. Place another, contrasting color of construction paper beneath a trimmed sheet.

7. Glue the top sheet into place, leaving a one/half inch border exposed.

8. Display the bordered prints around the classroom. Post a few on a bulletin board along with the dust jacket from A CHAIR FOR MY MOTHER.

Something to think about
Let the children write or dictate captions for the back of their pictures to tell about the special family event depicted.

STORY STRETCHER

For Art And Creative Dramatics: Blue Tile Diner In Our Class

What the children will learn
To decorate the classroom

Materials you will need
Butcher paper, crayons, markers, stapler, construction paper, scissors, tape, laminating film or clear contact paper

What to do

1. Show the children the cover of A CHAIR FOR MY MOTHER. Recall that this is the diner where the girl's mother works, and where Josephine, the boss, sometimes pays the girl for doing extra jobs.

2. Ask the children to decorate part of the classroom like the Blue Tile Diner.

3. Make a large mural on butcher paper showing the grill, cash register, stacks of dishes and all that is depicted in the background.

4. Edge the mural with blue construction paper.

5. Make a sign that says, "Blue Tile Diner."

6. Staple the Blue Tile Diner mural onto a bulletin board.

7. Push some of the class tables under the bulletin board and place chairs on the outside.

8. Let each child make a place mat by drawing an outline of a place setting, including a plate, fork, knife, spoon, napkin, glass, cup and saucer.

9. Encourage each child to decorate the plate with a special design.

10. Laminate the place mats with laminating film or cover them with clear contact paper.

11. Serve snacks at the Blue Tile Diner.

Something to think about

To extend the activity, add a waitress uniform, aprons, chef's hat, name tags, menus, signs announcing specials.

STORY STRETCHER

For Mathematics: Guesstimate The Amount Of Money

What the children will learn

To estimate the amount of money and then count it

Materials you will need

Large clear plastic or glass jar with slit cut in the lid, pennies, index card, marker, scraps of paper, pencils, large envelope

What to do

1. Place the "money jar" in the mathematics center. Put a few pennies and other loose change into the jar.

2. Print on an index card, "Guess how much money is in this jar. Write your answer on a piece of paper and put it in the envelope." Tape this sign to the side of the jar.

3. After a day or two, count the money and find out who came closest to the correct amount.

4. Make the closest guesser the class accountant for the "Payment in Pennies" story s-t-r-e-t-c-h-e-r below.

Something to think about

Continue the activity after the children start earning money and adding to the jar each day. Appoint a new accountant each day, based on the new guesstimates.

STORY STRETCHER

For Mathematics And Social Studies: Purchasing Power—Shopping For A Chair

What the children will learn

To comparison shop

Materials you will need

Newspaper ads, want ads, community bulletin boards, catalogs

What to do

1. Talk with the children about the big purchase in A CHAIR FOR MY MOTHER.

2. Collect a few newspaper ads from furniture stores and ask the children to locate other sources of information about chairs for sale. Encourage them to look in the want ads, on community bulletin boards and in catalogs.

3. Gather ads from as many different places as possible.

4. Ask the entire class to decide what kind of chair they would like to purchase if they could buy a chair.

5. Let small groups of children scour the ads and decide on where to find the best bargains. Remind the children that price and quality should be considered.

Something to think about

Survey the parents to see if any work for or own a furniture store. If possible, take a field trip to a furniture store. Let the children see the whole operation, from ordering, loading, shipping and unpacking to sales. Ask a salesperson to show the children how to make a consumer decision based on quality.

STORY STRETCHER

For Social Studies: Payment In Pennies

What the children will learn

To earn money for class jobs

Materials you will need

Large clear plastic or glass jar with slit cut in the lid, chart paper, marker, scraps of paper

What to do

1. If you already have a coin collection, use these.

2. Save a few dollars in pennies as payment for class jobs.

3. Count out all the pennies, for example, 500 pennies for $5.

4. Mound the pennies on a table. Tell the children that this is the money they can earn and contribute to the class money jar.

5. Ask the children how this money might be spent. There are many ideas: for a popcorn party, class decorations, blank tapes for the listening station, a gift for the community volunteer who comes to their class, a contribution to a community fund-raiser. Ask them before they begin working to decide what they will do with the money they earn.

6. With the children's help, write up a list of class jobs and the payment for each job.

7. Let the children rotate the jobs among themselves so that each has an opportunity to earn pennies for the class money jar.

8. At the end of the week, count the pennies in the jar and decide whether or not to continue the project the next week.

Something to think about

Do not enter the penny payment project with a preconceived notion as to what the class should do with the money it earns. Let them decide.

References

Bunting, Eve. (1989). **THE WEDNESDAY SURPRISE**. Illustrated by Donald Carrick. New York: Clarion.

Cairo, Shelley. (1985). **OUR BROTHER HAS DOWN'S SYNDROME**. Photographs by Irene McNeil. Toronto, Canada: Annick.

Christiansen, C. B. (1989). **MY MOTHER'S HOUSE, MY FATHER'S HOUSE**. Illustrated by Irene Trivas. New York: Atheneum.

Joosse, Barbara M. (1991). **MAMA, DO YOU LOVE ME?** Illustrated by Barbara Lavallee. San Francisco: Chronicle.

Williams, Vera B. (1982). **A CHAIR FOR MY MOTHER**. New York: Greenwillow.

Additional References for Families

Carlson, Nancy. (1991). **A VISIT TO GRANDMA'S**. New York: Viking. *Tina and her parents visit Grandma in her new Florida condominium and are surprised to find that she is very different from when she lived on the farm.*

Fox, Mem. (1989). **SHOES FROM GRANDPA**. Illustrated by Patricia Mullins. New York: Orchard Books. *In this rhyming story, family members describe the clothes they intend to give Jessie to go with the shoes from Grandpa.*

Garza, Carmen Lomas. (1990). **FAMILY PICTURES. CUADROS DE FAMILIA**. San Francisco: Children's Book Press. *The author describes in bilingual text and illustrations her experiences growing up in a Hispanic community in Texas.*

Griffith, Helen V. (1986). **GEORGIA MUSIC**. Illustrated by James Stevenson. New York: Greenwillow. *A little girl and her grandfather share two kinds of music, that of his mouth organ and that of the birds and insects around his cabin. The girl misses the music when she has to return from summer vacation, and she misses grandfather, too.*

Mora, Pat. (1992). **A BIRTHDAY BASKET FOR TIA**. Illustrated by Cecily Lang. New York: Macmillan. *With the help and interference of her cat Chica, Cecilia prepares a surprise gift for her great-aunt's ninetieth birthday.*

FAMILY STORIES FROM THE PAST

My Great-Aunt Arizona
Bigmama's
When I Was Little
The Quilt Story
Tar Beach

5
FAMILY STORIES FROM THE PAST

MY GREAT-AUNT ARIZONA

By Gloria Houston

Illustrated by

Susan Condie Lamb

Arizona was born in the Blue Ridge Mountains on Henson Creek, in a log cabin built by her father. Arizona grows to be a tall girl who loves to pick flowers, to read, to sing and to dance. Jim is Arizona's brother, and they have fun in the mountains during every season of the year. Arizona loves her one-room "blab" school and knows she wants to be a teacher when she grows up. She becomes a teacher in the same one-room school that she and her brother attended as children. She loves the school, planting flowers, reading to the children and teaching them about all the faraway places they will go when they grow up. Eventually she marries, but continues to teach. Every year at Christmas, her class plants a tree on the playground. For fifty-seven years, Arizona teaches the boys and girls and plants the trees until they grow in rings around Riverside School. Susan Condie Lamb's colorful illustrations are a joyful tribute to a magnificent story that will inspire every teacher who ever hugged a child and taught about faraway places.

Read-Aloud Presentation

Ask the children if they have aunts or great-aunts. Tell them that a great-aunt would be their grandmother's or grandfather's sister. Read the title of the book, MY GREAT-AUNT ARIZONA. Wonder aloud how she got the name Arizona. Look at the cover and ask the children if this is a story set in the present, the future or the past. Read MY GREAT-AUNT ARIZONA from cover to cover without pausing for discussion. At the end, if you have a favorite teacher who inspired you to teach, tell the children about that teacher.

STORY STRETCHER

For Art: Mountain Scenes

What the children will learn
To paint and draw from photographs

Materials you will need
Photographs or postcards or calendars showing real mountain scenes, sponges, plastic margarine tubs, thinned tempera paints, paper, brushes

What to do
1.   Look at the mountain scenes on the photographs, postcards or calendars.

2.   Look through Susan Condie Lamb's illustrations of the Blue Ridge mountains in MY GREAT-AUNT ARIZONA.

3.   Have the children compare the photographed scenes with Lamb's illustrations, which depict the colors, textures, mountains, valleys, roads and streams of the Blue Ridge Mountains.

4.   Call attention to how the artist seemed to sponge on color. Demonstrate how to do this by dipping a sponge in dark green paint and pressing it onto paper. See whether the sponge painting reminds them of the green valleys in the book illustrations.

5.   Let the children experiment with painting and ask them to draw and paint mountain scenes. Remind them that their illustrations are like Susan Condie Lamb's: they are representations and do not have to be realistic.

Something to think about
Leave the photographs and paints out for the children to explore on their own. Studies of creativity indicate that children need time to explore and experiment before they are ready to pursue the creative possibilities of a medium.

STORY STRETCHER

For Cooking And Snack Time: Blue Ridge Mountain Apple Pies

Materials you will need
Dried apples, pie crust, brown sugar, cinnamon, butter, deep fryer, plates, napkins, forks, cartons of milk

What to do
1.   With parent volunteers, plan a tasting party of Blue Ridge Mountain Fried Apple Pies.

2.   Make fried apple pies by shaping pie crust into a five-inch circle.

3.   Onto one half of the circle, spoon about a tablespoon of a mixture of dried apples, butter, brown sugar and cinnamon.

4.   Fold over the pie crust and close by pressing the fork tines around the edge of the crust.

5.   Deep fry just long enough to brown the crust.

6.   Drain on paper towels.

7.   Sprinkle with brown sugar.

8. Serve hot with cold milk.

Something to think about
Use a canned apple pie filling if dried apples are not available.

For Games: Playing Tag

What the children will learn
To enjoy simple old-fashioned games

Materials you will need
None

What to do
1. Almost all children have played tag. Have them think up variations of tag that could go along with MY GREAT-AUNT ARIZONA. For example, in a drop-the-handkerchief version of tag, you could drop an apron, a flower, a hair ribbon or an old shoe behind the runner's back.

2. Vary the tag game further by suggesting that the runners gallop like a mule, run while pretending to rock a baby in their arms, crawl backwards, jump like frogs.

Something to think about
Explore with the children why games were simpler in Great-Aunt Arizona's day.

For Social Studies: Where Are The Blue Ridge Mountains?

What the children will learn
To locate the Blue Ridge Mountains in North Carolina and Virginia

Materials you will need
Maps of the United States and North Carolina and Virginia, travel brochures from national parks and from North Carolina and Virginia, atlas, encyclopedia

What to do
1. Show the children your location on a map of the United States. Point out where the Blue Ridge Mountains are.

2. Look at maps of North Carolina and Virginia and follow the Blue Ridge Parkway.

3. Read about the Blue Ridge Parkway in the encyclopedia and look at the travel brochures.

Something to think about
Find out whether or not there really is a Henson Creek in the Blue Ridge Mountains and a village named "Wing."

For Science And Nature: Planting Great-Aunt Arizona's Trees

What the children will learn
To care for and plant an evergreen

Materials you will need
Potted evergreen tree, shovel, water

What to do
1. Secure permission from school officials to plant a tree.

2. Tell the children that Great-Aunt Arizona planted Christmas trees each year in honor of her students. Tell them that you want to plant a tree in their honor.

3. Invite a nursery owner to assist with the project.

4. Have the children interview the nursery owner to find out which species of evergreen grows best in your area.

5. Purchase the tree and have it delivered to the school.

6. Keep it inside the classroom for a week or two.

7. Let the children decorate the tree in honor of Great-Aunt Arizona with brightly colored cutouts of flowers and birds.

8. Dig a hole for the tree following the nursery owner's directions. Involve all the children in the digging.

9. Plant the tree ceremoniously by letting each child add a shovel full of soil. Remove the decorations.

10. Continue caring for Great-Aunt Arizona's tree.

Something to think about
Involve the children in as much of the experience as possible.

FAMILY STORIES FROM THE PAST

BIGMAMA'S

By Donald Crews

Donald Crews takes the reader back to the 1940s, to the Florida country home of his Bigmama. Though tired from a train ride of three days and two nights, the children are thrilled to visit every inch of the house, barn, chicken coops, sugar cane pit, pond, boat, farm and acreage all around, and to discover that everything is the same. Donald digs worms hidden under the sugar cane pulp and goes fishing. Satisfying and reassuring memories are captured to help a new generation understand the importance of going home to Bigmama's and Bigpapa's. Crews portrays the extended family with warmth and affection, even giving us a glimpse of his own self-portrait at the end.

Read-Aloud Presentation

Ask the children what they call their grandmothers. Tell them any affectionate names you have for your grandmothers. Show the cover of BIGMAMA'S and explain to the children that it illustrates children riding on a train and celebrating as their destination nears. They will spend the summer at Bigmama's in Cottondale, Florida. Read BIGMAMA'S. Encourage the children to recall any visits to relatives who live in the country. Help the children understand that BIGMAMA'S takes place in the countryside of the 1940s, and that country life has changed since Donald Crews was a little boy. This story is a family story from the past. If your students have little experience with country life, they may assume that all people in the country have outdoor toilets and slaughter chickens, and that every family has horses.

STORY STRETCHER

For Art: Countryscapes Or Scenes From The Country

What the children will learn
To draw a scene from their lives in the country or from a remembered visit to the country

Materials you will need
Drawing paper, crayons, marker, colored pencils, pastel chalks

What to do
1. Look through the illustrations in BIGMAMA'S and discuss all the things in the pictures that one would not usually see in a city.

2. Ask the children to make countryscapes—scenes from the country.

3. Encourage the artists to select a variety of drawing materials to achieve the textures they desire.

Something to think about
Looking at other people's drawings or paintings does not encourage children to copy, but rather inspires them to think of possibilities.

STORY STRETCHER

For Mathematics: Ordering From A Catalog

What the children will learn
To calculate costs and decide whether a toy comes from the era of the story

Materials you will need
Mail order catalogs, pencils, note pads

What to do
1. Read the passage in BIGMAMA'S in which Donald Crews describes their checking to see that everything was the same in the house, including the "Sears Roebuck" catalogs.

2. Ask children if their families order anything from catalogs.

3. Bring a few popular catalogs to the classroom.

4. Suggest that the children find toys they would like. There is one rule, however: a similar toy must have been available in the 1940s. Ask the children to think of toys the children in the story might have played with. Dolls, for example, and toy trucks, cars and trains, but not electronic or mechanical toys requiring batteries.

Something to think about
Do not allow the children to use calculators to figure out cost. Explain that calculators were not available to children when this story took place.

For Music and Movement: Train Songs

What the children will learn
Traditional train songs

Materials you will need
Chart paper, marker

What to do
1. Observe that Donald Crews and his family probably played games and sang to pass the time on their long three-day train ride to Cottondale, Florida.

2. Teach the children a few traditional train songs like "She'll Be Coming 'Round the Mountain," "Down by the Station" and "Working on the Railroad."

3. Print the words to the songs on chart tablet paper.

4. Read through the songs and sing them, asking the children to join in.

5. Change words in the songs to fit the story. For example, since there are no mountains in Florida, and Cottondale is located in the Florida panhandle, sing, "She'll be coming into Cottondale when she comes."

Something to think about
If any parents know traditional African-American train songs, invite them to come to class to teach the songs and explain their cultural significance.

For Social Studies: Where Is Cottondale, Florida?

What the children will learn
To locate Florida on a map of the United States

Materials you will need
Maps of the United States and Florida, push pins, yarn or string

What to do
1. Help older children find Cottondale, Florida, in the panhandle, just south of Interstate 10.

2. Help the children calculate how long it would take to drive from their home to Florida. Call AAA or another automobile club for maps, directions and time estimates.

3. Help younger children find Cottondale by first pointing out the state where they live and placing a push pin in that location. Then place a push pin on Cottondale, Florida, and show the children how to tie a string from their location to the place where Donald Crews spent his boyhood summers.

Something to think about
Geographic perspective is not easy for young children. Help them understand distance by telling them how long it would take riding in a car to travel from their school to Cottondale.

For Writing Center: "I Remember When" Stories

What the children will learn
To transcribe and interpret a favorite family story

Materials you will need
Tape recorder, cassette tape, chart tablet, writing paper, pencils, art supplies, materials for binding a book

What to do
1. Invite a grandparent who has lived in the country to come to class. Show him or her BIGMAMA'S.

2. Ask the grandparent to recall a special event from his or her childhood.

3. Tape-record the grandparent's conversation with the children.

4. The next day, listen to the tape with a small group of children.

5. Let the children retell the story in their own words by taking turns dictating sentences to you.

6. Write the dictated sentences on chart tablet paper.

7. When the children have finished, go back through the dictated story and let them help you edit it.

8. Type the story on paper, leaving room for illustrations.

9. Allow the children to illustrate the story, then bind it into a durable book for the classroom library. (See the appendix for directions for binding a book.)

Something to think about
Third graders might tape-record stories their grandparents tell and then write shorter versions of them.

5
FAMILY STORIES FROM THE PAST

WHEN I WAS LITTLE

By Toyomi Igus

Illustrated by Higgins Bond

During the summer, Noel visits his Grandpa Will, who takes him fishing. They enjoy each other's company. Grandpa Will reminisces about how the lake was when he was little. He surprises Noel when he tells the child that he had no washing machine, no telephone and no television. Noel can't imagine life without cartoons. Grandpa Will's fond memories and their shared enjoyment of fishing help Grandpa and Noel realize that some simple pleasures never change. Higgins Bond's beautifully realistic illustrations in acrylics capture the warmth, the humor and the special bonds in this family story. The black-and-white pencil sketches reflect the past in a real treasure of a story with a gallery of memorable pictures.

Read-Aloud Presentation

Introduce the children to Grandpa Will and Noel by showing the first illustration in the book of the two of them walking down the lane with their fishing gear. Show the children the cover of the book and the realistic drawing of grandfather and grandson fishing from the pier. Read WHEN I WAS LITTLE. Pause occasionally to point out the signs of the city encroaching on the country, like the high-rise apartment building across the lake, the condo on the lake shore and the jet plane flying overhead. After reading WHEN I WAS LITTLE, note how the artist portrayed scenes from the past in black and white, while scenes from the present are in color. Invite the children to talk about their parents or grandparents telling them stories of another era.

STORY STRETCHER

For Art: Remembering Pictures

What the children will learn
To experiment with drawing in pencil and charcoal

Materials you will need
White drawing paper, scraps of paper, soft-leaded pencils, charcoal, tissue paper, hair spray

What to do
1. Look at Higgins Bond's illustrations of WHEN I WAS LITTLE. Note how the scenes that Grandpa Will remembers are drawn in black and white.

2. Demonstrate how to use the side of a soft-leaded pencil to create shading.

3. Encourage the children to experiment with pencil shading, then introduce them to charcoal. Show the children how to use the points and sides of the charcoal. Demonstrate how to use tissue to smudge the charcoal, creating shading and shadows.

4. Let the children experiment with the charcoal on scraps of paper before using the drawing paper.

5. Spray the finished drawings with hair spray to keep the pencil and charcoal from rubbing off.

Something to think about
Experiment with pastel chalks, with which many of the same techniques are useful.

STORY STRETCHER

For Classroom Library: Tapes Of Old Radio Shows

What the children will learn
To listen and create a story in their minds

Materials you will need
Tapes of old radio shows, tape player

What to do
1. Visit a public library and listen to audiotapes of old radio shows. You may find these in the section for commuters who listen to tapes on their way to work.

2. Ask the librarian to help you find a comedy or adventure story that your students would enjoy.

3. Show the children the illustration of Grandpa Will as a little boy listening to the radio with his family.

4. Play the tape of the radio program.

5. Let the children talk about how they use their imaginations when they don't have television pictures to rely on.

Something to think about
Avoid radio shows which stereotype African-Americans or other racial or ethnic groups.

For Music and Movement: Fats Waller Records And Rapping

What the children will learn
To compare music from the present to music from the past

Materials you will need
Recordings of Fats Waller or other famous African-American artists from the past, contemporary rap song recording

What to do
1.   Read the passage in WHEN I WAS LITTLE in which Grandpa Will tells Noel about how his Uncle Hoot used to pretend to be a deejay playing Fats Waller records.

2.   Play a Fats Waller record.

3.   Play a rap record.

4.   Let the children decide which recording they like best.

Something to think about
Survey the class and find out whether or not they have favorite recording artists. Use artists who make recordings for children.

For Social Studies: Washing Clothes, The Old-Fashioned Way

What the children will learn
To wash clothes on a washboard

Materials you will need
Cotton shirts and blouses, detergent, wash tub, washboard, water, clothes line or wooden clothes drying rack

What to do
1.   Look at the illustration of Grandpa Will's grandmother washing clothes in a wash tub with a washboard.

2.   Set up the wash tub and board. Demonstrate how the person washing the clothes scrubbed them against the board.

3.   Let the girls and boys take turns washing clothes.

4.   Hang the clothes on a line to dry or on a wooden drying rack.

Something to think about
Discuss the fact that this method of washing and drying clothes takes no electrical energy, and thus is good for our environment.

For Special Event: Going Fishing

What the children will learn
To fish

Materials you will need
Fishing gear

What to do
1.   Arrange to go fishing at a local pond or lake.

2.   Select parent volunteers and grandparents who enjoy fishing and can be enthusiastic instructors for the children. Ask them to bring along their fishing gear.

3.   Secure parental permissions, arrange for transportation and determine whether fishing licenses are required.

4.   Enjoy the day.

Something to think about
If you cannot take your students fishing, bring an old fishing boat into the playground, add bamboo canes and let them pretend.

FAMILY STORIES FROM THE PAST

THE QUILT STORY

By Tony Johnston

Illustrated by Tomie dePaola

A pioneer mother stitches a quilt of shooting stars for a little girl named Abigail. The quilt keeps her warm as the family travels west in a covered wagon. It provides comfort when they settle into a new home. When the girl grows up, she puts the quilt away in the attic. There a family of mice sleep on the quilt and gnaw holes in it. Later a raccoon hiding in the attic scratches holes in the quilt. Years later, a kitten climbs into the attic and curls up comfortably on the quilt. The little girl who finds the kitten also discovers the old quilt. Her mother repairs the quilt, and once again it is loved and comforts a child as she moves into a strange new house. Tomie dePaola's illustrations capture the story with warmth and color.

Read-Aloud Presentation

Bring a quilt to class and place it across your lap. If you know the history of the quilt, share it with the children. Point out the patterns in the quilt. Show the cover of THE QUILT STORY. Call attention to the pattern of shooting stars, the checkerboard, the hearts, the doves. Tell the children that the quilt in this story is older than they are, older than their parents, even older than their grandparents. Read THE QUILT STORY. Pause after the passage in which the girl grows up and stores the quilt in the attic. Let the children predict what will happen to the quilt. Continue reading. Pause at the end of the story to compare the colors and shades of the quilt on the last page with the one on the first.

STORY STRETCHER

For Art: Stenciling Patterns

What the children will learn
To choose and arrange stencils artistically

Materials you will need
Construction paper, scraps of paper, sponges, scissors, tempera paint in primary colors, plastic margarine tubs, stencils

What to do
1.   Show children how to cut sponges into small pieces, one for each color of tempera paint.

2.   Pour tempera paint into margarine tubs.

3.   Place a stencil over a scrap of paper and show the children how to dapple the sponge in the paint, then press it onto the stencil.

4.   Lift the stencil to see the shape underneath.

5.   Encourage the children to experiment with many different shapes and patterns. Call attention to the shapes in Abigail's quilt.

Something to think about
As an alternative to stencils, use the ends of thread spools, small plastic construction blocks, even wheels from toy cars. Dab them in the paint and print with them.

STORY STRETCHER

For Classroom Library: A Comfy Quilt To Curl Up And Read With

What the children will learn
To find a special place to enjoy reading

Materials you will need
Library books, comfortable chairs or cushions, the class reading quilt

What to do
1.   Celebrate the class quilt by placing it in the classroom library.

2.   Sit on the quilt, using it as a story quilt when telling a fantasy story.

3.   Drape it across the arms of a comfortable reading chair.

Something to think about
The classroom library should be an inviting place with cozy and comfortable fabrics. Consider making a favorite author quilt or favorite book quilt.

STORY STRETCHER

For Creative Dramatics: Packing And Moving

What the children will learn
To dramatize a family moving

Materials you will need
Packing boxes, newspapers, packing tape, markers

What to do
1.   Plan to move one area of your classroom. Pretend that this requires a long move across town or across the state.

2. Let the children pack up one learning center, wrapping the equipment and supplies in newspaper, packing them in boxes, taping the boxes shut and labeling them.

3. Ask volunteers to include personal possessions.

4. Pack the quilt that you had on your lap when you read THE QUILT STORY.

5. Make the move very long by having the children move the center all the way around the school, going outside and returning to your classroom.

Something to think about
Children like the added drama of the move when objects actually leave the classroom. To make it more realistic, talk with the principal and other teachers to see if there is an area which needs moving, and involve your children in packing, moving and unpacking.

STORY STRETCHER

For Mathematics: Patterning

What the children will learn
To match fabric samples and create closed and open designs

Materials you will need
Variety of fabric or wallpaper samples, pinking shears

What to do
1. Ask parent volunteers for yards of old fabric that they do not plan to use.

2. Let the children assist in cutting 30 to 40 fabric or wallpaper swatches, approximately six inches square, using pinking shears. Make sure there are at least two of each kind of fabric or wallpaper swatch.

3. After all the swatches are cut, let the children arrange them to create open and closed patterns.

Something to think about
Younger children can simply match the fabric swatches, while older students can create elaborate horizontal, vertical and diagonal patterns.

STORY STRETCHER

For Special Project: Making A Class Quilt

What the children will learn
To cut and sew quilt pieces

Materials you will need
Cardboard square, pencil, fabric scraps or quilt pieces, scissors, pins, liquid embroidery or embroidery thread, embroidery needles, sewing machine, quilt backing

What to do
1. Invite a quilter to come to class and assist with this special project.

2. Make a cardboard pattern for the squares of cloth.

3. Place the fabric flat on the table, place the pattern over the fabric, draw around the pattern and cut out the fabric.

4. Cut more fabric squares.

5. Let each child embroider his or her name on a quilt square.

6. Arrange the fabric squares in a pleasing pattern.

7. Pin the squares together.

8. Sew the squares together.

9. Have the quilter show the class how to attach the backing to the quilt.

10. When the class quilt is finished, place it in the library area of the classroom.

Something to think about
Younger children can write their names in liquid embroidery. Third graders can learn to embroider their names with thread.

FAMILY STORIES FROM THE PAST

TAR BEACH

By Faith Ringgold

Cassie Louise Lightfoot is only eight years old, but in her dreams she flies above her home in Harlem. She flies over all of New York City, above a building her father helped to build. Her father longs to be a member of the union, because then he could earn more money. Cassie Louise makes her dreams for her family and herself come true. As she flies, she imagines having ice cream every night for dessert, owning the ice cream factory, bringing all the neighbors up to the roof—Tar Beach—for a picnic. In the end, she takes her little brother BeBe flying, then returns to Tar Beach to awaken on the quilt where she has been sleeping. Faith Ringgold's lovely, lively, vibrant illustrations sweep the reader of the book away through this creative adventure inside a dream world where children's memories and fantasies come together. The pages are edged like the quilt pieces in the artist's quilt painting of the same name, "Tar Beach."

Read-Aloud Presentation

Ask the children if they have ever dreamed that they were flying. Talk about having dreams in which our wishes come true. Look at the cover illustration of TAR BEACH and call attention to the girl who flies near the bridge, her pigtails sailing in the air. Let the children look at the cover and imagine as much as they can about the story. Ask the children where the story takes place. Where is Tar Beach? What time of the year is it? Who is the main character? Read TAR BEACH without interruption, then let the children tell you what they like about the story. Answer questions about the significance of Cassie Louise's father not being allowed to be a member of the union. Look back through the illustrations at the many ways Faith Ringgold uses quilts.

STORY STRETCHER

For Art: Paintings Of Dream Flying

What the children will learn
To experiment with a multi-media approach to painting

Materials you will need
Acrylic paints, brushes, plastic margarine tubs or meat tray palettes, thick paper, scissors, glue, pencils

What to do
1. Read the last page of the book, which describes Faith Ringgold's family and her life as a storyteller and artist.

2. Call attention to the description of the acrylic paints and canvas paper that the artist used to illustrated TAR BEACH.

3. Ask the children to paint scenes that they would see if they flew anywhere they wanted to go.

4. From scraps of construction paper, have the child cut and paste a self-portrait of a figure in flight.

5. Glue this figure in place flying over the scene.

Something to think about
Display the acrylic paintings in the art area. Try other experiments, like gluing fabric to the flying figures to make clothing.

STORY STRETCHER

For Cooking And Snack Time: Cassie Louise's Ice Cream

What the children will learn
To make homemade ice cream

Materials you will need
Ice cream freezer, ice, milk, eggs, flavoring, bowl, long-handled wooden spoon, measuring cups and spoons, ice cream salt, ice cream scoop, small bowls, spoons

What to do
1. Read the directions for operating the ice cream freezer and the recipe to figure out the recommended quantity of ingredients for the freezer.

2. Measure and mix the ingredients. Pour this mixture into the freezer.

3. Pack the freezer in ice and add salt on top of the ice in the amounts recommended by the freezer manufacturer.

4. Let the children take turns cranking the freezer and adding salt to the ice.

5. Check on the freezing process, showing the children how to check the consistency of the mixture.

6. Serve the ice cream for a snack, and while the children are enjoying it, read the story of TAR BEACH again.

Something to think about
Make ice cream with an old-fashioned hand-cranked freezer and with a new motorized one. Compare the taste. Name the children's favorite, Cassie Louise Ice Cream. (Adapted from Raines, S. C., & Canady, R. J. (1992). STORY S-T-R-E-T-C-H-E-R-S FOR THE PRIMARY GRADES. Mt. Rainier, MD: Gryphon House. 168-69.)

For Music and Movement: Up, Up And Away

What the children will learn
To move in response to music

Materials you will need
Recordings of songs like "Up, Up and Away In My Beautiful Balloon" or "Up On the Roof," tape or record or compact disc player

What to do
1. Let children experiment with moving as if they were flying through the air.

2. Play some flying music and pretend alongside the children.

3. Stop the music and ask someone to tell what she or he is flying over.

4. Start the music again and continue the flight, pausing every few minutes to have someone describe what she or he sees.

Something to think about
If you have children who do not want to participate, that is fine. Encourage them, but do not insist. However, do not let them make fun of other children who are flying and dreaming.

For Social Studies: Cityscape

What the children will learn
To build representations of cities

Materials you will need
Sand table, sand, cardboard boxes, rocks, construction paper, glue, tape, staplers, scissors, tempera paints, brushes, liquid detergent, interlocking blocks, other construction blocks

What to do
1. Look at the city scenes in TAR BEACH. Point out to the children the skyscrapers and the George Washington Bridge.

2. Show the children how to make a skyscraper from a box. Place a large rock, block or heavy book inside the box. Close the box and paint it like a skyscraper, using tempera paint mixed with a drop of liquid detergent. Let the box dry and place it in the sand. There is the first skyscraper.

3. Encourage the children to add other buildings made of cardboard boxes, interlocking blocks and other construction blocks.

4. See if the children can adapt the materials to improvise a George Washington Bridge. They can build towers and connecting roads, and string yarn from tower to tower to make suspension cables.

5. Encourage the children to continue adding to the cityscape.

Something to think about
Ask two of the cityscape artists to create Tar Beach atop one of the buildings.

For Writing Center: Flying Stories

What the children will learn
To write an adventure story patterned after TAR BEACH

Materials you will need
Writing paper, pencils, writing folders, art supplies for illustrations, book binding materials

What to do
1. Talk with the children about using sketches and key words as the basis for brainstorming a story. Practice the brainstorming strategy by leading the children through this thinking exercise.

2. With the children who would like to write flying stories, look at TAR BEACH and point out how Faith Ringgold constructed the story with a surprise opening scene.

3. Ask the children to imagine a surprise opening scene they would like for their own story. Where would they be flying? Encourage the children who respond to sketch something or to write key words to remind them later of the scene they are imagining.

4. Return to the TAR BEACH book and observe that the next section is about how Cassie came to fly. Cassie was lying on TAR BEACH on a quilt, and she felt magical, like she owned everything she could see.

5. Have the children imagine a scene in which they are lying on a magic quilt. Where will they be lying? What will they see from the magic quilt? Ask the children to sketch something or to write key words to remind them later of the scene they are imagining.

6. Return to the TAR BEACH book and note that the next section is about the George Washington Bridge, how Cassie's father helped to build it and how she loves looking at it.

7. Ask the children to imagine a special place, a place that someone they know helped to build, or a place they like to go. Where is it? Ask the children to sketch or to write to remind them later of the scene they are imagining.

8. Return to the TAR BEACH book and note that Faith Ringgold wrote about a second special place, the Union Building.

9. Ask the children to imagine a second special place and sketch or write as a reminder.

10. By this time, the writers should be well on their way to a flying story. Let them continue brainstorming, creating several more scenes before the end of the story, by inviting a brother, sister or friend to go flying with them.

11. Edit the stories over the course of a few days.

12. Work with the children to publish and bind their stories so that the class can enjoy them in the classroom library. (See appendix for directions on book binding.)

Something to think about
For first graders who are less proficient writers, suggest they draw several scenes and dictate the story to the teacher, parent volunteer, or an older student. Some first graders will be able to construct a whole story, using invented spelling.

References

Crews, Donald. (1991). **BIGMAMA'S**. New York: Greenwillow.

Houston, Gloria. (1992). **MY GREAT-AUNT ARIZONA**. Illustrated by Susan Condie Lamb. New York: HarperCollins.

Igus, Toyomi. (1992). **WHEN I WAS LITTLE**. Illustrated by Higgins Bond. Orange, New Jersey: Just Us Books.

Johnston, Tony. (1985). **THE QUILT STORY**. Illustrated by Tomie dePaola. New York: G. P. Putnam's Sons.

Ringgold, Faith. (1991). **TAR BEACH.** New York: Random.

Additional References for Family Stories From The Past

Bunting, Eve. (1988). **HOW MANY DAYS TO AMERICA?: A THANKSGIVING STORY**. Illustrated by Beth Peck. New York: Clarion. *Refugees from a Caribbean island embark on a dangerous boat trip to America where they have a special reason to celebrate Thanksgiving.*

Cech, John. (1991). **MY GRANDMOTHER'S JOURNEY**. Illustrated by Sharon McGinley-Nally. New York: Bradbury Press. *A grandmother tells an intriguing story about a rescue by Gypsies, her life in early twentieth century Europe and her good fortune in coming to America.*

Howard, Elizabeth Fitzgerald. (1991). **AUNT FLOSSIE'S HATS (AND CRAB CAKES LATER)**. Illustrated by James Ransome. New York: Clarion. *Sarah and Susan share tea, cookies, crab cakes and stories about hats when they visit their favorite relative, Aunt Flossie.*

Medearis, Angela Shelf. (1991). **DANCING WITH THE INDIANS**. Illustrated by Samuel Byrd. New York: Holiday House. *While attending a Seminole Indian celebration, a black family watches and joins in several exciting dances.*

Tan, Amy. (1992). **THE MOON LADY**. Illustrated by Gretchen Schields. New York: Macmillan. *Nai-nai tells her granddaughters the story of her outing, as a seven-year-old girl in China, to see the Moon Lady and be granted a wish.*

NEIGHBORHOODS

Everybody Cooks Rice
Three Stalks of Corn
Uncle Willie and the Soup Kitchen
Dinosaurs to the Rescue! A Guide to Protecting Our Planet
A Country Far Away

EVERYBODY COOKS RICE

By Norah Dooley

Illustrations by Peter J. Thornton

While searching door-to-door for her little brother, Anthony, who is late for dinner, Carrie visits a series of neighbors. In the process, she learns about each family's work, customs and dinner. Each family invites Carrie to taste the dinner they are cooking. They each cook rice, but coming from different parts of the world, prepare it in different ways. The rice dishes include Barbados black-eyed peas and rice, Puerto Rican yellow rice with tumeric, Vietnamese nuoc cham—a fish sauce over rice, Chinese tofu and vegetables cooked with rice and Haitian creole rice with hot peppers, chives and red beans. When Carrie gets home, Anthony is waiting, but she is not hungry anymore because she has tasted so many meals made with rice. Peter J. Thornton's colorful full-page illustrations alternate with full pages of text. The book ends with a set of recipes from Carrie's neighbors.

Read-Aloud Presentation

Show the cover of the book with its colorful wooden frame houses, and talk about the neighborhood pictured. Discuss why it looks like a neighborhood in which children would enjoy living. Talk with the children about foods their families cook often. Read EVERYBODY COOKS RICE. Make a chart of all the neighbors: where they came from before settling on Carrie's street, how many people are in the families, what kind of work they do, and of course, their favorite rice recipes.

STORY STRETCHER

For Art: Making Colorful Houses

What the children will learn
To make a three-dimensional house structure

Materials you will need
Cardboard boxes in various shapes and sizes, scraps of cardboard, construction paper, markers, staplers, scissors, craft knives, tempera paints, liquid detergent or thinned glue, plastic margarine tubs, brushes, table or sand table.

What to do
1. Tell the children who are interested in creating a special art project that for the study of neighborhoods the class needs a display of colorful houses.

2. Show the children the illustrations from EVERYBODY COOKS RICE. Discuss how the neighborhood in the book is similar to or different from the neighborhoods where they live.

3. Brainstorm ways to turn the cardboard boxes into houses. Older children can cut holes in the boxes for windows and doors. Younger children can create windows and doors from construction paper instead.

4. Paint the boxes with tempera paint that has been mixed with either a drop of liquid detergent or thinned glue in the small margarine tubs.

5. Allow a day for the houses to dry before attaching the construction paper doors and windows.

6. Set the houses on a table or in a sand table.

Something to think about
Older children can cut windows and doors using craft or Exacto knives. Always supervise the children closely who are using craft knives. Show them how to place the cardboard flat on a table for cutting. Place scrap cardboard underneath to protect the table top.

STORY STRETCHER

For Classroom Library: Display Of Carrie's Neighborhood

What the children will learn
To create a neighborhood community

Materials you will need
Houses from the art story s-t-r-e-t-c-h-e-r, cardboard, contact paper, construction paper, markers, scissors, stapler, glue, construction blocks

What to do
1. Observe that Carrie's street is only one part of the neighborhood.

2. Read EVERYBODY COOKS RICE and note other locations that are mentioned, like the places where family members work—the video store, gift shop, community center.

3. Ask the children to think of other places in their communities, like the park, school, church,

synagogue, library, grocery, fire station, police station, hospital, pharmacy. Continue the discussion without turning the neighborhood into a town or a city. Explain that neighborhoods may be limited by facilities or by geographic boundaries.

4. Ask the children to make other houses, shops, schools and community buildings to represent a neighborhood.

5. Display the model neighborhood in the classroom library area along with the books for the unit on neighborhoods.

Something to think about
Try to create a neighborhood similar to the area in which your school is located.

For Cooking And Snack Time: Carrie's Neighborhood Rice

What the children will learn
To prepare and eat an unfamiliar rice dish

Materials you will need
Rice, wok or saucepan, recipe ingredients listed in the book, chart paper, marker, measuring cups and spoons, trays, hot plate or range, forks, chopsticks, plates, napkins

What to do
1. Read all the rice recipes, select one that you think your students would like and prepare it for them.

2. Make a large chart of the recipe so the children can follow it easily.

3. Assemble small teams of children to work together. Divide responsibilities for collecting ingredients, measuring, mixing, cooking, serving and clean-up.

Something to think about
Invite parents to prepare rice recipes with teams of children assisting them, and have a

recipe-tasting party. For a simpler story s-t-r-e-t-c-h-e-r, prepare wild rice and white rice and compare the tastes.

For Social Studies: Locating Carrie's Neighbors

What the children will learn
To locate the countries where Carrie's neighbors lived before coming to the United States

Materials you will need
World map, push pins, construction paper, marker, different colors of yarn

What to do
1. Pretend that Carrie's neighborhood is your neighborhood.

2. Read EVERYBODY COOKS RICE and locate each family's home before they came to America on the world map.

3. Make tiny signs from construction paper with each family's name on it.

4. Push the pin through the tiny sign at the location of the family's former country.

5. Select children to represent the different families in EVERYBODY COOKS RICE. Have each child tie a piece of yarn to the push pin at their family's former country.

6. Tie the ends of all the yarn together to represent everyone coming together in one neighborhood.

Something to think about
If you live in a multicultural neighborhood with recent immigrants, try the same exercise using families from your own neighborhood.

For Writing Center: Publishing Favorite Rice Recipes From Our Neighborhood

What the children will learn
To collect, organize, collate and publish rice recipes

Materials you will need
Rice recipes from parents and grandparents, index cards, photocopies, cardboard, contact paper, scissors

What to do
1. Write a column for the parent newsletter asking parents to send in favorite family rice recipes. Attach an index card for them to return to school.

2. Instruct the parents to write all the ingredients at the top of the card and to write directions for preparation, in numbered steps, at the bottom.

3. As the cards come in, read the recipes with the children and let them decide whether each is an appetizer, main dish, side dish or dessert.

4. Ask a parent volunteer to type the recipes and run photocopies. Leave space at the bottom of each page for the children to add an illustration of their family eating rice.

5. Bind the recipes and illustrations into a permanent book for the classroom collection. (See the directions for book binding in the appendix.)

Something to think about
Make a collection of recipes for the children's favorite snacks. Invariably some parents want copies. If a parent group wants to pay to photocopy the collection for other parents, encourage them to do so.

THREE STALKS OF CORN
By Leo Politi

In this reprint of a popular 1976 book, THREE STALKS OF CORN takes the reader into the California neighborhood of Barrio de Pico Viejo, where Angelica and her grandmother live. Like many of their neighbors, they have a vegetable and herb garden. As Grandmother watches over their three stalks of corn, she teaches Angelica the legends of the corn. They enjoy the corn fresh or ground into flour for tortillas. They use it to make corn-husk dolls and colored corn necklaces. The book is filled with the scenes of an active neighborhood, a loving family of daughter and grandmother cooking together, a community fiesta in the park. Grandmother is invited to teach the other students how to make traditional Mexican foods. The book ends with recipes for enchiladas and tacos. Politi's illustrations are wonderful line drawings, filled with detail, delicate shading, and stylized figures of the residents.

Read-Aloud Presentation

If you have any Spanish speakers among your students, ask them to teach the class phrases for greeting, counting and colors. If you live where there are street addresses in Spanish, call attention to these. Show the children the cover of THREE STALKS OF CORN and tell them that this family is composed of just two people—a grandmother and her granddaughter, Angelica. Discuss with the children whether the story takes place in the city or in the country. They will probably guess in the country, since the cover shows Angelica with the corn. Read THREE STALKS OF CORN and call attention to the neighborhood scenes, especially the fiesta activities. Announce that, like Grandmother, they will cook the traditional Mexican foods of tacos and enchiladas.

STORY STRETCHER

For Art: Simple Corn-Husk Dolls

What the children will learn
To make corn-husk dolls

Materials you will need
Corn husks of various colors from a craft store or real dried corn husks colored with food coloring, tongue depressors, glue, colored markers

What to do
1. Buy corn husks of various colors at a craft store or color dried corn husks by soaking them in water with different food colorings.

2. Allow the husks to dry thoroughly on paper towels after soaking in food coloring.

3. Cut animal or human shapes from the corn husks as if they were sheets of paper.

4. Glue the shapes onto tongue depressors.

5. With colored markers, draw faces on the wide end of the tongue depressors.

6. Encourage children to make dolls like the characters in the book or like Grandmother's corn husk puppets.

Something to think about
Invite a craftsperson who works with corn husks to come to class and demonstrate how to make figures or to experiment with forms. One technique is to take heavy craft wire, wrap it with corn husks and shape it by wetting with white glue.

STORY STRETCHER

For Cooking And Snack Time: Tacos And Enchiladas

What the children will learn
To prepare Mexican dishes

Materials you will need
Recipe ingredients found at the back of THREE STALKS OF CORN, chart tablet, marker, mixing bowls, knives, trays, plates, forks, napkins

What to do
1. Print the recipes for enchiladas and tacos on large sheets of chart tablet paper.

2. Divide the class into groups and let each make either enchiladas or tacos.

3. Since some children will have experience making these foods, compare the modern way of making tacos, with already prepared taco shells, to the traditional way of wrapping flour tortillas around meat and sauce

and dropping them into a hot fryer until the tortilla puffs.

Something to think about
Invite a parent or grandparent who makes tortillas to teach the children to cook them the way that Angelica's grandmother does.

STORY STRETCHER

For Creative Dramatics: Mexican Puppet Theater

To improvise a puppet play based on characters seen in the book

Materials you will need
Corn husk dolls from the art story s-t-r-e-t-c-h-e-r

What to do
1. Look at the page of THREE STALKS OF CORN where Angelica and Grandmother are playing with corn husk puppets.
2. Let the children play with their corn husk puppets and improvise dialogue and action.

Something to think about
For younger children, make paper puppets of Angelica and her Grandmother and other neighborhood residents. Let them act out the book, rather than create a play.

STORY STRETCHER

For Mathematics: Patterns In Necklaces

What the children will learn
To make patterns and string kernels of corn

Materials you will need
Dried corn or beads of various colors, needles and thread or string

What to do
1. Read the passage in the book in which Grandmother shows Angelica how to make a necklace of dried corn.

2. Prepare dried kernels of corn by sticking holes through them with a needle.

3. Encourage the children to create different patterns with the corn as they string it onto thread.

4. As an alternative, string wooden or plastic beads onto string.

Something to think about
When the children have finished their corn or bead necklaces, make prints of the color patterns they have created. Give groups of children index cards and crayons. Have each child call out the pattern on his or her necklace, while the rest of the group makes crayon marks on their cards to represent the pattern. They can use these directions to make necklaces like those of their friends.

STORY STRETCHER

For Writing Center: Script For The Puppet Theater

What the children will learn
To turn their improvisations into spoken words

Materials you will need
Corn-husk puppets from the art story s-t-r-e-t-c-h-e-r, paper, pencils

What to do
1. Ask a small group of children who enjoyed the creative dramatics with the corn-husk puppets to turn their improvisations into a script.

2. Help the children recall what they did in their improvisation by encouraging them to think in terms of scenes.

3. Let each child become the dialogue writer for his or her character, in conjunction with a group leader.

4. Leave the children to negotiate their writing together.

5. Edit to produce a finished script.

6. Read the script to the other children and let them try it out.

Something to think about
If your students are familiar with both English and Spanish, let them act out the story in both languages. Encourage English speakers to use some Spanish in their scenes.

....

UNCLE WILLIE AND
THE SOUP KITCHEN

By DyAnne DiSalvo-Ryan

....

"Sometimes people need help," is the message of UNCLE WILLIE AND THE SOUP KITCHEN. The story is told in the voice of a young boy who helps his Uncle Willie by volunteering at a soup kitchen on his day off from school. The boy is a bit scared by the man who rummages through the garbage looking for aluminum cans, and by the woman who sleeps on a park bench. Uncle Willie helps the boy see these people as neighbors who need help. In the process, we also learn how a neighborhood supports a soup kitchen, with donations from merchants, churches and individuals. DiSalvo-Ryan's story and illustrations are sensitive yet straightforward, showing the feelings a child would have if fortunate enough to have an Uncle Willie who helps him appreciate other people.

Read-Aloud Presentation

Cover the title of the book, but show the illustrations of Uncle Willie and the boy seated at a table. Ask the children what they think these two are doing. (It looks like a restaurant or a school cafeteria.) Then read the title, UNCLE WILLIE AND THE SOUP KITCHEN. Discuss what a soup kitchen is. Read UNCLE WILLIE AND THE SOUP KITCHEN, pausing briefly at the first illustrations of the Can Man. Let one or two children talk about what they would feel if they saw the Can Man coming. Just like other children, the boy was curious, sad and a little scared. Read on, then pause and discuss how the boy must have felt when he saw the woman sleeping on the park bench. At the end of the book, discuss the importance of the soup kitchen in their lives, including its importance to Uncle Willie and the boy who tells the story.

STORY STRETCHER

For Art: Have A Nice Day Posters

What the children will learn
To decorate a bright and cheerful poster

Materials you will need
Newsprint, tempera paints, brushes, easels, posterboard, scissors, glue, hole punch, yarn or fishing wire, markers

What to do
1. Read the passage in UNCLE WILLIE AND THE SOUP KITCHEN in which the soup kitchen is described as decorated with "Have a nice day" posters.
2. Ask the children who come to the art center to paint "Have a nice day" posters on newsprint.

3. When the posters have dried, cut strips of posterboard and glue them onto the top and bottom of the posters.
4. Let the children print along the bottom on the posterboard, "Have a nice day."
5. Punch holes in the top of the posters an inch or two in from the sides.
6. String yarn or fishing wire through the holes and tie to make a poster hanger.
7. Give the "Have a nice day" posters to the soup kitchen when donating cans of food.

Something to think about
Make thank-you posters for soup kitchen volunteers. For more durable posters, use posterboard and poster paints.

STORY STRETCHER

For Cooking And Snack Time: Sharing Our Soup

What the children will learn
To prepare a vegetable soup

Materials you will need
Large soup pot, cutting boards, knives, vegetable peelers, vegetables

What to do
1. Read the passage from UNCLE WILLIE AND THE SOUP KITCHEN that describes the vegetables that go into the soup.
2. Ask the cafeteria manager to give the children a vegetable soup recipe which would make one large pot of soup.
3. Compare the recipes, making sure that all the vegetables Uncle Willie mentions are added.
4. Purchase the vegetables.
5. Scrub the vegetables and allow them to drain.

6. Set up the cutting board for chopping vegetables.

7. Organize the children into pairs so that each pair is chopping or peeling vegetables.

8. Ask the cafeteria manager or worker to demonstrate how to chop vegetables easily and safely.

9. Show the children how to use vegetable peelers.

10. Assemble the soup and take it to the cafeteria for cooking.

11. Donate the soup to a soup kitchen.

Something to think about
Pour some of the soup into a crock pot and let it simmer in the classroom for the children to smell. Reserve some soup for the children to eat, recalling how Uncle Willie and the boy ate a bowl of soup before serving the others.

STORY STRETCHER
For Social Studies: Canned Food Harvest

What the children will learn
The satisfaction of knowing that their family is helping a neighbor in need

Materials you will need
Large heavy-duty cardboard box, newsletter to parents

What to do
1. Contact a local soup kitchen or another organization that helps the poor and find out how they prefer to receive donations of canned food.

2. Talk with the children about how they can help their neighbors who are hungry by donating cans of food.

3. Compose a newsletter to parents telling them about the project.

4. Set up the collection box for the canned food and leave it up for a week.

5. Invite a representative of the organization to come to the school, or deliver the box to them.

Something to think about
According to the preface in UNCLE WILLIE AND THE SOUP KITCHEN, one in every eight people is poor. Many are children. Not all of them are homeless. Working poor who cannot make enough to cover all their expenses also visit soup kitchens. If you have children who have eaten at soup kitchens, be aware of and respect their feelings. Some may volunteer to talk about the soup kitchen, but others may be embarrassed.

ANOTHER STORY STRETCHER
For Social Studies: Assisting Volunteers For A Day

What the children will learn
To understand what volunteers do, and how to do a volunteer job well

Materials you will need
Chart paper, marker, camera, film, bulletin board

What to do
1. Invite the principal or assistant principal to come to the classroom and list all the jobs that volunteers in the school do.

2. Make a chart of the jobs and the names of the volunteers.

3. Pair children from your classroom with volunteers who need assistants for a day.

4. Take pictures of the children and their partners doing their volunteer jobs.

5. Make a bulletin board display about the school volunteers.

Something to think about
It would be wonderful if everyone had an Uncle Willie to teach them about the neighborhood soup kitchen. If possible, invite volunteers from a soup kitchen to bring photographs of what they do, in order to show the children that your community responds to people who need help.

STORY STRETCHER
For Writing Center: Thank You Letters To Volunteers

What the children will learn
To know what to write in a thank you note and to express their appreciation in words

Materials you will need
Note paper, pencils, envelopes

What to do
1. Read a thank you note to the children, one which you wrote or received.

2. Have the children write thank you notes to the school volunteers they assisted.

3. Encourage the children to state at least one thing they learned about volunteering or about the job the volunteer does.

Something to think about
The children might also enjoy designing and decorating their own thank you notes.

DINOSAURS TO THE RESCUE! A GUIDE TO PROTECTING OUR PLANET

By Laurie Krasny Brown

and Marc Brown

These imaginary creatures offer solutions that neighborhoods can adapt to protect our planet. Reduce, reuse and recycle—the environmental 3R's—is the motto of these dinosaurs. Their advice includes things that children can easily do. The dinosaurs, with their humor and their funny names (like Slobosaurus), make the advice memorable as well as important. In this book, one of a series of humorous dinosaur books, Laurie Krasny Brown and Marc Brown have succeeded in sending a clear and important message calling on good neighbors to save the planet.

Read-Aloud Presentation

Children are often quite knowledgeable about ways they can help save the planet. Ask them to name some things they do or their families do. Write their good environmental habits on the chalkboard. Read DINOSAURS TO THE RESCUE! A GUIDE TO PROTECTING OUR PLANET, and add additional ideas to the list. Let the children brainstorm ways that the members of their classroom neighborhood could help save the planet. Add their suggestions to the list and make plans to start carrying them out right away.

STORY STRETCHER

For Cooking And Snack Time: Natural Packaging Fruits

What the children will learn
To choose snacks that do not include a lot of packaging

Materials you will need
Fruits, bowl

What to do
1. Purchase an assortment of fruits for snack time.

2. Let the children peel their fruits, but instead of throwing the peelings in the trash, ask them to leave the peelings in a bowl.

3. After the children have eaten their fruits, add the cores and stems to the bowl.

4. Save the fruit peels, cores and stems for composting. Explain to the children what it means that their snacks are biodegradable. See the science and nature story s-t-r-e-t-c-h-e-r.

Something to think about
Suggest that the children look at DINOSAURS TO THE RESCUE! and compare their snacks to the wrapped ones in the illustrations. All their fruit snacks are biodegradable.

STORY STRETCHER

For Mathematics: Saving, Sorting And Cashing In

What the children will learn
The value of recycling

Materials you will need
Recycling bins for tin, aluminum, newspaper, paper, cardboard, plastics and green, brown and clear glass

What to do
1. Contact the community recycling director and find out which materials can be recycled for cash.

2. Collect cans, newspapers, paper, cardboard, glass and plastics.

3. Organize a recycling effort in your classroom by planning for the collection and storage of materials until they can be recycled. Stress cleanliness.

4. When materials that can be recycled for cash are collected, let the class take them to the recycling center.

5. With the small profits from the recycling, purchase materials for the classroom to make recycling easier. For example, buy an aluminum can crusher.

Something to think about
Earning money by recycling materials is not easy because it takes huge quantities to make much money. Children should learn to appreciate recycling for the natural resources it saves.

For Social Studies: Our Neighborhood's Plan For Recycling

What the children will learn
To recycle materials

Materials you will need
Recycling materials from the mathematics story s-t-r-e-t-c-h-e-r

What to do
1. Talk about the 3R's of reduce, reuse and recycle. Encourage children not to buy snacks or other products with a lot of packaging. Discuss ways to reuse items rather than discarding them. Plan a recycling project.

2. Invite the manager of the community's recycling program to come to class to talk about ways children can help in their families.

3. Plan a field trip to the recycling center and involve all the children in putting materials in the appropriate bins.

Something to think about
Write a newsletter to parents informing them about the project and asking permission for their children to go on the recycling center field trip. Include the 3R's of protecting our environment and ideas for ways that families can save energy, water and oil. Print the newsletter on recycled paper.

For Special Project: Cleaning Up And A Litter Watch In Our Neighborhood

What the children will learn
To take positive steps to clean up their neighborhood and discourage littering

Materials you will need
Heavy paper bags or recyclable plastic ones

What to do
1. Select a neighborhood spot to pick up litter, such as the school grounds, a park or a stream. Avoid areas with heavy traffic like roads or parking lots.

2. Let pairs of children work together, one picking up and the other holding the bag, then alternating jobs.

3. Make a mound of the trash bags and help the children to see that litter takes a lot of time and effort to clean up.

4. Organize a litter watch. Have children who live near the area let the class know when another clean-up day is required because the place has become littered again.

Something to think about
Contact city officials and ask them to place no littering signs on the site.

For Science And Nature: Composting

What the children will learn
To recycle household food wastes that will biodegrade

Materials you will need
Wire container, large garden fork

What to do
1. Invite the county extension agent or another resource person from your neighborhood to come to the class to demonstrate how to compost household food wastes.

2. Begin a compost pile on the school grounds using a simple design that meets local health codes.

3. Make composting a regular routine by composting the peelings from the children's daily snacks.

4. When the compost is ready, use it to fertilize plants and shrubs on the school grounds.

Something to think about
Involve all the teachers at your grade level and take turns caring for the compost.

A COUNTRY FAR AWAY

By Nigel Gray

Illustrated by

Philippe Dupasquier

Two boys, one black and one white, awake on opposite sides of the world. Each goes through parallel experiences: eating, helping with family chores, celebrating the last day of school before summer, riding bikes, experiencing Mom having a baby, swimming, going shopping, having photographs taken, playing soccer, staying up late and looking at pictures of a country far away. They look at pictures of each other and wish they could be friends. In spite of their different neighborhoods, the boys have much in common. Each page is split horizontally: the top section shows the African boy, the middle contains the text and the bottom section shows the boy from a Western culture, probably the United States. Dupasquier's detailed and colorful illustrations bring home the truth that we share many commonalities.

Read-Aloud Presentation

Show the children the cover of A COUNTRY FAR AWAY and discuss whether or not they think these two boys have much in common. Make sure all the children can see the illustrations easily, because the similarities of their lives are revealed not by the text, but by the pictures. After you have read the book once, go back and ask several children to point out the comparison pictures. For example, both boys are drawing, but one on a chalk board and the other on a computer.

STORY STRETCHER

For Art: Drawing In Chalk And On The Computer

What the children will learn
To draw using chalk and a graphic design computer software program

Materials you will need
Chalkboard, chalk, pastels, computer, graphics software, printer

What to do
1. Look at Dupasquier's illustrations of the two boys making drawings, one using a computer and the other a chalkboard and chalk.
2. Let the children experiment with both.
3. Load the computer software and help the children draw and paint with it.
4. Print the finished products.
5. Discuss the pros and cons of each artistic medium.

Something to think about
The chalk is more portable than the computer and printer. The chalkboard drawing has to be erased, however, while the printer can reproduce the drawing. One

costs little and the other costs a great deal, comparatively.

STORY STRETCHER

For Classroom Library: Stories For Entertainment

What the children will learn
To retell a tale for entertainment

Materials you will need
Variety of flannel board stories, construction paper tickets

What to do
1. Show the children the illustrations of the two children enjoying stories.
2. Ask several children who enjoy storytelling to tell a story without props, or to select a story from the classroom library flannel board collection.
3. Schedule a storytelling day and have stories throughout the day.
4. At the first morning group time, let the children select the time of day for storytelling by the color of the ticket they choose, for example, green for morning group time, yellow for morning break, red for center time, blue for afternoon break.
5. Ask each storyteller to choose an assistant to take up tickets.

Something to think about
Teach the children a story from an African culture.

STORY STRETCHER

For Games: Soccer

What the children will learn
To play soccer at a rudimentary level

Materials you will need
Soccer ball, field, goals

What to do
1. Explain the positions: goalie, half-backs, full-backs and forwards or strikers. The goalie

tries to keep the opposing team from kicking the soccer ball into the net and scoring. Half-backs are the second line or mid-fielders, who play either offense or defense. Full-backs are defensive and protect the goals. Forwards play at the front line near the opposition's goal and try to score.

2. Demonstrate how to dribble the ball with the feet, how to pass and how to shoot to make a goal. Each goal wins one point.

3. Assemble teams to include both boys and girls.

4. Tell the children that in many parts of the world, soccer is called "football." It is one of the games most universally played and enjoyed by adults and children throughout the world.

Something to think about
Invite the physical education teacher or a volunteer soccer coach to help demonstrate this popular sport. Do not demonstrate head passes unless you have seasoned soccer players. Never allow children to choose sides, because the unpopular or less athletic are always the last chosen.

STORY STRETCHER
For Social Studies: Comparison Chart Of Neighborhoods

What the children will learn
To compare similar and contrasting activities

Materials you will need
Chalkboard and chalk or chart paper and marker

What to do
1. Make a comparison chart of the neighborhoods where the two boys live. Use three sheets of chart tablet paper or mark three columns on the chalkboard.

2. Label the columns, "what we do," "what is the same," "what is different."

3. With a small group of children, go through the book and fill out the chart.

4. After the comparison chart is finished, ask a child to retell the book without looking at the illustrations.

Something to think about
Leave the comparison chart on display in the library area with other books about neighborhoods. Let children who are interested draw illustrations and post them all around the chart.

STORY STRETCHER
For Writing Center: Adding A Third Child To The Story

What the children will learn
To see how they are similar and how they are different from the two boys

Materials you will need
Drawing or typing paper, paper cutter, stapler

What to do
1. Cut sheets of paper horizontally to create half-page strips like the ones in A COUNTRY FAR AWAY.

2. Create a page to correspond to each page of the book.

3. Let the children draw and write so as to show and tell how they are different from and similar to the two boys in the book.

4. Staple the pages together in order.

5. Have the children read their books as if they were extensions of A COUNTRY FAR AWAY.

Something to think about
Ask two children who come from very different cultures to write about their similarities and

differences. Children who live in the city and those who live in the country can also write a story together.

ANOTHER STORY STRETCHER
For Writing Center: Pen Pals By Computer Or By Mail

What the children will learn
To describe themselves in writing a simple letter

Materials you will need
Addresses from pen pal columns in teacher magazines, envelopes, pens, class pictures, computers, access to educational computer network for electronic mail

What to do
1. Take instant print photographs of the children.

2. Read part of a letter from one of your friends. Discuss how special it makes you feel to receive a letter.

3. Show the last page of A COUNTRY FAR AWAY and guide the children toward deciding that there are ways for the two boys to communicate.

4. Contact a teacher listed in one of the pen pal columns in teacher magazines and confirm that his or her classroom is still available.

5. Show the children a copy of the magazine. Talk about pen pals, how they write to each other and sometimes establish friendships by mail.

6. Brainstorm with the children what they want to tell their pen pals about themselves.

7. Demonstrate how to communicate by way of electronic mail.

8. Devise a schedule for communicating that will allow

every child to become involved in the e-mail project.

Something to think about
Both these activities require preparatory work by the teacher. The school librarian is a good source for magazines with pen pal columns. Worldwide Friendship International, 3749 Bryce Run Road Suite A, Randallstown, MD 21133 is a good source for pen pal information. Or "adopt" a class in a nearby school as pen pals. If you do not have access to an electronic mail system, contact the person at the school district office in charge of technology. She or he can usually provide a demonstration.

References

Brown, Laurie Krasny and Brown, Marc. (1992). **DINOSAURS TO THE RESCUE! A GUIDE TO PROTECTING OUR PLANET**. Boston: Little Brown.

DiSalvo-Ryan, DyAnne. (1991). **UNCLE WILLIE AND THE SOUP KITCHEN**. New York: Morrow.

Dooley, Norah. (1991). **EVERYBODY COOKS RICE**. Illustrated by Peter J. Thornton. Minneapolis: Carolrhoda.

Gray, Nigel. (1988). **A COUNTRY FAR AWAY**. Illustrated by Philippe Dupasquier. New York: Orchard.

Politi, Leo. (1976, 1993). **THREE STALKS OF CORN**. New York: Macmillan.

Additional References for Neighborhood

Chalofsky, Margie, Finland, Glen and Wallace, Judy. (1992). **CHANGING PLACES: A KID'S VIEW OF SHELTER LIVING**. Mt. Rainier, MD: Gryphon House. *A collection of poignant personal narratives from children who have lived in homeless shelters.*

Derros, Arthur. (1992). **THIS IS MY HOUSE**. New York: Scholastic. *Text and illustrations depict the different types of houses lived in by children all over the world. On each page "This is my house" will appear in the appropriate native language.*

Root, Phyllis. (1992.. **THE OLD RED ROCKING CHAIR**. Illustrated by John Stanford. New York: Arcade Publishing. *An old rocking chair is recycled through a neighborhood, broken down bit by bit as young and old find various uses for it, until it ends up as a tiny footstool in the hands of the original owner.*

Wallner, Alexandra. (1992). **SINCE 1920.** New York: Doubleday. *As the years pass a quiet country house is overtaken by the growing city, until the granddaughter of the original homeowner helps to restore the neighborhood to its former beauty.*

Wheatley, Nadia and Rawlins, Donna. (1992). **MY PLACE**. Brooklyn: Kane/Miller. *Depicts life in Australia at different times in its development by viewing one place in different years while moving backwards from 1988-1788.*

ENDANGERED ANIMALS

Tigress
Look Out for Turtles!
Prince William
World Water Watch
Will We Miss Them? Endangered Species

ENDANGERED ANIMALS

TIGRESS

By Helen Cowcher

A tigress and her cubs prowl the boundaries of a wildlife sanctuary. Just beyond the sanctuary, goat herders leisurely watch their herd. Suddenly, they hear a monkey shriek, sounding the danger signal, but it is too late, a goat is dead. The herdsman warns the others and notifies the ranger. Later, a stray camel is killed. The herdsmen and ranger devise a clever plan to drive the tigress and cubs far back into the sanctuary. Helen Cowcher's boldly dramatic paintings cover the facing pages with unusual perspectives. These glowing pictures illuminate a powerful story of animals in conflict with humans and a peaceful resolution achieved.

Read-Aloud Presentation

Talk with the children about what we mean by a sanctuary, a preserve, a conservation area. Discuss why animals need a safe place for protection. Read TIGRESS without pausing until the passage in which the herders and the ranger are trying to think of a way to protect the goats and camels without threatening the tigress and her cubs. See whether the children can think of solutions. Finish the story and relish the clever decision that the herders and the ranger devise. Announce the story s-t-r-e-t-c-h-e-r-s that the children may choose.

STORY STRETCHER

For Art: Droplets, Watercolor Effects

What the children will learn
To load paints onto the watercolor brush and to create a textured effect

Materials you will need
Watercolors, watercolor paper, masking tape, brushes, water, paper towels

What to do
1. Tape the watercolor paper to the table with masking tape. Tape all around the edges.

2. Show the children how to load the paint onto the brush.

3. Demonstrate how to create a watercolor background bysmoothly gliding the brush across the paper without retracing the strokes already made.

4. Let the children experiment with the watercolors.

5. Allow the watercolor backgrounds to dry.

6. Show the children the watercolor backgrounds in Helen Cowcher's paintings. Notice the marks that texture the paper and look like water spots.

7. Deliberately drop a few drops of water onto the dried paper.

8. Let the paper dry again, and notice the textures created.

9. Demonstrate how to use a drier brush, barely moistening the watercolor paints, and painting with them much like tempera paints.

Something to think about
Allow the children to create their own scenes with favorite animals or endangered animals or animals found in TIGRESS. If an artist wants to paint something else entirely, allow him or her to do so.

ANOTHER STORY STRETCHER

For Art: Night Scenes

What the children will learn
To paint with colors which convey night

Materials you will need
Watercolor paints (dark blues, browns, purple, blacks, white), brushes, water, margarine tubs, paper towels, scrap paper, full sheets of watercolor paper, masking tape

What to do
1. Look closely at the night scenes that show the tigress and cubs in silhouette, coming down the hill, and the herders hidden behind the thorn bushes.

2. Call attention to the different colors, shades and tints that the artist used to create the suspenseful and mysterious night scene.

3. Encourage the children to experiment with the watercolor paints by adding white to lighten the tint.

4. Let them experiment with shading blue or purple by adding black to the mixture.

5. After the children have experimented, help them prepare their watercolor canvas by taping it down on the table, placing masking tape over all the edges.

Something to think about
Some children may be interested in trying to create the illumination that makes the tree trunks seem to glow. Show them how to paint the trunks in white first, then paint over the white with a darker color.

STORY STRETCHER

For Classroom Library: Dramatic Reading For A "Book On Tape" Recording

What the children will learn
To read a story with a sense of drama

Materials you will need
Audiotape cassette recorder, stapler, listening station, jack, headphones

What to do
1. Ask five children who seem particularly interested in the story to help you make a "dramatic" tape recording for the listening station.

2. One child makes the page-turning signal. The child holds a stapler near the microphone of the tape recorder and snaps the stapler to signal the turning of a page.

3. Seat the children in a circle at a table around the recorder. One child reads, then passes the book to the next child to read.

4. Rehearse the reading of the story so that all the children are comfortable with their passages.

5. Tape-record the story, including instructions at the beginning to explain the page-turning signal.

6. Listen to the tape and decide where to add more drama, where

to quiet the voices, where to shriek or to sound worried.

7. Record the story again and listen again.

8. During the second recording, listen with the headphones on and ask one child to turn the pages, just as children would do who are listening to the book on tape.

Something to think about
If you have a small bell, jingle it to make the page-turning signal. Also jingle it whenever the text says, "Goat bells jingle as they scramble over the rocky hillside."

STORY STRETCHER

For Cooking And Snack Time: Goat's Milk Or Goat's Cheese

What the children will learn
To taste unfamiliar foods

Materials you will need
Goat's milk or goat's cheese, crackers, apple juice, cups, napkins, cheese spreader or knife

What to do
1. Talk with the children about why the herders value their goats so highly—as the source of milk and cheese for their families.

2. Take a small swallow of goat's milk.

3. Slice or spread goat's cheese on crackers and serve with apple juice.

Something to think about
Serve a variety of cheeses, offering the goat's cheese as only one choice. If the children have a strong aversion to tasting these foods, do not push them, but do encourage them.

STORY STRETCHER

For Writing Center: Tigress And Cubs Adventure

What the children will learn
To use their previous knowledge to compose another adventure

Materials you will need
Writing paper, pencils, colored pens

What to do
1. Discuss how curious the ranger must be, wondering whether or not the tigress and her cubs are safe in the sanctuary. Invite them to imagine an adventure in which the ranger searches for the tigress and cubs.

2. Ask the children to brainstorm what might happen. After only a few comments, stop them and send them off to write, letting their individual imaginations take them into a story.

3. When the children finish writing, ask them to place their compositions in their writing folders.

4. Call editing conferences, during which children read their stories aloud. Let each group comment on the parts of the stories they find most exciting and intriguing. Compliment the children on descriptive or moving language.

5. During the editing conference, ask each listener to pose one question to the writer/reader, such as, "What did the ranger take with him into the sanctuary when he followed the tigress and her cubs?"

6. The writer can then decide whether or not to answer the question in redrafting the story.

7. Continue redrafting and editing until the writers are ready to publish their stories in book form. (See the directions for book binding in the Appendix.)

Something to think about
Not all stories need to be edited to final form. Encourage the children to select from among their compositions the ones with the most story potential.

LOOK OUT FOR TURTLES!

By Melvin Berger

Illustrated by Megan Lloyd

Turtles live longer than any other animal because they have remarkable survival skills. Both land and sea turtles can live almost anywhere and eat almost anything. Amazing facts are offered about the red-footed tortoise, desert tortoise, Marion's tortoise, diamondback terrapin, loggerhead turtle, wood turtle, eastern box turtle, common snapping turtle, green turtle, eastern mud turtle, leatherback turtle, Galapagos turtle, eastern painted turtle, Kemp's ridley turtle, and spotted turtle. The reader learns about turtle habitats and ways we can protect them. LOOK OUT FOR TURTLES! is a part of the Roma Gans Let's-Read-and-Find-Out Science Book series. As the publisher explains, these books are written with an understanding of how young children think: with texts brief enough for them to cope with, yet complex enough to challenge them. Megan Lloyd's realistic watercolor illustrations are nature art for elementary age children at its best.

Read-Aloud Presentation

Show the children an illustration in the book of a turtle found in your geographic location. Let the children share any personal experiences they have had with turtles, such as seeing them in their backyards, on the side of the road or at the zoo. Read LOOK OUT FOR TURTLES! and ask the children what they think the title means. The children will probably think that the title means to watch out or a turtle might bite them. Read the book and guide the children towards understanding the title's message, that even though the turtle is a survivor, some species have become endangered. Note that the book also calls turtles, "tortoises" and "terrapins." Land-dwelling turtles are often called tortoises. Terrapin is usually used with the name "diamondback."

STORY STRETCHER

For Art: Patterns Of Shells

What the children will learn
To recognize, describe and produce patterns that look like turtle shells

Materials you will need
Light brown or green construction paper, scissors, pastel chalks, colored pencils, hair spray

What to do
1. Cut large shapes like turtle shells from light brown or light green construction paper.

2. Ask the children to look through the illustrations of the turtles and describe the patterns found on their shells. Explain and use the term "geometric patterns."

3. Be sure to call attention to the eastern painted turtle, eastern box turtle and red-footed tortoise, or

another turtle that lives in your geographic location.

4. Ask the children to make turtle-like patterns on the construction paper shapes using pastel chalks or colored pencils or a combination.

5. When the artists are finished, spray their patterns with hair spray to prevent smudging.

Something to think about
Explain to the children why they should *never* paint or carve the shell of a real turtle.

STORY STRETCHER

For Classroom Library: Turtles In Reality And In Fantasy

What the children will learn
To compare what is real and what is not, and to think about how fantasy is often based on reality

Materials you will need
Various turtle stories like Aesop's Fable of "The Tortoise and the Hare," chart tablet, marker

What to do
1. Make a chart with two columns. Label one column "reality" and one column "fantasy based on reality."

2. Read to the children who come to the library corner Janet Steven's adaptation of Aesop's Fable "The Tortoise and the Hare."

3. After reading the fable, discuss the story's basis in the observation that land turtles move very slowly.

4. Write the title of the fable in the column "fantasy based on reality."

5. Show the children LOOK OUT FOR TURTLES! and have them decide in which column to write the title of the book.

Something to think about
Find Native American stories
which include turtles, such as the
retold story of FIRE RACE by
Jonathan London. Read an African
tale like HOW THE TURTLE
GOT ITS SHELL: AN AFRICAN
TALE by Sandra Robbins. Also
consider reading TORTOISE
SOLVES A PROBLEM by Avner
Katz.

STORY STRETCHER

For Mathematics: How Many Turtle Eggs In A Clutch?

What the children will learn
To recognize, count and prove
quantity

Materials you will need
Cotton balls, container

What to do
1.   Have the children who are
interested find the description of
the green turtle in LOOK OUT
FOR TURTLES! Read that
section again.

2.   Discuss the female turtle's
habit of laying 150 eggs.

3.   Let the children take cotton
balls from a bag or container and
try to guess how many 150 is.

4.   Depending upon how many
cotton balls you have, let the
children pile them up, then count
to see if they have close to 150.

5.   Ask the children to count out
exactly 150 cotton balls and place
them in the science display area
with a sign that states, "Green
turtles lay up to 150 eggs in a
clutch."

Something to think about
Let the children investigate other
comparisons of measurement
made in the book, like the
comparisons between the speed of
a human being and a tortoise on

land, and a human being and a sea
turtle swimming.

STORY STRETCHER

For Science And Nature: Studying A Turtle

What the children will learn
To observe the habits of a turtle at
close range

Materials you will need
A turtle, protected outdoor
environment, water supply, note
pads, pencils

What to do
1.   Contact a zoo director or
naturalist in your community.

2.   Arrange for a turtle to live in a
protected area of the school
grounds.

3.   Let teams of children study
the turtle by observing its behavior
over the course of a week.

4.   Each week the teams can
answer simple questions: "Where
is the turtle?" "Has the turtle
moved from one place to another
since yesterday at this time?"
"What is the turtle doing?" "What
is the turtle eating?"

5.   When the naturalist comes to
take the turtle back to its natural
environment, let the children tell
the naturalist what they have
observed and ask any questions
they have.

Something to think about
For the length of the study, place
the turtle in a fairly small area,
such as an atrium. If the school
yard natural environment offers
the turtle sufficient protection and
food supply, let the turtle live
naturally on the grounds. If it is
not possible to have the turtle on
the grounds, or you fear it would
not be safe, contact a pet store and
arrange for a turtle and a terrarium
to visit for a week.

STORY STRETCHER

For Science Display: Amazing Facts, True Or False

What the children will learn
To recall interesting facts and
realize that some facts which
sound amazing are true, while
others are false

Materials you will need
Index cards or Post-it notes,
markers, two empty tissue boxes

What to do
1.   Have a group of writers recall
amazing facts from LOOK OUT
FOR TURTLES!

2.   Let the writers check their
recollections in LOOK OUT FOR
TURTLES! and print them onto
cards.

3.   Ask the writers to think up
false and funny statements, such
as, "Green sea turtles turn green
because they eat green algae."
After the statement print, "Place
this statement in the box marked
'true' or the box marked, 'false.'"

4.   Let the writers think of funny
statements such as, "Ninja turtles
once lived and now appear on
Saturday morning cartoons."

Something to think about
Make a chart from page 31 of
LOOK OUT FOR TURTLES!,
which states what children can do
to help turtles survive.

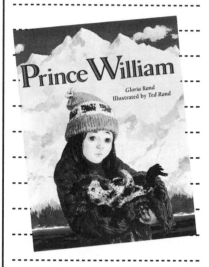

PRINCE WILLIAM

By Gloria Rand

Illustrated by Ted Rand

PRINCE WILLIAM is based on the true-to-life environmental disaster which occurred in Prince William Sound, Alaska. When a tanker crashes and spills millions of gallons of oil into the water, sea animals and birds suffer, and the pristine shoreline is spoiled. Denny, a little girl, is the main character in the drama, as she and her mother try to save a seal pup. Saving the seal, named Prince William, requires heroics. The reader also sees volunteers working to save the shoreline and the animals of sea and shore. The story is told sensitively yet accurately. The wonderfully expressive illustrations by Ted Rand highlight the beauty of Alaska and the perils threatening our environment.

Read-Aloud Presentation

Ask the children to look at the cover of PRINCE WILLIAM and tell what the little girl is feeling. The expression on her face shows that she is worried, probably about the seal she cradles in her arms. Introduce the little girl as Denny and the seal as Prince William. Read PRINCE WILLIAM and pause periodically to let the children predict what Denny and her family will do to help with the clean-up operation.

STORY STRETCHER

For Art: Before And After Pictures

What the children will learn
To illustrate sequential views of the same location

Materials you will need
Drawing and painting paper, crayons, markers, colored pens, paints, brushes

What to do
1. Have the children imagine the shoreline of Prince William Sound before the oil spill and draw or paint what they imagine, based on the impressions they gained from Ted Rand's illustrations.

2. Ask the children to create a second picture showing the oil spill and its effects on the same location.

Something to think about
Some children may prefer to illustrate a favorite scene from the book. Remember to allow children to choose their subjects. Whenever you ask children to make a drawing or painting, make it clear that they may draw or paint something else if they choose.

STORY STRETCHER

For Classroom Library: Reading About The Real Prince William Sound Oil Spill

What the children will learn
To compare newspaper accounts to what they learn from a fiction book based on fact

Materials you will need
Newspaper accounts of Prince William Sound and the Alaskan oil spill, chart paper, marker

What to do
1. Go to the public or school library and find 1989 newspaper reports on the Exxon oil tanker spill in Prince William Sound. Make a few photocopies.

2. On a large sheet of chart paper or the chalkboard, construct a two-column chart. At the head of the first column write "Book," and at the head of the second column print "Newspaper."

3. Read PRINCE WILLIAM again. Ask the children to list facts they learned from the book, including new terms like "containment booms."

4. Distribute the photocopied newspaper accounts and read them to the children.

5. After they listen to the newspaper accounts, let the children add facts and terms they learned to the chart.

Something to think about
Conduct this activity with a small group of children in the library corner of the classroom. At a large group session, have the small group share with their classmates what they learned. Invite the other classmates to come to the library corner the next day. Read a different newspaper account to them and try to add to the information.

Something else to think about
If possible, locate newspapers both from your own community and from Alaska that reported the oil spill.

STORY STRETCHER

For Mathematics: How Much Does It Cost To Feed Them?

What the children will learn
To calculate the cost of feeding wild animals in captivity

Materials you will need
Index cards, markers

What to do
1. Read the story of PRINCE WILLIAM again, pausing at each point where the text mentions an animal. Write the animal's name on an index card. For example, on the first page, the reader is told that Denny's father is away setting containment booms around the salmon fish hatchery to protect the salmon fry. Print on the card, "salmon fry."

2. The following birds and animals are mentioned:

   Seal pup
   Birds
   Otters
   Gulls
   Murres
   Kittiwakes
   Deer
   Bear and cubs
   Wolverines
   Eagles
   Herring

3. Read the end of the book where the authors describe how school children in Alaska helped buy food for the animals being cared for during the clean-up.

4. Telephone the education director of a zoo in a nearby city. Explain to the director that you want the children to learn how much it costs to care for a wild animal during a clean-up effort.

Give the director the list of animals.

5. Encourage the children to call the director and inquire about how much each animal eats per day, or how much it costs to feed an animal per day.

6. Have the children calculate how much it costs to care for an animal during a clean-up, both for one week and for ten weeks.

Something to think about
Many zoos make these calculations as part of their fund-raising activities. At the end of the book, there is a note that children in Alaska collected recyclable paper and cans, and sold popcorn to make money to help feed the animals. Call a recycling center and find out how much paper and cans the children would have to sell to feed each animal.

STORY STRETCHER

For Science And Nature: Oil Spills

What the children will learn
The difficulty of cleaning up oil spills

Materials you will need
Water table or child's plastic swimming pool, water, quart of oil, can opener, plastic wrapping tape, small pieces of fake fur, fabric

What to do
1. Talk with the children about how tankers carry oil and explain that once oil spills, it is very difficult to contain.

2. Fill the water table or plastic swimming pool with water.

3. Puncture a hole in the side of an oil can and place it in the water.

4. Invite the children to observe that the can leaks oil much like an oil tanker with a punctured hull.

5. Give the children pieces of plastic wrapping tape, twisted into a rope-like strand, and ask them to try to contain the oil slick.

6. Give the children small pieces of fake fur.

7. Let them float the fabric on the water and watch as it absorbs oil.

8. Dispose of the oily water at an oil recycling center.

Something to think about
Let the children try to clean the oil from the fabric.

STORY STRETCHER

For Writing Center: To Inquire About The Environment

What the children will learn
To write for information to answer their questions

Materials you will need
Paper, pencils, envelopes

What to do
1. Secure the address for the Chamber of Commerce, Prince William Sound, Alaska, or another location where an oil spill has occurred.

2. Let the children write for tourism information about Prince William Sound and ask how the area looks now.

3. When the children receive a response, have them write to thank the chamber and perhaps also to ask more questions.

Something to think about
If your school is connected to an electronic communication network, locate a school on the network in Alaska and ask questions about the oil spill and its effects.

WORLD WATER WATCH

Michelle Koch

WORLD WATER WATCH
By Michelle Koch

Beginning with the poem, "Watch over the world, watch over the water," the book teaches about animals who live in the oceans and upon the seashores around the world. Each animal is introduced by a child who is watching it. The text includes sea otters in Alaska, green sea turtles in Mexico, penguins in Antarctica, fur seals in Chile, polar bears in Norway, and humpback whales in Maui. The text alternates between larger and smaller print, the larger describing where the animals live and what the child sees, and the smaller offering interesting facts, including the ways in which governments and environmental agencies are trying to help the animals. Koch's illustrations are in watercolor, charming in their simplicity, most covering two facing pages. The cover features six smaller panels portraying the animals.

Read-Aloud Presentation

Show the children WORLD WATER WATCH. Ask them to identify the six animals on the cover: polar bear, whale, penguin, seal, sea otter and green turtle. Read the opening poem, which laments that these animals are dying because of problems in their habitat, the oceans. Write the names of the animals on the chalkboard, and ask the children to listen closely so they can "add-a-fact" about each animal. After the reading, add information about each animal on the chalkboard.

STORY STRETCHER

For Art: Colorful Watercolor Habitats

What the children will learn
To mix watercolors to create tints and shades

Materials you will need
Watercolors, brushes, palettes, scrap paper, watercolor paper, masking tape

What to do
1.   Note how Michelle Koch portrays each of the six oceans in a different color, and uses paint to portray the choppiness or stillness of water.

2.   Let the children experiment with mixing paint to create different watercolor tints and shades.

3.   Demonstrate how to mix watercolors by mixing a small amount of each color in a different area on the palette.

4.   Place the watercolor paper on a table top and tape it down along each edge.

5.   Ask the children to paint an ocean of their choice, depending on which animal most interests them. For example, if they are most interested in the polar bear, they should paint the ocean off the coast of Norway.

Something to think about
Taping paper down with masking tape allows it to dry evenly, without the crinkling caused when some sections of paper absorb more water than others.

STORY STRETCHER

For Classroom Library: Six Animals, Six Voices

What the children will learn
To read a simple text and follow along with the reader of a more complicated text

Materials you will need
Tape recorder, cassette tapes, listening station, jack, headphones, glass, fork

What to do
1.   With six interested children, look closely at the design of WORLD WATER WATCH. The text in large print is sufficiently simple for most second and third graders to read easily, and with practice, most first graders can read it.

2.   Let the children select an animal to read about from the six mentioned in the text. You should read the more difficult information in smaller print.

3.   Plan to tape-record the book. Ask one child to record the page-turning signal: a fork tapped against the side of a glass placed near the tape recorder microphone.

4.   Let one child introduce the book by stating the title, naming the animals pictured on the cover, and reminding listeners about the page-turning signal.

5. After the recording is made, place it in the listening center in the classroom library.

Something to think about
Since there are three boys and three girls in the book who keep watch over the oceans, find three boys and three girls to make the tape recording.

For Science And Nature: Danger Floating In The Ocean

What the children will learn
To identify which objects float

Materials you will need
Water table, tray, various metal or wooden or plastic classroom objects, plastic rings from six-packs, small pieces of wood, fishing wire, two reusable plastic containers, index cards, tape, marker

What to do
1. Fill the water table with water.
2. Let the children collect a variety of objects made of metal, wood and plastic from around the classroom.
3. Add objects such as small pieces of wood, fishing wire, tin cans and plastic rings from six-packs. Place all these objects on a tray near the water table.
4. Let the children experiment to see which objects float and which ones sink, and place the objects in the appropriate containers.
5. Tape an index card to each of the reusable plastic containers. On one card write, "Sink," on the other, "Float." After their experiments, sort the objects.

Something to think about
Talk with the children about the harm caused in the oceans by floating objects, which sea

creatures either mistake for food or become tangled in and die.

For Social Studies: Seas, Gulfs, And Oceans Of The World Water Watch

What the children will learn
To locate seas and ocean habitats

Materials you will need
World map or globe, Post-it notes

What to do
1. Gathering small groups of children at a time, read WORLD WATER WATCH again, pausing after each animal to point out on the map or globe the country where each child lives and the ocean where each animal lives.
2. On a Post-it note, write a sentence about the country and the ocean. For example, after hearing about the sea otters that live in the ocean bordering the little girl's home in Alaska, the children could compose the sentence, "The sea otters are swimming in the Gulf of Alaska."
3. Place the Post-it notes in the book on the appropriate pages.
4. At another read-aloud presentation the same day, read the information that the children added to the text.

Something to think about
Other examples of sentences include the following: The green sea turtles are swimming in the Gulf of Mexico. The penguins are diving in the Indian Ocean. The Juan Fernandez seals are lounging on the rocky shore of the South Pacific Ocean. The polar bears are floating on icebergs in the Norwegian Sea. The humpback whales are blowing plumes of water as they swim and dive in the Pacific Ocean.

For Writing Center: Write To An Environmental Organization

What the children will learn
To write for information

Materials you will need
Paper, pencils, envelopes, stamps

What to do
1. Talk with the children about environmental organizations that try to protect the animals and the oceans. Many of these organizations have branches for children.
2. Identify three or four organizations and invite the children to write for information about their special interests. For example, some may be interested in research, as is the Cousteau organization, or interested in saving a specific animal, as is Save-the-Whales.
3. Let the children decide which organization to write to, based on their interests.
4. Demonstrate the correct letter form.
5. Edit their letters.
6. Let the children address and stamp the envelopes and mail their letters.

Something to think about
Write to the National Audubon Society, 700 Broadway, New York NY 10003 or to the Center for Environmental Information, 50 West Main Street, Rochester NY 14614. For the return address, use the school address to prevent the children's home addresses from being placed on mailing lists. Some organizations sell their mailing lists to make money.

ENDANGERED ANIMALS

WILL WE MISS THEM? ENDANGERED SPECIES

By Alexandra Wright

Illustrated by Marshall Peck III

A sixth grader from Countryside Elementary in Newton, Massachusetts, Alexandra Wright, wrote WILL WE MISS THEM? ENDANGERED SPECIES. She describes where endangered animals live, why they are vanishing, interesting facts and any special needs they have. The animals discussed include the bald eagle, elephant, blue whale, panda, Galapagos tortoise, mountain lion, whooping crane, grizzly bear, manatee, muriqui, rhinoceros, mountain gorilla and crocodile. The book also includes a world map showing habitats and a few encouraging words about protection of wildlife. Marshall Peck III's brightly colored illustrations in acrylic show animals in a variety of natural poses and native surroundings.

Read-Aloud Presentation

Engage the children in discussion of the implications of the title, WILL WE MISS THEM? Lead the discussion into consideration of endangered species. Read WILL WE MISS THEM? ENDANGERED SPECIES. Point out on the map the endangered animal species nearest your home. After reading the book, announce that it was written by an author who is in the sixth grade. Turn to the back dust jacket cover and read about Alexandra Wright and the illustrator, Marshall Peck III.

STORY STRETCHER

For Art: Animal Cutouts

What the children will learn
To make a drawing using the most effective medium

Materials you will need
An array of art supplies, such as tempera, watercolor, acrylic paints, paper, brushes, crayons, colored pencils, markers, charcoals, pastel chalks, hair spray, construction paper, posterboard, scissors, stapler, hole puncher, yarn or string

What to do
1. With the children who come to the art center, look at Marshall Peck's illustrations. Ask the children which art medium they would choose to portray the different animals. For example, watercolor might be a good choice for the whale, which swims under water. Colored pen might be a good choice for the whooping crane, and pastel chalk and charcoal for the grizzly in its cave.

2. Let the children sketch or paint any animal using any medium or mix of media that they choose.

3. Ask the children to cut out the animals they have drawn or painted.

4. Glue or staple a small posterboard tab at the top of each animal. Punch a hole in the posterboard and thread yarn through it to make a loop.

5. Use the animal cutouts in the "Sorting By Habitat Bulletin Board" story s-t-r-e-t-c-h-e-r.

Something to think about
Finish charcoal and pastel chalk drawings by lightly spraying with hair spray to keep them from smudging.

STORY STRETCHER

For Classroom Library: Riddle Writers Write Animal Riddles

What the children will learn
To confirm their knowledge about animals

Materials you will need
Large index cards, markers, copy of WILL WE MISS THEM? ENDANGERED SPECIES

What to do
1. With a small group of children, write out riddles based on the information in WILL WE MISS THEM? ENDANGERED SPECIES. There are fascinating facts about each animal in the book.

2. Have the children read the book and decide what would make a good riddle.

3. Create riddle cards and answer cards. Write a question on a riddle card. On an answer card, restate the question as an answer. For example, the riddle card might read, "What animal can spot small animals moving in a field a mile away?" The answer card could reply, "When bald eagles fly in search of their dinner, they can

spot small animals moving in a field a mile away."

4. Leave the riddle cards in the classroom library with the endangered animal books.

5. Ask the riddle writers to continue making new riddle cards as the class learns more about endangered animals from other books.

Something to think about
For younger children, simplify the questions and answers. You can also devise a simple system which they can use to check their answers. Make riddle puzzles by cutting the index cards into two puzzle shapes which fit together.

STORY STRETCHER

For Science And Nature: Sorting By Habitat Bulletin Board

What the children will learn
To determine the habitats of endangered species

Materials you will need
Bulletin board, butcher paper, scissors, colored chalks, crayons, markers, animal cutouts from the art story s-t-r-e-t-c-h-e-r, push pins, small step stool

What to do
1. Staple butcher paper onto two bulletin boards.

2. On one bulletin board, make long, sweeping lines with colored chalk to create the habitats of sky, flatland, mountains, cave, rocky seashore, ocean.

3. On the second bulletin board, make long, sweeping lines with colored chalk to represent rain forest, jungle, water hole, marshland.

4. Let the children color in the habitats with crayons and markers.

5. Place many push pins into the different habitats.

6. Place the animal cutouts near the bulletin boards. Let the children put the cutouts onto the bulletin board habitats where they belong.

7. Encourage many different arrangements: the bald eagle could be placed in the sky and in the trees near the mountains.

Something to think about
You do not have to be an artist to make these bulletin boards. Even faint lines will be sufficient to remind the children of the habitats that they are supposed to represent. The step stool allows the children to reach high enough to place the eagles in the sky and the muriqui near the top of the rain forest canopy.

ANOTHER STORY STRETCHER

For Science And Nature: Visiting A Zoo

What the children will learn
More about endangered animals and the role the zoo plays in protecting species

Materials you will need
Transportation, field trip permission forms, volunteers

What to do
1. Arrange a class visit to the zoo by talking with the education director of the zoo ahead of time. Ask the education director to come to your class to talk before the visit, if possible, and also to greet the children on the day of the class visit.

2. Obtain maps of the zoo before the visit and show the children the path the class plans to take through the zoo.

3. On the maps, mark the locations of endangered animals you have studied.

4. Prepare parent volunteers to supervise and interact educationally with the students. With first graders, plan to have one volunteer for every two children. With second and third graders, plan one volunteer per four children.

5. Either ask a parent volunteer who is a good photographer to take pictures of the endangered animals, or purchase slides in the gift shop. Ask another parent to take candid photographs of the children.

Something to think about
One of the most difficult challenges for a teacher on a field trip is that children are likely to become over-stimulated with the excitement of being at the zoo. Plan ahead to include time and space for relaxation.

STORY STRETCHER

For Writing Center: Writing Thank You Letters To The Zoo

What the children will learn
To write a thank you note and to express their feelings

Materials you will need
Construction paper, colored pencils, markers, large mailing envelope

What to do
1. Ask each child to fold a piece of construction paper in half, vertically or horizontally, to make a thank you note.

2. On the outside of the thank you notes, write the words, "Thank You," and decorate the words with different colors or shading.

3. On the inside of the thank you note, ask the children to write their appreciation to the zoo for protecting animals from extinction, or for building a more natural habitat or for researching the best care of endangered species.

4. Somewhere on the note, ask the children to sketch one of their favorite animals.

5. Mail the thank you notes in the large envelope to the education director of the zoo.

Something to think about
Older children can cut shapes in the construction paper and place their drawing of the animal inside, where it can be seen through the cutout.

References

Berger, Melvin. (1992). **LOOK OUT FOR TURTLES!** Illustrated by Megan Lloyd. New York: Harper Collins.

Cowcher, Helen. (1991). **TIGRESS**. New York: Farrar, Straus, and Giroux.

Koch, Michelle. (1993). **WORLD WATER WATCH**. New York: Greenwillow.

Rand, Gloria. (1992). **PRINCE WILLIAM**. Illustrated by Ted Rand. New York: Henry Holt.

Wright, Alexandra. (1992). **WILL WE MISS THEM? ENDANGERED SPECIES**. Illustrated by Marshall Peck III. Watertown, MA: Charlesbridge.

Also Mentioned in this Chapter

Aesop. (1984). **THE TORTOISE AND THE HARE**. Adapted by Janet Stevens. New York: Holiday House.

Katz, Avner. (1993). **TORTOISE SOLVES A PROBLEM**. New York: HarperCollins.

London, Jonathan. (1993). **FIRE RACE: A KARUK COYOTE TALE**. Illustrated by Sylvia Long. San Francisco: Chronicle.

Robbins, Sandra. (1990). **HOW THE TURTLE GOT ITS SHELL: AN AFRICAN TALE**. Illustrated by Iku Oseki. New York: Berrent Publications.

Additional References for Endangered Animals

Cowcher, Helen. (1990). **ANTARCTICA**. New York: Farrar, Straus, and Giroux. *Examines the dangers faced by penguins and seals, including danger from humans.*

Kitchen, Bert. (1992). **SOMEWHERE TODAY**. Cambridge, Massachusetts: Candlewick Press. *Describes unusual animal rituals of work, play, courtship and survival.*

Lewin, Ted. (1990). **TIGER TREK**. New York: Macmillan. *Riding on the back of an elephant, the author tours a wildlife park in India, observing the hunting behavior of a mother tiger.*

Schoenhess, John. (1991). **BEAR**. New York: Philomel. *Searching for his mother, a young bear finds his own independence.*

Uchitel, Sandra. (1992). **ENDANGERED ANIMALS OF THE RAINFOREST**. Illustrated by Serge Michaels. Los Angeles: Price Stein Sloan. *Describes the characteristics of tropical rain forests, examines the plight of endangered rain forest animals and discusses how readers can help save these threatened areas.*

OCEANS

The Magic School Bus on the Ocean Floor
Is This a House for Hermit Crab?
An Octopus Is Amazing
Sam the Sea Cow
Whales

THE MAGIC SCHOOL BUS ON THE OCEAN FLOOR

By Joanna Cole

Illustrated by Bruce Degen

When Ms. Frizzle announces a class trip to the ocean, the children think she means a day at the beach, but Ms. Frizzle drives the Magic School Bus right into the ocean. The class explores the intertidal zone (where the tide meets the shore), the continental shelf (where the land slants down and is covered by the ocean), the deep ocean floor (where little light reaches), and the coral reef, before returning to shore. The Magic School Bus changes into a submarine, a submersible, a glass-bottom boat and a giant surfboard. When the children return, Ms. Frizzle's classroom is also transformed, becoming a giant science display that explains everything the children have learned. Readers will recognize Bruce Degen's trademark illustrations. The Cole and Degen combination is magical, and the mix of fact, humor and fantasy makes this an excellent book with which to launch a study of the oceans.

Read-Aloud Presentation

Recall with the children other MAGIC SCHOOL BUS adventures, such as THE MAGIC SCHOOL BUS AT THE WATERWORKS, THE MAGIC SCHOOL BUS INSIDE THE EARTH, THE MAGIC SCHOOL BUS INSIDE THE HUMAN BODY, THE MAGIC SCHOOL BUS LOST IN THE SOLAR SYSTEM. Often the mere sight of a Magic School Bus book will bring applause. Ask the children what they like so much about the Magic School Bus series of books. Read THE MAGIC SCHOOL BUS ON THE OCEAN FLOOR without pausing to read the children's written reports or the classroom charts on the sidebars. After reading, first let the children comment on the story, then ask everyone to write in their learning logs at least one amazing fact they learned from the book. Of course, if you live near an ocean, plan a trip there.

STORY STRETCHER
For Art: Factual Ocean Murals

What the children will learn
To present information in an aesthetically pleasing manner

Materials you will need
Butcher paper, stapler, masking tape, colored pencils, chalks, markers

What to do
1.   With the children, decide on a number of different ocean murals. Examples might include an ocean food chain, intertidal zone, continental shelf, ocean floor, coral reef, the ways fish move or a favorite fish.

2.   Talk with the students about making the information on the murals accurate and, because it

will decorate the room, aesthetically pleasing as well.

3.   Cut table-length strips of butcher paper. Let the paper hang off the edge and tape it down to the sides of the table.

4.   Let teams of children work on each mural.

5.   When the murals are complete, trim the edges and hang them around the room for the children to study.

Something to think about
For a related story s-t-r-e-t-c-h-e-r, create a Ms. Frizzle print using liquid embroidery to paint an ocean scene on old T-shirts.

ANOTHER STORY STRETCHER
For Art: Fish Mobiles And Balloons

What the children will learn
To improvise a three-dimensional representation

Materials you will need
Construction paper, tissue paper, newspaper, coat hangers, fishing wire, tempera paints, brushes, balloons, markers, glue, tape, stapler, gift wrap ribbon

What to do
1.   Look near the end of the book at the artistic representations of fish that Ms. Frizzle's students create.

2.   Have the children brainstorm ways to show the beauty of fish.

3.   Demonstrate how to make a fish mobile by cutting fish shapes from construction paper and gluing them around the edges, leaving a small opening through which crumpled newspaper can be stuffed.

4.   Let the children also experiment with decorating the balloons to create jellyfish and

octopus. Tie strings on the balloons and let them float in the air.

5. Create fish mobiles by stapling fishing wire onto the construction paper fish and tying the wire from a coat hanger.

Something to think about
Plan a huge Magic School Bus display by covering a bulletin board with yellow construction paper and inviting the children to decorate it.

STORY STRETCHER

For Classroom Library: "I Have Always Wondered"

What the children will learn
To find answers to their questions

Materials you will need
Reference books on the ocean, chart tablet, marker

What to do
1. Begin the "I Always Wondered" activity by thinking aloud. For example, say "I always wondered why the sea is salty."

2. Ask the children to think of questions they always wondered about and write them on chart tablet paper.

3. Find as many of the answers as possible in the margins of each page of the book, where the reports and charts made by Ms. Frizzle's class are printed. Search for other answers in books read as a part of this unit and in reference books.

4. Begin another chart of "Amazing Facts," such as "Whale sharks are not whales."

5. Include a third set of questions, but instead of labeling them "Ms. Frizzle's questions," insert your name.

Something to think about
Ms. Frizzle's classroom offers an excellent example of the many ways children can investigate a topic, even without the Magic School Bus.

STORY STRETCHER

For Mathematics: Sorting Seashells And Coral

What the children will learn
To name and categorize seashells and coral

Materials you will need
Small baskets or boxes, many seashells and coral, index cards, markers

What to do
1. Help the children identify a number of seashells by comparing them to the drawings in THE MAGIC SCHOOL BUS ON THE OCEAN FLOOR.

2. Ask the children to categorize the seashells by a number of different attributes, such as size, shape, whether people regard the animal as a food.

Something to think about
Older children may be able to categorize the seashells by whether the animals live in the intertidal zone, on the continental shelf or on a coral reef.

STORY STRETCHER

For Science Display: Salting The Water

What the children will learn
To create a three-dimensional display of different geological formations

Materials you will need
Aquarium, plastic pan or dish about 12" X 12," two-pound boxes of salt, spoons, pebbles, sand

What to do
1. To illustrate how salty most of the ocean is, fill a 12" X 12" pan or dish with water. Let the children pour in two pounds of salt and taste the water.

2. Pour the salt water into the aquarium.

3. Let groups of children take turns creating geological formations in the aquarium by adding sand and pebbles. Encourage the groups to make their representations demonstrate that what looks like an island above the water is really a mountain top. They can create the intertidal zone, the continental shelf and the mountains and valleys of deep ocean.

Something to think about
If resources are available, invite a pet store owner to help the children establish and monitor a salt water aquarium.

OCEANS

IS THIS A HOUSE FOR HERMIT CRAB?

By Megan McDonald

Illustrated by S.D. Schindler

In this beautifully illustrated book, the reader follows a hermit crab searching for a new house because he has outgrown his. He tries on a rock, a rusty old tin can, a piece of driftwood, a plastic pail and an already occupied fiddler crab shell. In the process, hermit crab becomes tangled in a fishing net and is swept out to sea where he is almost eaten by a prick-lepine fish. But finally, hermit crab finds a snail shell for a new home. S.D. Schindler's illustrations are beautiful pastel chalks on deeply textured paper.

Read Aloud Presentation

Talk with the children about "outgrowing" their clothes. What do they notice when their clothes have gotten too little? Mention some piece of clothing you use to wear which was a favorite piece and how disappointed you were when it no longer fit. Discuss how some people say they have "outgrown" their houses. Let the children decide what that might mean. When a grandparent comes to live with them, when a new baby is born, when the children grow and accumulate toys and books, then it may become a tight squeeze at home. Tell the children that hermit crab has something which he has outgrown and has a problem to be solved. Read IS THIS A HOUSE FOR HERMIT CRAB?

STORY STRETCHER

For Art: Watery Pastel Chalks

What the children will learn
Materials you will need
Paper towels, water, pastel chalks

What to do
1. Sprinkle a few drops of water onto a paper towel, just enough to dampen it.
2. Spread the paper towel out flat.
3. Draw seascapes on paper towels using pastel chalks.
4. Leave the paper towels to dry overnight.
5. Display the chalk drawings of the ocean around the classroom.

Something to think about
Use coarse brown paper towels and white paper towels. Wetting the toweling allows the colors from the chalks to go deeper into the paper fibers.

ANOTHER STORY STRETCHER

For Art: Driftwood And Seashell Centerpieces

What the children will learn
To arrange objects found in nature as part of a pleasing display

Materials you will need
Driftwood or small tree branch, sand, seashells, baskets, colorful cloth or place mats

What to do
1. Place the materials in the art center.
2. Ask several children to arrange the materials to create a centerpiece for the snack table.
3. Add additional objects, like interesting rocks or pebbles.
4. On other days, have other children make new displays using the same objects.

Something to think about
As the art displays take shape, talk with the children about symmetrical and asymmetrical balance, about the greater appeal of groupings composed of threes and fives. Observe their natural sense of the attributes of a pleasing display.

STORY STRETCHER

For Classroom Library: Flannel Board Story

What the children will learn
To recall the sequence of events

Materials you will need
Flannel board, felt or construction paper and colored pencils, old emery boards, scissors, glue, pencil, large resealable plastic bag, masking tape

What to do

1. Have the children create a flannel board story of the book by looking through the illustrations and deciding what pieces they would need to make to retell the story. At a minimum these should include Hermit crab, old shell, rock, old tin can, driftwood or large piece of bark, pail, fiddler crab shell, pricklepine fish and snail shell.

2. Let the children decide whether to make the flannel board pieces out of felt or construction paper.

3. Roughly sketch the pieces in outline on felt and cut them out. If construction paper is used, the children can draw and color the pieces, cut them out, then glue old pieces of emery board to the backs of the pieces to make them adhere better to the flannel.

4. Store the flannel board pieces in a large resealable plastic bag. Place a strip of masking tape across the plastic bag and print the title of the story on the masking tape.

5. Place the flannel board, the story pieces and the book in the class library area.

Something to think about
Teachers often think of flannel board stories as only appropriate for younger children. If the third graders feel that flannel board stories are too young for them, ask them to make one for the kindergartners and first graders, and use it to tell the story to the younger children. We also find flannel board stories are excellent for students of English as a second language.

For Classroom Library: Puppet Show With Hermit Crab

What the children will learn
To improvise dialogue using puppet and props

Materials you will need
Gardening glove, pipe cleaners, permanent markers, rock, driftwood or bark, tin can, plastic pail, snail shell, crab shell, fishing net, plastic eyes from a craft store (optional), glue (optional), construction paper and tongue depressors or wooden spoons (optional)

What to do

1. Read the back jacket cover of IS THIS A HOUSE FOR HERMIT CRAB? which tells the reader that Megan McDonald is a librarian who wrote the book when she created a puppet story to teach children about hermit crabs.

2. Let the children create their own hermit crab puppet from a gardening glove which they decorate using pipe cleaners for tentacles, drawing eyes or gluing on plastic eyes. An alternative is to make a stick puppet out of construction paper and glue it onto a tongue depressor or wooden spoon.

3. Assemble the props: the rock, old tin can, driftwood or bark, plastic pail, crab shell, fishing net, construction paper cutout of pricklepine fish, snail shell

Something to think about
Extend the puppet show story s-t-r-e-t-c-h-e-r by asking third graders to write a script for their puppet show.

For Science Display: Hermit Crab Visits The Classroom

What the children will learn
To observe the way hermit crabs move and eat

Materials you will need
Aquarium, sand, hermit crab, chopped-up raw fish, raw shrimp in the shell

What to do

1. Visit a pet store and purchase a hermit crab. Ask the owner for specific directions about how to care for the hermit crab.

2. Set up the aquarium with the sand, feeding dish and a small piece of wood for the crab to burrow near.

3. Have the children decide on a name for the hermit crab and plan for its care and feeding.

4. Place the aquarium in the science display area for the children to observe.

5. Ask the students to write their observations in their science learning logs and add illustrations.

Something to think about
Plan for what you will do with the hermit crab after the unit is over. One of the best ideas is to pass the crab onto another classroom. Or plan to return the hermit crab to a city aquarium or to the pet store owner.

AN OCTOPUS IS AMAZING

By Patricia Lauber

Illustrated by Holly Keller

The ability of an octopus to camouflage itself by changing colors, even becoming striped or spotted, is truly amazing. Known also for its ability to stave off an attacker with a cloud of ink, the octopus is amazing in the ways it eats, moves and cares for its young. Octopuses in aquariums have been observed solving problems like how to open clams or twist off jar lids, and interacting with the people they come to recognize. AN OCTOPUS IS AMAZING is a Let's-Read-and-Find-Out Science Book inspired by Roma Gans, Professor Emeritus of Childhood Education, Teachers College, Columbia University. Holly Keller's simple black-line and painted drawings give objects a distinct edge, which makes it easy for children to see them during group read-aloud sessions.

Read-Aloud Presentation

Talk with the children about what they already know about the octopus. Perhaps some have seen an octopus in an aquarium. List on the chalkboard the facts the children already know. Read the title, AN OCTOPUS IS AMAZING, and tell the children that this is a factual book. Every statement in the book is true, even though some are amazing. After reading the book, invite the children to add to their list of what they know about the octopus.

STORY STRETCHER

For Art: Camouflage Collage

What the children will learn
To show how the octopus uses camouflage for survival

Materials you will need
Construction paper, glue, brush, sand, rocks, pebbles, shells, tissue paper, paints, paintbrushes, markers, crayons, colored pens, scissors

What to do
1.   Ask the children to make at least three octopuses and show them in various colors or patterns of camouflage.

2.   Paint a line of glue along the bottom of the sheet of construction paper and sprinkle with sand. Shake off any excess.

3.   Have the children cut out the octopuses and glue them onto the construction paper.

4.   Add pebbles, rocks and shells.

5.   Cut seaweed shapes from tissue paper and glue them onto the collage.

Something to think about
Consider making a diorama of the octopus and its sea home by placing these materials inside a shoe box and displaying it by turning the box on its side.

STORY STRETCHER

For Mathematics: Comparisons Of Size

What the children will learn
To measure, compare and represent different lengths

Materials you will need
Butcher paper, scissors, masking tape, yardsticks, rulers, crayons, tempera paints, brushes

What to do
1.   Show the illustration near the front of the book of four octopuses, on the page titled, "There are more than 150 known kinds of octopus."

2.   Have the children read the measurements given on this page, then cut lengths of butcher paper a few inches longer than the measurements. For example, the common octopus is usually 30 inches long. Cut a piece of butcher paper 32-34 inches in length. The giant octopus is 17 feet long; cut the paper 18 feet long.

3.   Let one child draw each octopus. The child drawing the seventeen-foot octopus will need your help.

4.   After the four octopuses are drawn, have pairs of children paint or color the dwarf octopus, the common octopus and the blue-fringed octopus.

5.   Involve the entire class in painting the giant octopus.

6.   Cut out the four octopuses and tape them up in the classroom.

Something to think about
Fold the giant octopus four times and work on about four to five feet at a time.

For Science And Nature: Octopus Defends Against Attack

What the children will learn
To study how the octopus protects itself against attackers

Materials you will need
Bottle of black or dark blue ink, small balloon, paper towels, rubber band, straight pin, aquarium, water, clear glass or plastic measuring cup

What to do
1. Have a child construct a balloon octopus by pouring ink into a balloon. Wipe off the mouth of the balloon with paper towels, blow additional air into the balloon and tie a knot.

2. Tie rubber bands around the tied-off knot so as to create tentacles for the octopus.

3. Float the balloon in the aquarium. Leave it there all day for the children to become curious about.

4. Remove a cup of water from the aquarium with a clear glass or plastic measuring cup.

5. Later, talk with the children about how the octopus survives in the ocean by using camouflage. The octopus has another defense mechanism, however, if an attacker like the moray eel approaches.

6. Have the children observe closely while one child holds the balloon underwater by grasping the rubber bands. Then give that child a straight pin (representing the moray eel's teeth) with which to puncture the balloon and, at the same time, release it. The ink will squirt from the balloon as it does from an octopus, and the octopus will be propelled forward through the water.

7. Count off the seconds and encourage the children to note how the ink disperses in the water—immediately, after fifteen seconds, thirty seconds, a minute, and so on. Compare the color of the water in the measuring cup to the color in the aquarium after the ink disperses.

Something to think about
Ask the children to write in their learning logs about the ways the octopus survives.

For Science Display: Reminders Of The Amazing Octopus

What the children will learn
To associate an amazing fact with an object

Materials you will need
Straw or siphon tube, suction cup from child's dart game, rice, ink bottle, jar with lid

What to do
1. Place the objects listed above in the science display area.

2. Ask the children to write in their science learning logs an amazing fact about the octopus that each object represents. For example, the grains of rice represent the 20,000 eggs the octopus lays, eggs that are about one-half the size of a grain of rice.

Something to think about
Let the children glue the grains of rice onto black construction paper to create the strings of the webs illustrated in the book.

For Writing Center: How To Write A Report On Sea Life

What the children will learn
To label types of information

Materials you will need
Chalkboard and chalk or chart tablet paper and markers

What to do
1. With a small group of children in the writing area, read AN OCTOPUS IS AMAZING again. Pause after each page, and invite the children to tell what information they have just heard. For example, page five defines and describes the octopus.

2. On the chalkboard or chart tablet, print, "definition that includes simple description."

3. Read on. After page six, write, "habitat—or where the octopus lives."

4. Continue on through the book, reading and labeling information. Other topics covered are survival or defense mechanisms, what and how the octopus eats, how it moves, longevity, how it cares for young and other amazing facts.

5. Help the children to see that this information is factual, the same type of information that they would provide if they were writing in a technical or scientific manner.

6. Let the children each choose a fish, invertebrate or shellfish that they would like to study. Have them read and find out more about their subject, and then write about it using the information labels they created based on AN OCTOPUS IS AMAZING.

Something to think about
Use the information labels for oral reports as well.

SAM THE SEA COW

By Francine Jacobs

Illustrated by Laura Kelly

This four-chapter adventure tells the story of Sam the sea cow. The book is based on the true story of a sea cow (or manatee) who became stuck in a sewer pipe and was named Sam by the media. The story tells of Sam's life from the minutes after he is born up until he is ready to mate. Sam's adventure includes an encounter with the blades of a motorboat, rescue from the sewer pipe, a stay in a marine park and finally his return to Crystal River in Florida. Additional factual information is provided about sea cows, as well as an address for the Save the Manatee Club. Laura Kelly's illustrations of plants, animals, insects and manatees are well-matched to the text. The full-color pages make this small book easily shared with a large group of children.

Read-Aloud Presentation

Read the explanation at the back of the book of why Francine Jacobs was inspired to write this story. Show the front cover of the book and explain to the children that the sea cow is also called the manatee. Pause between each of the four chapters to let the children predict what will happen to Sam. After reading the entire book, ask the children to think about why these animals have become endangered. Announce the story s-t-r-e-t-c-h-e-r-s planned for SAM THE SEA COW.

STORY STRETCHER

For Art: Mural Of SAM THE SEA COW

What the children will learn
To plan and create a cooperative art project

Materials you will need
Newsprint, colored pencils, bulletin board, construction paper

What to do
1.   With a group of eight children, plan a bulletin board for the hallway that will tell the story of SAM THE SEA COW.

2.   Read the story again and plan a major scene for each of the four chapters.

3.   Let pairs of children work together. Make each pair responsible for one chapter.

4.   Have each pair of artists make a small sketch of what they want to do on a larger scale.

5.   Divide the mural into five sections by drawing lines across the butcher paper. In the first section, print the title of the book.

6.   Let each pair of artists create their section of the mural.

7.   After each section has been sketched and painted, staple the mural to the hallway bulletin board.

Something to think about
If younger children are working together, cut the sections of the butcher paper apart, then staple them together once completed. They will have less difficulty dealing with a smaller strip of paper.

STORY STRETCHER

For Mathematics: Numbers Tell A Story

What the children will learn
To use numbers to represent the various parts of the story

Materials you will need
Large index cards, colored markers, hole punch, yarn

What to do
1.   Distribute twelve index cards and markers to a small group of children.

2.   Read SAM THE SEA COW. Every time a number is mentioned, have the children write it on an index card.

3.   After the story is finished, have the children retell the story using the index cards as prompts.

4.   Link the story together by punching two holes in the top and in the bottom of each index card. Make the holes about an inch in from either side of the cards.

5.   Thread yarn through the holes and tie the cards together so that they are aligned vertically.

6.   Since only ten cards are needed for the numbers, ask the children to draw a picture of Sam as a baby on the top card and as an adult on the bottom card.

7.   Let the children tell their number stories to listeners in the library area. Ask a child to retell the story at another read-aloud session.

Something to think about

With older students, continue adding numbers from the factual information provided at the end of the story.

STORY STRETCHER

For Science And Nature: Sam's Water Hyacinths

What the children will learn

To observe the growth patterns of water plants

Materials you will need

Aquarium or child's plastic swimming pool, water hyacinths, plant food

What to do

1. Visit a nursery and find specimens of water hyacinths.

2. Explain to the nursery owner or worker what you are trying to help the children understand.

3. Set up a water habitat for the hyacinths using an aquarium or a child's plastic swimming pool.

4. Maintain the plants and feed them as directed.

5. Observe the growth patterns and measure the changes every two to three days.

6. Ask the children to note in their science learning logs what they are learning.

Something to think about

If possible, visit a water garden or botanical garden which has water hyacinths and other plants that live in rivers, swamps and marshy areas.

STORY STRETCHER

For Writing Center: Writing The News Release About Sam The Sea Cow

What the children will learn

To write a report using who, what, where, when, how

Materials you will need

Chalkboard and chalk or chart tablet paper and markers

What to do

1. With a small group of children in the writing area, pretend that they are newspaper reporters who have heard about a manatee stuck in a sewer pipe. They must write an article that will cause their readers to want to help the sea cow.

2. On the chalkboard or chart paper, print, "who," "what," "when," "where" and "how."

3. Invite the children to write a newspaper article, based on the story in the book, about the manatee's first becoming stuck, another article explaining his rescue, another article about his release into the Crystal River.

4. As an alternative, let the children write their reports as if they were radio or television newscasters.

Something to think about

Consider having the children write a scientific or technical report on manatees using the list of questions from the writing center story s-t-r-e-t-c-h-e-r for AN OCTOPUS IS AMAZING.

ANOTHER STORY STRETCHER

For Writing Center: Communicating With The Save The Manatee Club

What the children will learn

To write for information about what the club does to help the manatee

Materials you will need

Map of Florida, paper, pencil, envelope, postage

What to do

1. Show the children the address in the back of SAM THE SEA COW, inviting readers to write for additional information about manatees.

2. Ask the children what they would want to know if they contacted the club, such as how much it will cost, what they will get, what the club does to protect the manatee, how much money the club raised last year and whether they can do anything to help if they don't live near the manatees.

3. Compose one class letter to the club asking these questions.

4. After the club receives your letter, no doubt they will send a brochure and catalog. Read this information and think of additional questions your class would like to have answered.

5. Call 1-800-432-JOIN during regular business hours and ask for someone who would be willing to speak to the class in a conference call.

6. Arrange the conference call ahead of time and place the call using a speaker phone, letting the children ask their questions.

7. Send a thank you letter to the person with whom the class spoke. If funds are available, join the club.

Something to think about

Of course, if you live near an aquarium or natural preserve with manatees, take the children to visit.

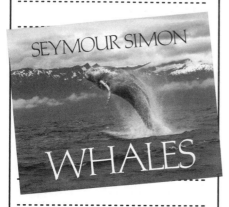

WHALES

By Seymour Simon

Photographs of whales accompany a text full of lively descriptions of the characteristics, habits and natural habitats of different whales. Beginning with the humpback, Simon clears up common misconceptions about whales. He explains how they breathe and their identity as mammals, and describes how scientists use the markings on flukes and tails to recognize individual whales. Additional information covers baby whales, nurturing of young, anatomy and different kinds of whales. Simon writes about the sperm, narwhal and orca, as well as the baleen whales like the right, gray, minke, blue and humpback. The book concludes with information about the International Whaling Commission. Simon's photographs are magnificent and majestic as well as informative.

Read-Aloud Presentation

Ask the children to imagine that they are on a ship, when suddenly a huge humpback whale careens alongside, arching its entire body up above the water, falling back into a giant belly flop, before sinking down below the waves. Show the children the cover photograph of WHALES. Read the entire book, pausing for the children to look closely at every picture. Ask each child to identify one whale he or she would like to learn more about. Have them write the name of that whale in their science learning logs.

STORY STRETCHER

For Art: Photographic Display

What the children will learn
To mount a photographic display

Materials you will need
Tempera paints, brushes, butcher paper or colored bulletin board paper, scissors, pictures of whales from nature magazines and brochures, construction paper, glue, stapler

What to do
1. Have the children paint the ocean on white butcher paper or staple colored bulletin board paper to a bulletin board.

2. Cut pictures of whales from nature magazines and brochures.

3. Have the children cut black construction paper 1/4 to 1/2 inch larger than each of the whale pictures.

4. Mount the magazine pictures by gluing them onto the black construction paper.

5. Staple or glue the mounted pictures onto the ocean background.

Something to think about
Make a small label for each print or number them and provide an identification key on a smaller poster.

STORY STRETCHER

For Classroom Library: Finding Out More From Whale Books

What the children will learn
To locate additional information

Materials you will need
Reference books or other children's books on whales

What to do
1. Collect as many different books on whales as you can find. Try to include realistic fiction, fantastic and factual books.

2. Leave the books on display in the classroom library for the children to browse through or to use in searching for information about the whale they selected to study in more detail.

3. After the children have had a few days to read the books, have them stage a "read-more" book report session. Several children can report on different books each day.

Something to think about
As an extension of this story s-t-r-e-t-c-h-e-r, compare the information found in realistic fiction, in fantastic and in factual books. Use Simon's WHALES as the example of a factual book. You could use Joanne Ryder's WINTER WHALE as an example of a fantastic book and Judy Allen's WHALE as an example of realistic fiction.

For Science And Nature: Amazing Facts Riddles

What the children will learn
To write riddles using facts

Materials you will need
Chalkboard and chalk or chart tablet paper and markers, large index cards, markers

What to do
1. List all the different whales mentioned in Simon's WHALES.

2. Form writing partnerships by assigning two children to write together about one kind of whale.

3. Have the writing partners read again about their particular whale, either in Simon's book or another from the class library.

4. Ask the partners to write a riddle card and an answer card about their whale. For example, on the riddle card, the partners could write, "Which kind of whale performs in marine parks?" On the answer card, they could write, "Orca or killer whale."

5. Mix up the cards and leave them in the science display area for the children to read and answer.

Something to think about
Let the writers make a riddle book, which can be bound and kept in the class library. The children can illustrate the book and provide the answers to their riddles at the back of the book.

For Social Studies: World Of Whales

What the children will learn
To locate on a world map the places where the whales Simon describes have been seen

Materials you will need
World map, Post-it notes, markers

What to do
1. As the children complete their writing in the writing center and their investigations in the library area, ask them to place Post-it notes on the ocean locations where various whales have been spotted.

2. Print the name of the whale on the Post-it note.

Something to think about
You can do this story s-t-r-e-t-c-h-e-r with younger children by reading WHALES again, pausing to locate each place mentioned.

For Writing Center: Revisiting The Text For More Information

What the children will learn
That a book filled with information will need to be read more than once

Materials you will need
Writing paper, stapler, pencils, notebooks or file folders

What to do
1. Construct science learning logs by stapling writing paper in file folders or notebooks.

2. Ask a small group of children at the writing center which whales they selected at the end of the read-aloud presentation.

3. One child might say the orca or killer whale. Read just that section of WHALES, then ask the child to write in the log what she or he wants to be sure to remember.

4. If the children are proficient readers, allow them to continue on their own, reading from WHALES and writing what they want to recall. If they are less proficient, read the information to them or record it on tape.

Something to think about
Ask every child to collect at least five specific facts about the whale they have chosen to study.

References

Cole, Joanna. (1992). **THE MAGIC SCHOOL BUS ON THE OCEAN FLOOR**. llustrated by Bruce Degen. New York: Scholastic.

Jacobs, Francine. (1979, 1991). **SAM THE SEA COW**. Illustrated by Laura Kelly. New York: Walker.

Lauber, Patricia. (1990). **AN OCTOPUS IS AMAZING**. Illustrated by Holly Keller. New York: HarperCollins.

McDonald, Megan. (1990). **IS THIS A HOUSE FOR HERMIT CRAB?** Illustrated by S.D. Schindler. New York: Orchard.

Simon, Seymour. (1989). **WHALES**. New York: HarperCollins.

Additional Books in THE MAGIC SCHOOL BUS series

Cole, Joanna. (1986). **THE MAGIC SCHOOL BUS AT THE WATER-WORKS**. Illustrated by Bruce Degen. New York: Scholastic.

Cole, Joanna. (1990). **THE MAGIC SCHOOL BUS IN THE HUMAN BODY**. Illustrated by Bruce Degen. New York: Scholastic.

Cole, Joanna. (1989). **THE MAGIC SCHOOL BUS INSIDE THE EARTH**. Illustrated by Bruce Degen. New York: Scholastic.

Cole, Joanna. (1990). **THE MAGIC SCHOOL BUS LOST IN THE SOLAR SYSTEM**. Illustrated by Bruce Degen. New York: Scholastic.

Additional References for Oceans

Allen, Judy. (1992). **WHALE**. Illustrated by Tudor Humphries. New York: Candlewick Press. *One night a young girl and her parents witness the seemingly magical rescue of a mother whale and her baby, exhausted from trying to outswim a spreading oil slick.*

DeSaix, Frank. (1991). **THE GIRL WHO DANCED WITH DOL-PHINS**. Illustrated by Debbi Durland DeSaix. New York: Farrar Straus Giroux. *A beautifully illustrated story of a girl who snorkels, whom a dolphin saves from a shark. That night she dreams of being a dolphin.*

Hirschi, Ron. (1991). **OCEAN**. Illustrated by Barbara Bash. New York: Bantam. *Various ocean animals describe their behavior and physical characteristics and ask the reader to guess what they are.*

Royston, Angela. (1992). **SEA ANIMALS**. Photographs by Steve Shott and Dave King. New York: Macmillan. *Eight sea animals are pictured and described, including the bullhead shark, sea horse, and sea gull.*

Ryder, Joanne. (1991). **WINTER WHALE**. Illustrated by Michael Roth-man. New York: Morrow. *Transformed into a humpback whale, a child experiences life in the ocean among other whales.*

PONDS, LAKES, RIVERS AND SWAMPS

Box Turtle at Long Pond
Tomorrow on Rocky Pond
The Lost Lake
Spoonbill Swamp
Come Back, Salmon

PONDS, LAKES, RIVERS AND SWAMPS

BOX TURTLE AT LONG POND

By William T. George

Illustrated by

Lindsay Barrett George

The reader visits Long Pond by tagging along with a box turtle for a day. The turtle awakes, forages for food, encounters other animals that live along the banks or drink from Long Pond. The reader sees the turtle as he suns on a rock, finds shelter during a rainstorm, eats worms and escapes from a raccoon by closing his shell. At the end of the day, the turtle searches for more food before hiding in the tall grasses, a camouflaged sleeping place. Lindsay Barrett George's beautiful yet realistic illustrations welcome the reader to the calm and excitement of a natural setting, helping us experience what it is like to live there.

Read-Aloud Presentation

Have the children recall LOOK OUT FOR TURTLES! from their endangered animal studies. Discuss some of the fascinating facts they learned about turtles. Read again the pages on the eastern box turtle. Show the children the cover of BOX TURTLE AT LONG POND and help them identify the turtle pictured as an eastern box turtle. Read the book. Pause before the illustration of the raccoon to place your hand over the turtle. Ask the children what will happen to a box turtle if a young raccoon comes too close. After reading, go back through the book, page by page, and let the children describe the natural surroundings.

STORY STRETCHER

For Art: Misty Morning Painting

What the children will learn
To use a watercolor technique

Materials you will need
Watercolors, heavy paper, small brushes, masking tape, paper towels, tissues, water

What to do
1.   Show the children the first of Lindsay Barrett George's illustrations of Long Pond and point out how the mist rises from the pond's surface.

2.   Tape the watercolor paper to a flat surface.

3.   Demonstrate how to wet the watercolor paper lightly by loading water into a brush and swishing it over the paper, then drying the paper with paper towels to leave a slightly damp surface.

4.   On a scrap of watercolor paper, paint some watercolors. Show the children how to crumple

tissue and paper towels and lightly touch these to the surface of the watercolor paper. The paint will be absorbed, leaving a whiter, lighter area with some color showing.

5.   Let the children experiment with these techniques, then encourage them to paint their own misty morning landscapes.

6.   Allow their landscapes to dry thoroughly and display them in the science center and the library area.

Something to think about
Plan to leave the watercolors out for several days to encourage the children to experiment. Experimentation leads children to paint with more confidence and creativity.

STORY STRETCHER

For Cooking And Snack Time: Turtle's Grapes

What the children will learn
To decide their preferences in grapes

Materials you will need
White grapes, red grapes, black grapes, wild grapes (if possible), scissors, napkins, chalkboard, chalk

What to do
1.   Have the snack helper wash the grapes and use the scissors to snip them into small bunches.

2.   Print at the top of the chalkboard, "white," "red," "black."

3.   Ask the children to sample all three varieties of grapes and to mark their preference on the chalkboard by making a hash mark under the color.

4.   Discuss the wild grapes that the box turtle ate and look at the illustrations of the turtle at the grape vines.

Ask the produce manager in a supermarket which grapes are the most popular.

STORY STRETCHER
For Science And Nature: Investigation Plots

What the children will learn
To sharpen their observation skills

Materials you will need
Yarn, note pads, pencils, paper bags, empty milk cartons

What to do
1. Before visiting a pond, talk with the children about how scientists gather information by observing and describing an area. If an area is too large to allow close observation of all the terrain, scientists observe smaller sections and generalize based upon these. Demonstrate for the children how to set up their investigation plots.

2. At the pond site, give each child a yard of yarn.

3. Have the child select a plot and mark it off by placing the yarn in a square with the ends meeting.

4. Each child then observes everything within their marked off area and takes field notes. Explain that field notes should contain a list or inventory of everything they see, sketches and notes of what happens.

5. Have the children collect three specimens or objects to represent their plot, such as a blade of grass, a twig, a pebble, loam. At the water's edge, collect water in a milk carton.

6. Create a science display for the science center in the classroom using specimens collected during the visit to the pond.

Something to think about
Older children could observe an undisturbed plot and write field notes, then use their hands or a stick to move objects and note the impact their actions have—causing grubs to dig further into the earth, for example.

STORY STRETCHER
For Special Event: Visit To A Pond

What the children will learn
To explore a natural environment leaving little evidence that they have been there

Materials you will need
Field trip permission forms, transportation, volunteers, naturally decomposing garbage bags, old clothes

What to do
1. Arrange for a visit to a pond. Inquire at nature centers if you live in an urban area.

2. Get parents to sign the field trip permission forms and instruct them to have their children dress in old clothes.

3. Prepare the volunteers for their responsibilities by telling them what you hope the children will learn from the visit.

4. Talk with the children about the investigations planned and the behavior expected of them.

5. Take paper or decomposing plastic garbage bags and pick up any litter found at the site.

6. Consult ahead of time with the naturalist or the pond owner about any areas that are off-limits because of nesting birds or other animals.

7. Mark out a trail or path so as not to disturb the grasses or other plants.

8. Plan for relaxation time to allow the children simply to enjoy being in a natural environment.

Something to think about
Help the children understand that they are visitors in the habitats of animals, their homes.

STORY STRETCHER
For Writing Center: Science Learning Log

What the children will learn
To synthesize information from reading, observing and sharing data

Materials you will need
Field notes from observations, writing folders, pencils, colored pens, crayons, markers

What to do
1. Assemble small groups of children around the science display and discuss the many different ways they learned about life at a pond and what they learned.

2. Invite the children to look at the specimens in the science display to remind them of what they observed. For instance, one child might see the leaf she placed in the display and remember how the grubs dug further into the earth after the leaves that covered them were lifted. Another child might look at a piece of bark and remember how solid the hollow log appeared until he touched it, and the log fell apart.

3. Ask the children to write in their science learning logs what they learned from visiting the pond. Encourage them to use their field notes and specimen samples and to talk with their friends.

4. Encourage the children to add illustrations.

Something to think about
Continue writing in learning logs to help children synthesize the information they acquire in each unit.

PONDS, LAKES, RIVERS AND SWAMPS

TOMORROW ON ROCKY POND

By Lynn Reiser

A child anticipates the family's fishing trip to Rocky Pond. The reader experiences the thrill the child feels about what tomorrow will bring. In the morning, they will see the mist rising from the water, loons calling and blueberries for breakfast. When they have collected everything on their long list of provisions, the family will trek through the woods, picnic near the water's edge, canoe on the pond, take a nap on a mossy bank and fish. While they fish, other animals fish, too, like the loon. Someone in the family will catch trout, and they will trek back to the cabin for a trout dinner before falling asleep to dream of another day on Rocky Pond. Lynn Reiser uses a black pen to add detail to the watercolor illustrations that bring the book to life.

Read-Aloud Presentation

Wear an old fishing hat or straw hat without telling the children what it means. Call attention to the cover of TOMORROW ON ROCKY POND and let the children describe what they see and what they infer about the story based on the cover. Call attention to the line of fish drawn as a frame around the picture of the two children decked out in their fishing gear. Look at the back cover and point out the picture of the loon. Discuss how excited you feel the night before you go on a trip. Let children talk about their excitement before going on a vacation or before someone special comes to visit. After reading TOMORROW AT ROCKY POND, place the fishing hat on one child's head and invite the children to the creative dramatics area of the classroom. Announce the story s-t-r-e-t-c-h-e-r-s based on TOMORROW AT ROCKY POND.

STORY STRETCHER

For Art: Symbols Frame A Picture

What the children will learn
To use a symbol that represents the main idea of an illustration

Materials you will need
An array of art supplies from which children can choose

What to do
1. Place the book jacket of TOMORROW ON ROCKY POND in the art center for the children to examine more closely.

2. Invite the children to draw or paint any picture they choose about a special trip they have taken, or would like to take, and to place a frame around the picture

that includes a symbol of that experience. On the cover of TOMORROW ON ROCKY POND, fish are used to frame the illustration.

3. Let the children choose any media they like to create their pictures and frames.

Something to think about
Be sensitive to the feelings of children whose families are not able to take vacations. You might focus instead on field trips that the class has taken.

STORY STRETCHER

For Cooking And Snack Time: Best Blueberry Muffins

What the children will learn
To follow directions in a recipe

Materials you will need
Chart tablet, marker, packaged blueberry muffin mix, water, milk, measuring cups and spoons, mixing bowl, wooden spoon, muffin tin, toaster oven

What to do
1. Make a large chart of the directions from the package for baking blueberry muffins.

2. Divide the class into small baking groups so that each child can help measure and mix.

3. Follow the directions on the chart. Bake several recipes.

4. Serve the muffins hot with cartons of milk.

Something to think about
If possible, bake a plain muffin mix and add fresh blueberries. On another day, make pancakes, adding blueberries to the mix and to the pancake topping.

For Creative Dramatics: Fishing Fun In Our Room

What the children will learn
To dress in fishing gear and recognize fishing equipment

Materials you will need
As many of the following items as possible: old shirts, fishing vests and hats, canoe or boat shoes, sunscreen, bug spray, sunglasses, backpacks, berry basket, thermos, life vests, float cushions, paddles, flashlights, fishing net, fishing rods or poles, fishing creel, canoe

What to do
1. Contact parents and grandparents for fishing gear, clothes and canoe.

2. As each family brings items, make a list of what they want returned and what you can keep.

3. Place the items in the creative dramatics area and let the children explore and play on their own, without teacher direction.

Something to think about
At the next read-aloud session, suggest that the children bring or wear something from the creative dramatics area. For the remainder of the unit, sit in the canoe while you read aloud from other books about ponds, lakes, rivers and swamps.

For Mathematics: Shopping For Fishing Gear

What the children will learn
To locate, price and calculate total costs of fishing gear

Materials you will need
Outdoor gear catalog, chalkboard, chalk

What to do
1. Look at the illustrations in TOMORROW ON ROCKY POND that show all the clothing, supplies and fishing gear the family took on their trip.

2. List these items on the chalkboard.

3. Have the children locate the items in the catalog, and write the price of each on the chalkboard.

4. Total the cost of the clothing, supplies and gear to outfit one person for the trip.

5. Extend the activity by determining the cost to outfit an entire family.

Something to think about
With older children, consider going to a camping store or neighborhood garage sale, and compare catalog, store and garage sale prices.

For Social Studies: Mapping An Adventure

What the children will learn
To draw a map which illustrates the highlights of an area

Materials you will need
Chart paper, butcher paper, markers, tape, tables

What to do
1. Spread a long length of butcher paper on a table or two tables pushed together for the children to use to make a map.

2. Look at the map the author made of the trip to Rocky Pond.

3. Read TOMORROW ON ROCKY POND and pause to allow one child to keep a list of places mentioned in the book.

4. Decide upon a central location, such as Rocky Pond, and draw that place on the map first.

5. Let the children add places until their map represents the Rocky Pond adventure.

Something to think about
Try varying the map the next day by asking the children to add illustrations of what the family did at each place on the map.

PONDS, LAKES, RIVERS AND SWAMPS

THE LOST LAKE

ALLEN SAY

THE LOST LAKE
By Allen Say

*When Luke spends the summer with his quiet father, he reads all the books he has brought with him and then becomes bored watching television. He cuts out magazine pictures of lakes and pastes them onto his bedroom wall. The magazine pictures cause his father to remember the hiking and camping trips **he** took with **his** father to their "lost lake." Outfitted in new hiking boots, Luke and his father go in search of the lost lake. They discover that the lake is no longer lost, but populated with lots of tourists. Undaunted, father and son hike on in search of a lake they can call their own. Even the trails are filled with hikers. Finally, compass in hand, they strike out to more remote mountain areas, where they camp, discover their own lost lake and learn to talk with each other. Allan Say's watercolor illustrations create the moods and capture the beauty, majesty and mystery of nature. The reader becomes involved in this reassuring quest for a peaceful natural environment, and for communication between father and son.*

Read-Aloud Presentation

Bring a hiking backpack or hiking boots to the group time. Let the children share with the group any of their hiking or camping experiences. Pass around photographs, postcards or travel brochures of lakes in your state. Ask the children what they do when they get bored. Read the scene in the book where Luke stares at the television, having finished all his books, wishing he could talk to his father. Let the children talk about what they would do if they were in Luke's predicament. Continue reading THE LOST LAKE. After reading, discuss the effects on the environment and our enjoyment of nature when too many people hike and camp in one area. Explore with the children the fact that some people prefer the excitement of a lot of people, while others prefer the serenity of a place like Lost Lake.

STORY STRETCHER

For Art: Night And Day At Lost Lake

What the children will learn
To compose a picture illustrating the effect of light

Materials you will need
Choice of art supplies, papers, paints, brushes, crayons, chalks, colored pens, markers

What to do
1. With the children who choose to work in the art center, look more closely at the daylight scene on the front cover of THE LOST LAKE, and at the night scene on the back cover.

2. In the daylight scene, notice how the illustrator shows the direction of the sun by placing some mountain faces in shadow and others in light.

3. In the night scene, note the light of the moon and the ways the illustrator has used blues, grays, blacks and other shades to show variations of light.

4. Ask the children to create both a day and a night scene of the Lost Lake, or of a favorite place they like to visit.

5. Display the pictures throughout the classroom.

Something to think about
Encourage children who are not interested in "night and day at Lost Lake" pictures to make a display of photographs, postcards and travel brochures.

STORY STRETCHER

For Cooking And Snack Time: Apricots

What the children will learn
To compare the flavors of fresh, canned and dried apricots

Materials you will need
Fresh apricots (if available), canned apricots, dried apricots, forks, napkins, bowls, trays

What to do
1. Have the snack helpers set up trays of fresh, canned and dried apricots.

2. Encourage the children to taste the apricots in all three forms and express their preferences.

3. If available, taste other foods that contain apricots, like apricot nectar, apricot preserves, trail mix with dried apricots.

Something to think about
In the book, Luke's father prepares a quick snack of salami and apricots. Let the children try this combination. He also has freeze-dried provisions. If possible, ask a camping supply

company for samples of freeze-dried foods.

For Mathematics: Shopping For Hiking And Camping Gear

What the children will learn
To locate, price and calculate total costs of hiking and camping gear

Materials you will need
Outdoor gear catalog, chalkboard, chalk

What to do
1. Read THE LOST LAKE again and look closely at the illustrations. Identify all the equipment that Luke and his father used on their hiking and camping trip.
2. List the items on the chalkboard.
3. Have the children locate the items in the catalog and write the price on the chalkboard.
4. Total the cost of clothing, supplies and gear to outfit both father and son for their trip.

Something to think about
With older children, consider going to a camping store or a neighborhood garage sale, then comparing catalog, store and garage sale prices.

For Social Studies: Locating Lakes

What the children will learn
To locate lakes nearby

Materials you will need
Push pins, map of the county or of a state or national park

What to do
1. Post the map on a large bulletin board in clear view and at the level of children's eyes.

2. Help them to distinguish the appearance of bodies of water on the map.

3. Place a push pin in the county map at your school's location, or place a push pin in the park map at the spot that marks the entrance.

4. Challenge the children to find the lake nearest the school or the park entrance, and another lake, which they would like to call "Lost Lake."

Something to think about
Help older children calculate distance by figuring the mileage from their school to the two lakes.

For Special Project: Setting Up A Tent

What the children will learn
To follow verbal directions and set up a tent

Materials you will need
Camera, camping equipment, tent, a person who knows how to set up a tent

What to do
1. Survey parents to find out who has a tent and who would be available to come to class to direct the children in setting up the tent.

2. Involve all the children in the process.

3. Add other camping equipment like a thermos, cooking and eating utensils, etc.

4. Read stories in the tent. Let the children select campfire games, sing campfire songs and tell campfire stories.

5. Take photographs during the tent activities and give some of them to the parents who helped with the tents.

Something to think about
If more than one parent volunteers a tent, place one inside the classroom and another outside.

SPOONBILL SWAMP

By Brenda Z. Guiberson

Illustrated by Megan Lloyd

A mother alligator and a mother and father spoonbill live with their babies in Spoonbill Swamp. The parents help their babies find food in the very active life of the swamp and mangrove thicket. Through vivid word and picture descriptions, we gain a sense of the urgency of the babies' needs and the instinctual care the parents give. The drama unfolds as the alligator's needs and the spoonbill's search for food bring them closer and closer together until snap—the mother alligator's powerful jaws close. Fortunately for the spoonbill, the alligator only catches a pink tail feather. Both return to the search for food for their young. Guiberson's excellent telling of nature's everyday drama is beautifully illustrated by Lloyd's watercolors with their spatter-painted backgrounds, rich textures and fluid washes of color. The pink spoonbill against the pink and golden sunset is particularly magnificent.

Read-Aloud Presentation

Recall with the children the different habitats and environments highlighted in the other books you have read for this unit. They include the box turtle's pond with its grassy banks, the high mountain location of Lost Lake, and the trek through the forest to Rocky Pond. Show the students the cover of SPOONBILL SWAMP and ask them what they know about swamps and wetlands. List what the children already know on the chalkboard. Ask them what else they would like to know and make a list of their questions. Read SPOONBILL SWAMP without pausing for discussion. Based on what they learn from SPOONBILL SWAMP, answer as many questions as possible. After reading, look back through the pages and admire the illustrations, especially the artist's use of color.

STORY STRETCHER

For Art: Luminescent Sunsets

What the children will learn
To mix watercolors that glow

Materials you will need
Watercolors (including florescent pinks, oranges, crimson), watercolor brushes, paper, water, containers, paper towels or sponges

What to do
1.   Let the children take their inspiration for mixing colors from Megan Lloyd's illustrations.

2.   Briefly demonstrate how to load watercolors onto brushes for dry effects, and how to wet the brushes with water to produce washes of color.

3.   Let the children experiment with mixing the florescent colors of sunset and sunrise at Spoonbill Swamp. Call attention to Lloyd's color separation for the sunrise and color overlapping for the sunset.

4.   Encourage the children to make illustrations of Spoonbill Swamp, if they like.

Something to think about
Also experiment with spatter painting. Load old toothbrushes with paint and draw your thumb across the bristles, spattering paint to add texture to a picture.

STORY STRETCHER

For Classroom Library: Drama On Tape

What the children will learn
To read with intonation that reflects the mood of a story

Materials you will need
Audiotape, tape recorder, stapler, listening station jack, headphones

What to do
1.   Ask four children to help tape-record SPOONBILL SWAMP for the library listening station. One will read the pages that feature the spoonbill, one will read the alligator's pages and one will read the italicized movement and sound words. The fourth will be the recorder, who is responsible for operating the tape recorder, checking volume and recording the page-turning signal by snapping a stapler near the microphone.

2.   Ask the children to rehearse.

3.   Plan to cue the readers by an agreed upon hand signal.

4.   Play the tape and let the readers decide whether they are pleased with its quality or want to record another.

5.   Place the book and the audiotape in the library area of the classroom.

Something to think about

Let storytellers record another retelling of SPOONBILL SWAMP on the other side of the tape. Let younger children use the illustrations to prompt their story retellings.

STORY STRETCHER

For Creative Dramatics: Moving Like The Inhabitants Of Spoonbill Swamp

What the children will learn
To imitate the movements of the alligator and the roseate spoonbill

Materials you will need
None needed

What to do
1. Read SPOONBILL SWAMP again. Pause at each description of movement, and try to move like the alligator and the roseate spoonbill.

2. Ask the children to join you in imitating the spoonbill and the alligator.

3. Continue with some children imitating the alligator and others, the roseate spoonbill.

4. Add to the mounting drama by reading very slowly about their near encounter.

Something to think about
Do not force children to participate, but rather encourage them. The best encouragement for children is for their teacher to move with them.

STORY STRETCHER

For Science And Nature: K-W-L About Alligator And Spoonbill

What the children will learn
To search for other answers to their questions about swamps

Materials you will need
Chart paper and marker or chalkboard and chalk, index card

What to do
1. Construct a K-W-L chart from the information the children shared during the read-aloud presentation of SPOONBILL SWAMP. Make three columns, labeling the first column "K" for what the children already "know," the second column "W" for what we "want" to know and the third column "L" for what we learn.

2. Assemble a small group of children to look at the book more closely. For example, ask the children to look at the spoonbill, describe it and think about how its physical features help it to survive in a swamp.

3. Add to the "L" column what the children learn by looking more closely at the roseate spoonbill, the alligator, nests, feeding grounds, other animals and plants in the swamp.

4. Place the chart in the science display area along with the book.

5. On a large index card, print directions for other children who come to the science area and want to add to the K-W-L chart. Use markers of a different color to add new information to the chart.

Something to think about
Ask the librarian for additional resources about swamps, marshes and wetlands. Place these resources in the science display area for the children to use to seek answers to their questions.

ANOTHER STORY STRETCHER

For Science And Nature: Swamp Aquarium

What the children will learn
To construct a mock swamp habitat and observe how the soil and water interact

Materials you will need
Aquarium, water, masking tape, soil, pebbles, sticks or straws, plants, minnows

What to do
1. On the first day, place water in the aquarium. Mark the water level with a strip of masking tape. Add soil and observe the rise in water level. Note how the soil sinks to the bottom of the tank.

2. On the second day, add pebbles and observe the new water level and the distribution of soil and pebbles.

3. On the third day, add more soil and pebbles so that the aquarium simulates the marshy banks of the swamps where the alligator's babies were born. Continue marking the water level by placing masking tape on the side of the aquarium.

4. On the fourth day, add more water to simulate the area where the roseate spoonbill stalked around on her long legs. Stand two sticks or straws in the water to simulate how the bird walks through the water catching fish in her bill.

5. If possible, replace the water with pond or swamp water and add plants and minnows.

Something to think about
The swamp aquarium can be as simple as water added to soil to show the children how saturated soil becomes with water or how soil settles to the bottom. Or the swamp aquarium can be as complex a system as you choose, with plants, minnows, frogs. If you want minnows, fish or tadpoles to live in the swamp aquarium, collect the water from a pond or swamp.

COME BACK, SALMON

By Molly Cone

Photographs by

Sidnee Wheelwright

COME BACK, SALMON is a Sierra Club book which chronicles how a group of dedicated school children adopted Pigeon Creek and brought it back to life. Jackson Elementary School students in Everett, Washington, reclaimed a stream where salmon had once spawned. Challenged by a fifth grade teacher, they cleaned up the stream, which had become a community dump choked with old tires, discarded furniture and other debris. The problems the project faced are told as accurately as their successes. COME BACK, SALMON is a realistic and exciting case of what a school can accomplish and what children can learn in any area of the curriculum. Sidnee Wheelwright's photographs bring home the reality of events.

Read-Aloud Presentation

From the cover of the book, read the description of COME BACK, SALMON: "how a group of dedicated kids adopted Pigeon Creek and brought it back to life." Discuss what might cause a stream to need to be brought back to life. Show the children the photograph of the stream when it was used as a garbage dump. Let the children talk about whether or not they have ever seen such an area in your community. Read each chapter of the book, then pause to summarize the main events. With younger children, consider reading the book in two sessions, stopping after chapter three. After reading the book, announce the environmental project your class or school has decided upon. With the children, chart out a plan of action. If possible, involve the entire school.

STORY STRETCHER
For Art: The Beauty We Save

What the children will learn
To photograph areas of beauty in their neighborhood

Materials you will need
Simple cameras, film, volunteers

What to do
1. Contact a photography club or a college photography class in the community.

2. Ask the club or class to help primary children learn to take good photographs.

3. Photograph areas of natural beauty in the neighborhood.

4. Photograph areas that could be beautiful, but are littered or used as dumps.

5. Continue the photographic essay throughout the special project story s-t-r-e-t-c-h-e-r below.

6. Display the photographs in the reception area of the school.

Something to think about
As an alternative art story s-t-r-e-t-c-h-e-r, look through the photographs of art and science displays in COME BACK, SALMON and make the fish mobiles or the signs for environmental clean-up areas.

STORY STRETCHER
For Mathematics: The Story Of Our Clean-Up Project

What the children will learn
To chart, graph and communicate various aspects of the special project using mathematics

Materials you will need
Chart paper, posterboard, markers, graph paper, construction paper, glue, array of materials for constructing posters

What to do
1. Use charts and graphs to keep track of the steps in the overall project plan, the number of children involved, the outside agencies involved and the amounts of money, time, supplies and equipment.

2. Each class should chart and graph information at the level appropriate to their students. Involve the children in collecting the data and deciding the best means for communicating it.

3. Make simple charts and graphs that communicate information at a glance to everyone involved, even the youngest children.

4. Construct more complex charts and graphs with the children to make the complexity of the task evident.

Something to think about
Children understand the importance of using mathematics as a tool for communication when they are involved in significant and specific projects, like the school environment project.

For Science And Nature: Aquarium As A Fish Hatchery

What the children will learn
To construct and maintain an aquarium fish hatchery

Materials you will need
Sturdy fish tank, air pump, filters, water, gravel, plants, food, fish eggs, thermometer, skimmers, plastic bags

What to do
1. Contact a fish hatchery in your state. Ask for someone to assist in your class project, or for printed instructions on how to prepare an aquarium for fish eggs.
2. Prepare the fish tank as directed.
3. Add the fish eggs.
4. Have the children watch the eggs and the developing embryos.
5. Monitor the water temperature as directed by the fish hatchery.
6. Once the fish have matured enough to survive in a stream, place them in plastic bags with water and give one fish to each child to release into the stream.

Something to think about
As you read in COME BACK, SALMON, maintaining a fish tank requires close monitoring. Plan to have the fish tank in an area where children from other classes can see the fish grow.

For Special Project: Environmental Clean-Up

What the children will learn
To be environmentally responsible citizens

Materials you will need
Determined by project planned

What to do
1. With the teachers and administrators at your school, decide on a significant environmental project for the school to undertake.
2. Construct a plan of action involving either your class or the entire school.
3. Use photographs, guest speakers, art projects, maps, flow charts, data in graphs and other media to communicate what the project is and its progress. Communicate the problems as well as successes.
4. Use school assemblies and small class gatherings to keep every child and parent informed.
5. Plan a significant role in the project for each class. Encourage each class to find their own ways to communicate about the project throughout all areas of the curriculum.
6. Celebrate your success in ways that involve the entire community.

Something to think about
The value of conducting significant projects is profound. They teach children that they can act constructively and can have an impact on society. Major projects also provide children with many opportunities for learning across different areas of the curriculum.

For Writing Center: Requesting Information From Environmental Agencies And Organizations

What the children will learn
To compose a letter asking for information about environmental issues

Materials you will need
Overhead projector, transparencies, marker, paper, pencils, envelopes, large envelopes, postage

What to do
1. With the class, compose a group letter to environmental agencies and organizations. Write the letter on overhead projector transparencies so that the children can see different drafts.
2. Ask each child to write the body of the letter, requesting information about something she or he wants to know, such as the names of fish that could live in a stream in our community, the biggest environmental problems in our state, or membership for children in the environmental organization.
3. Demonstrate how to address envelopes. Place the children's letters and envelopes into a large envelope and mail them.
4. When the agency or club answers, write thank you letters.

Something to think about
Write to the National Wildlife Federation, 1400 16th St. N.W., Washington, DC 20036 or the US Department of the Interior, Fish and Wildlife Service, 1849 C Service, 1849 C St. N.W., Washington, DC 20240. Ask your school or community librarian for other suggestions.

References

Cone, Molly. (1991). **COME BACK, SALMON**. Photographs by Sidnee Wheelwright. San Francisco: Sierra Club.

George, William T. (1989). **BOX TURTLE AT LONG POND**. Illustrated by Lindsay Barrett George. New York: Greenwillow.

Guiberson, Brenda. (1992). **SPOONBILL SWAMP**. Illustrated by Megan Lloyd. New York: Henry Holt.

Reiser, Lynn. (1993). **TOMORROW ON ROCKY POND**. New York: Greenwillow.

Say, Allen. (1989). **THE LOST LAKE**. Boston: Houghton Mifflin.

Also Mentioned in this Chapter

Berger, Melvin. (1992). **LOOK OUT FOR TURTLES!** Illustrated by Megan Lloyd. New York: HarperCollins.

Additional References for Ponds, Lakes, Rivers and Swamps

Berger, Melvin. (1992). **LOOK OUT FOR TURTLES**! Illustrated by Megan Lloyd. New York: HarperCollins. *Describes the remarkable turtle that can live almost anywhere, eat almost anything, range in size from tiny to gigantic and live longer than any other animal.*

George, Jean Craighead. (1969, 1991). **THE MOON OF THE ALLIGA-TORS**. Illustrated by Michael Rothman. New York: HarperCollins. *Describes an alligator's desperate search for food in the Florida Everglades during the month of October.*

George, William T. (1991). **FISHING AT LONG POND**. Illustrated by Lindsay Barrett George. New York: Greenwillow. *While fishing for bass, Katie and her grandfather observe a deer, an osprey, a goose, and other pond visitors.*

Lewin, Ted. (1992). **WHEN THE RIVERS GO HOME**. New York: Macmillan. *Describes life in the marsh in Brazil known as the Pantanal.*

Wallace, Karen. (1993). **THINK OF A BEAVER**. Illustrated by Mick Manning. Cambridge, Massachusetts: Candlewick Press. *Pictures and rhythmic text provide a close-up look at the habits and homes of North American beavers.*

TREES AND RAIN FORESTS

The Lorax
The Gift of the Tree
Someday a Tree
Save My Rainforest
Welcome to the Green House

THE LORAX
By Dr. Seuss

A child goes to the wise Once-ler in search of answers to the question of what happened to the Truffula trees. The tale is told in Seuss rhyme with many double messages. The answer is clear, however: the Truffula trees disappeared because the Once-ler's company was greedy and did not allow time for the trees to grow and replace themselves. They were warned by a character named the Lorax, but no one listened when he said that cutting down the trees would cause problems for the environment and all the creatures that lived in the Truffula tree forest. The Once-ler company thought it was more important to make "thneeds," meaning "something-that-all-people-need." Soon there were lots of "thneeds," but no trees. The last hope is one Truffula seed and a good citizen who might make it grow. This environmental tale, told by Dr. Seuss in his venerable style, is surely relevant today.

Read-Aloud Presentation

Show the children the cover of THE LORAX and tell them that the little creature with the beard gives advice that everyone should heed. Ask them to listen for the Lorax's advice. Read THE LORAX, pausing after the first "thneed" has been knitted. Ask the children to predict what they think will happen next. When the Lorax appears in the story, ask if they think anyone will listen. Continue reading, pausing after the last Truffula tree has been cut down and ask the children what they think will happen. At the end of the story, ask what the Lorax meant when he said, "I speak for the trees." What did the trees want him to say?

STORY STRETCHER

For Art: An Imaginative Place Where Truffula Trees Grow

What the children will learn
To use their imaginations to create a new kind of tree

Materials you will need
Cotton balls, yarn, popsicle sticks, pipe cleaners, felt, tissue paper, fabric, glue, stapler, construction paper

What to do
1. Look again at the illustrations in THE LORAX and discuss how Dr. Seuss used his imagination to create a new tree, the truffula tree.
2. Ask the children to use their imaginations to create new trees.
3. Let the children invent the new trees using materials found around the classroom.

Something to think about
Invent new names for the trees. Print tiny signs for each tree and its inventor.

STORY STRETCHER

For Cooking And Snack Time: Truffula Fruits

What the children will learn
To distinguish among the flavors of different grapes

Materials you will need
Scissors, napkins, green grapes, black grapes, red grapes

What to do
1. Call the grapes "truffula fruits." Let the cooking and snack helpers wash them.
2. With scissors, snip small bunches from the larger bunches.
3. Ask the children to decide which flavor of truffula fruit they like best. Ask them which is sweetest, which is tartest.

Something to think about
Bring kiwi, nectarines or another fruit the children rarely see and call it truffula fruit.

STORY STRETCHER

For Science And Nature: Planting A Truffula Tree

What the children will learn
To plant and take care of seedlings

Materials you will need
Seedlings, trowel, top soil, compost or rich soil, flower pots or plastic containers, rulers

What to do
1. Secure enough seedlings from the county extension office or an environmental project to give one to every child.

2. Prepare a bed for the seedlings by mixing top soil with compost or rich soil, turning it into the bed with the hand trowel.

3. Measure the growth of the seedlings on the first of each month.

4. After the seedlings have grown for several months, transplant them into flower pots or plastic containers.

5. Give one to each child for a family tree-planting ceremony.

Something to think about
If some children do not have places to plant trees, ask for space on the school grounds or in a park.

STORY STRETCHER

For Writing Center: Speaking For The Trees

What the children will learn
To compose a passionate speech about caring for the environment

Materials you will need
Chalkboard, chalk, pencil, paper

What to do
1. Read again the passage in the story where the Lorax proclaims that he speaks for the trees.

2. Brainstorm with the children a list of things you think the Lorax might have said when he talked with the "Once-ler," who would not listen to his speech.

3. Let the children write their speeches.

4. Encourage the children to give their speeches.

Something to think about
On another occasion, let the Lorax speak for the animals who were driven from the Truffula forest, or for the birds or the fish. Or write about what the Lorax would say if he came to our town.

ANOTHER STORY STRETCHER

For Writing Center: The Return Of The Lorax

What the children will learn
To think constructively and write a message of hope

Materials you will need
Chalkboard, chalk, writing paper, pencils

What to do
1. Extend the story of the Lorax by asking the children to write about what happened after the child planted the Truffula tree seed.

2. Invite them to imagine the new world once the forest returns.

3. Let them pretend that the Lorax, who lives far away, hears news of the Truffula trees beginning to grow.

4. Encourage the children to write a scene in which the Lorax comes back and is greeted by the Once-ler, who has longed for his return.

Something to think about
Make a mural of "The Return of the Lorax."

TREES AND RAIN FORESTS

THE GIFT OF THE TREE

By Alvin Tresselt

Illustrated by Henri Sorensen

Alvin Tresselt helps the young reader see the life in an old tree that has lived in the forest for over 100 years. The insects, birds and animals it has sheltered and fed are testimony to its boundless worth. The text is not poetry, but the language is poetic, as in the phrase, "rich rain of acorns." The gift of the tree is the life it brings, even as it dies during a hurricane whose winds slash through the forest. We see the way the tree and the forest creatures depend upon each other. In the end, a tiny acorn sprouts to carry on the life of the proud tree. Originally published in 1972 and reissued in 1992, the book is timely and timeless. Sorensen's illustrations are as splendid as Tresselt's words. Each tells the story of the natural cycle in a realistic, yet respectful approach to the subject.

Read-Aloud Presentation

Open the book and flatten out the dust cover to let the children see that on the back is a beautiful painting of the forest. Invite them to note the season of the year. In addition to the deer and the birds on the cover, ask the children what other animals they might see if they visited this forest. Keep a chart tablet nearby, and as you read the book, ask one child to list the animals, birds and insects. At the end of the book, let the children share their observations.

STORY STRETCHER

For Art: Leaf Rubbings

What the children will learn
To create rubbings

Materials you will need
Variety of leaves, newspaper, newsprint, crayon, charcoal, pastel chalk

What to do
1.   During the nature walk, collect a variety of fallen leaves.

2.   Arrange the leaves in interesting patterns.

3.   Place newsprint over the leaves.

4.   Hold a piece of charcoal, pastel chalk or crayon on its side and rub it, on the newsprint, over the leaves.

5.   Display the leaf rubbings around the room.

Something to think about
Arrange some leaves with identification labels for the science center.

ANOTHER STORY STRETCHER

For Art: Twig Pictures

What the children will learn
To incorporate an object they find into a picture

Materials you will need
Fallen twigs, construction paper or posterboard, glue

What to do
1.   Ask the children to place a twig randomly on a piece of paper or posterboard. Glue the twig in place.

2.   After the glue has dried, ask the children to make pictures that incorporate the twig. For example, if the twig is placed across the top of a page, it could look like a tree branch in front of a window.

3.   Allow the children to think of many imaginative alternatives.

Something to think about
To reinforce this activity, have the children use three, then five twigs in a design.

STORY STRETCHER

For Mathematics: Hugging A Tree

What the children will learn
To use parts of their own bodies to measure trees

Materials you will need
None needed

What to do
1.   Ask the children to find trees that they can measure with different parts of their bodies.

2.   Let the children brainstorm a few examples: a tree as big around as a hug, a tree as short as a hand, a tree as tall as an arm is long.

3. Have the volunteers write down at least one inventive measurement per child during a walking field trip.

Something to think about
Upon returning from the field trip, discuss the usefulness of using parts of the body to measure other things.

For Science And Nature: Loam, A Natural Compost

What the children will learn
To use loam (naturally decomposing materials made by falling leaves) as planting material

Materials you will need
Acorns, loam, trowels, milk cartons, scissors

What to do
1. Cut the tops off milk cartons.

2. Have the children fill a milk carton with loam collected during a walking field trip.

3. Plant acorns collected on the trip.

Something to think about
Compare the growth of acorns in various soils—loam, potting soil, fertilized soil, over-watered and under-watered soil.

For Science And Nature: A Walk In The Forest

What the children will learn
To enjoy the beauty of trees and recognize various stages of growth and decay

Materials you will need
Parent volunteers, paper grocery bags, leaves, twigs, pebbles, other interesting objects found along the way, milk cartons, loam

What to do
1. Schedule a field trip or walking excursion into a wooded area.

2. If possible, arrange for groups of children to walk on different nature trails to allow them to enjoy the pleasure of discovery without interruptions from the entire class.

3. Spend at least five minutes sitting in a quiet spot and simply listening to the sounds of nature.

4. Do the mathematics story s-t-r-e-t-c-h-e-r during the walking field trip.

5. Bring back leaves and twigs for art and science displays.

6. Fill a milk carton with loam collected under a tree.

7. Look for sprouting acorns in the loam.

8. Bring the sprouting acorns back to the classroom for the science display center.

Something to think about
If you have a wooded area near your school, consider taking four or five children at a time with you for a special walk, rather than making it a class trip.

SOMEDAY A TREE

By Eve Bunting

Illustrated by Ronald Himler

A beloved oak tree, hundreds of years old, provides a dreamy place for picnics, storytelling and lazy naps for Alice, her mother and their dog Cinco. Unfortunately, the tree is poisoned by someone who dumps chemicals. Even though the neighbors try to save it, and well-wishers bring it cards, bouquets, scarves and even a get-well balloon, nothing can save the tree. Early one morning after a gentle rain, Alice goes to the tree and plants a ring of acorns around its roots. Ronald Himler's soft watercolor illustrations set just the right tone for this touching story.

Read-Aloud Presentation

Spread a large, colorful tablecloth on the floor in the read-aloud area of the classroom. Hide the book SOMEDAY A TREE in a picnic basket. Ask the children where their favorite picnic spots are. Pull the book from the basket and, showing its cover, ask the children where this family's favorite picnic spot is. To sustain the drama of the story, read SOMEDAY A TREE without pausing, . Let the children express their dismay at anyone poisoning a tree. Remind them that the father said it was probably an accident. Ask the children to talk about their favorite trees.

STORY STRETCHER

For Art: Circle Pictures

What the children will learn
To compose a picture in the shape of a circle

Materials you will need
Large paper plates with smooth edges, pencils, newsprint or manilla paper, easels, tempera paints, brushes, scissors

What to do
1.   Look at the dedication page and at the back cover of SOMEDAY A TREE. Notice the circle painting of the tree.

2.   Ask the children to place a large paper plate on a sheet of newsprint or manilla paper and draw around the plate to make a circular shape.

3.   Attach the newsprint or manilla paper to the easel. Invite the children to paint their pictures.

4.   Once the paint is dry, let the children cut out their circle pictures.

Something to think about
To make more permanent displays of circle pictures, glue paper onto round pizza boards.

STORY STRETCHER

For Cooking And Snack Time: Picnic Under The Tree

What the children will learn
To make picnic snacks

Materials you will need
Apple juice, cheese, crackers, napkins, picnic basket, large tablecloth

What to do
1.   Spread a large tablecloth on the ground under a tree.

2.   Invite the children to have their snacks with you.

Something to think about
While the children are casually snacking, talk about the beauty of the tree and read SOMEDAY A TREE again.

STORY STRETCHER

For Science And Nature: Planting A Circle Of Acorns

What the children will learn
To plant acorns

Materials you will need
Acorns, basket, trowels

What to do
1.   Look under an oak tree for acorns.

2.   Collect acorns.

3.   Select an old oak tree and plant a circle of acorns around it just as Alice did.

Something to think about
Create a ceremony to honor the occasion of planting the acorns. Read a poem, sing a song and dance around the tree.

For Special Event: D.E.A.R. Time Under The Story Tree

What the children will learn
To enjoy the pleasure of reading a favorite book while relaxing under a tree

Materials you will need
Array of books from the classroom

What to do
1. At D.E.A.R. time, "Drop Everything and Read" time, ask the children to bring their favorite books or a new book they are reading and meet you at the story tree.

2. Once all the children are settled under the tree, begin reading your own book silently and invite the children to do the same.

3. After ten to fifteen minutes of quiet reading, ask one child to show the others a special picture from his or her book. Ask another child to find an interesting phrase the author uses. Ask someone else to recommend a humorous book and read a funny part.

Something to think about
Make the story tree a special event several times a month. Encourage leisurely enjoyment of stories.

For Writing Center: My Special Tree

What the children will learn
To express their special feelings in writing

Materials you will need
Paper, pencils, colored pens, markers, crayons

What to do
1. With the children who are interested in writing stories about their special trees, explain that the author of this book is Eve Bunting. Encourage the children to imagine that the author must enjoy trees and probably even has a special tree. Let them discuss a tree that is special to them.

2. Encourage the children to write about their special tree, whether a real or imaginary one. They can write about a special tree they wish they had.

3. After the children have written their stories, guide them through listening conferences during which they read their stories to each other and take questions. The writer then can choose whether to add to his or her story by answering the questions.

4. Continue the editing process by asking the children to revise their stories if they think they have the beginning of a good story. Let those who do not feel that their stories are promising, begin writing about something else.

5. Edit the stories to final form and ask the children to make illustrations to accompany them.

Something to think about
Plan a time at the story tree to let the writers read their stories.

SAVE MY RAINFOREST

By Monica Zak

Illustrations by

Bengt-Arne Runnerstrom

English version by Nancy Schimmel

SAVE MY RAINFOREST is the true story of eight-year-old Omar Castillo and his determination to save the Lacandona rain forest of southern Mexico. Omar tries to communicate with the president of Mexico about the urgency of saving the rain forest. Unable to reach the president, Omar sets off on a pilgrimage to save the rain forest by marching there. His father decides to go with him, and they have many adventures along the way earning enough money to eat. Omar delivers his message to the governor. When they return to Mexico City, Omar and his father set up a red tent in the plaza near the president's balcony. He sees the president, who promises to save the birds and animals and stop cutting the rain forest. Runnerstrom's illustrations are pencil drawings washed in watercolors of many hues.

Read-Aloud Presentation

Show the children the photograph of the real Omar Castillo carrying the flag. Then turn to the front cover of the book and point out the artist's portrait of Omar Castillo. Read the book from cover to cover without stopping. The drama of the story and its compelling message will hold the children's attention. After finishing the book, read the message on the last page from the real Omar Castillo, in which he asks other children to join him in helping to save the rain forest and its animals.

STORY STRETCHER
For Art: Making A Flag

What the children will learn
To design a flag to represent their environmental concerns

Materials you will need
Newsprint, pencils, old pillow cases, newspapers, acrylic fabric paints, yardsticks, stapler

What to do
1. Look at the illustration in SAVE MY RAINFOREST that shows Omar and his father marching along the roadway carrying a flag. Point out to the children that the symbol and the message are simple: a tree with the words, "Save My Rainforest."

2. Encourage the children to plan a simple and direct message about an environmental issue that concerns them. Suggest they sketch their designs on paper first.

3. Use a pencil to sketch the outline of the design on an old pillowcase.

4. Slip newspaper between the layers of fabric and paint the designs with fabric paint.

5. After the designs dry, staple the flags onto the yardstick flag poles.

Something to think about
As an alternative, let the children paint designs on old T-shirts.

STORY STRETCHER
For Cooking And Snack Time: Omar's Birthday Cake

What the children will learn
To bake a cake

Materials you will need
Box of cake mix, eggs, water, vegetable oil, cake pans, bowl, mixer, spatula, oven, chocolate icing, nine candles, cartons of milk

What to do
1. Bake the cake on the day that the musicians are scheduled to play Mexican music.

2. Follow the recipe on the cake mix box.

3. Divide the responsibilities so that each child is able to help with mixing, decorating or serving.

4. Serve the cake with cold milk to drink.

Something to think about
If you cannot bake a cake, serve some of the other snacks that people in the villages gave Omar: pineapple juice, oranges, tortilla chips.

STORY STRETCHER
For Music And Movement: Mexican Party Music

What the children will learn
To enjoy music from Mexico

Materials you will need
Guest musicians

What to do
1. Invite musicians from the Mexican-American community to come to your classroom for a celebration of Omar Castillo.

2. Encourage the musicians to talk about learning to play their instruments when they were children.

3. Ask them to teach the children "Happy Birthday" in Spanish.

4. If possible, serve a chocolate cake with nine candles, as in the story.

Something to think about
In the story, Omar's father wakes him with "Las Mañanitas" on his harmonica. Ask the musicians to play "Las Mañanitas."

STORY STRETCHER

For Social Studies: Locating Omar's Rain Forest

What the children will learn
To find the Lacandona Rain Forest on a map of Mexico

Materials you will need
Map of Mexico, push pins, yarn, green construction paper, scissors

What to do
1. Post a map of Mexico in the library corner of the classroom.

2. Mark the location of Mexico City with a push pin.

3. Locate Tuxtla Gutierrez on the map, showing the place Omar and his father reached after walking thirty-nine days. Place a push pin at Tuxtla.

4. String a length of yarn from Mexico City to Tuxtla and then from Tuxtla to Lacandona.

5. Cut a small tree or leaf from green construction paper. Attach it to a push pin and mark the location of the Lacandona Rain Forest.

Something to think about
Read accounts of the earthquake in Mexico City, which happened while Omar and his father were on their journey.

STORY STRETCHER

For Writing Center: Writing For Environmental Information

What the children will learn
To write a letter requesting information

Materials you will need
Paper, pencils, envelopes, large manuscript-sized envelope, stamps

What to do
1. Read the message to the reader found at the bottom of the last page of the book. It tells where to write to request more information.

2. Teach the children the correct letter form and how to address envelopes.

3. Include a self-addressed stamped envelope and write requesting information to Rainforest, Volcano Press, P.O. Box 270, Volcano, CA 95689.

Something to think about
Just as Omar wrote a letter to his president, encourage the children to write to our president, at The White House, 1600 Pennsylvania Avenue, Washington, DC 20500, to express their concerns about environmental issues.

10

TREES AND RAIN FORESTS

WELCOME TO THE GREEN HOUSE

By Jane Yolen

Illustrated by Laura Regan

Jane Yolen communicates the beauty, mystery and wonder of the rain forest in wonderful rhyme. Her eloquent and accurate descriptions introduce the reader to the inhabitants of this fragile ecosystem. She helps the reader appreciate the color, climate, weather and sounds of the rain forest. The last two pages offer a refrain that young children will enjoy chanting together. This is Laura Regan's first children's book. Her illustrations in gouache capture the splendid rain forest colors and the mysteries of camouflage.

Read-Aloud Presentation

Construct a K-W-L chart with the children, listing all the things they already "know" about the rain forest and the things they "want" to know. Read WELCOME TO THE GREEN HOUSE and add to the chart by listing what they "learned" from the reading. After constructing the chart, read the last two pages of WELCOME TO THE GREEN HOUSE again and encourage the children to repeat the lines after you. Print these lines on chart paper for the classroom library and for the children to read on their own. Introduce the other rain forest books you have collected for the children to look at during free reading time. At another read-aloud session, present Helen Cowcher's RAINFOREST and compare the animals included in that book to those in WELCOME TO THE GREEN HOUSE.

STORY STRETCHER

For Art: Rain Forests Are Every Shade Of Green

What the children will learn
To shade and tint greens

Materials you will need
Display table, collection of green art supplies (many different shades of green construction paper, green crayons, green pencils, green chalk, etc.), tempera paints (green, black and white), brushes, newsprint, easels

What to do
1. With the children who are working at the art center, collect all the art supplies in the class room that are any shade or tint of green.

2. Look through all of Laura Regan's illustrations in WELCOME TO THE GREEN HOUSE.

3. Have the children choose different art supplies and create as many different shades and tints of green as they can to represent the greens of the rain forest.

4. Demonstrate how to shade green with black tempera and to tint with white.

5. Make a display of the rain forest greens for the art center bulletin board.

Something to think about
Connect the art story s-t-r-e-t-c-h-e-r with the science story s-t-r-e-t-c-h-e-r by inviting the children to think about which animal or bird could hide near this color and be camouflaged.

STORY STRETCHER

For Music And Movement: Rain Forest Creatures On The Move

What the children will learn
To move like the rain forest animals

Materials you will need
Chart tablet paper, marker

What to do
1. Read WELCOME TO THE GREEN HOUSE again and list all the animals and birds.

Slow, green-coated sloth
Quick-fingered capuchin
Blue hummingbird
Golden toad
Waking lizards
Silver fish
Coral snake
Howler monkey troop
Golden lion tamarin
Keel-billed toucans
Wild pigs
Chorusing frogs
Boat-billed herons
Fluttering bats
Kinkajous
Prowling ocelot

2. Let the children move like they think these birds and animals

11/30/05
06:08 pm

m:Month-by-month arts & crafts :
cember, January, February
e Date 12/28/2005,23:59

m:Out and create! For all seasons : easy
ep-by-step projects that teach scissor skills
e Date 12/28/2005,23:59

m:The storytime craft book
e Date 12/28/2005,23:59

m:450 more story stretchers for the
mary gra for activities to expand
ldren's favorite books
e Date 12/28/2005,23:59

would move. If they cannot decide, refer back to the text.

Something to think about
Plan another session for the children to interpret the movement of flowers and plants during different times of the day and different weather conditions (vines inching their way around the trees, for example, or orchids holding on during a violent downpour).

For Music And Movement: Connected To...

What the children will learn
To chant the names of the rain forest animals

Materials you will need
List of rain forest animals from previous story s-t-r-e-t-c-h-e-r, tagboard, scissors, marker

What to do
1. Discuss the rain forest ecology as an environment where all the species support each other, like a chain.

2. If the children do not know the old childhood song, "The head bone's connected to the neck bone. The neck bone's connected to the chest bone," then teach it to them.

3. Ask the children to sing the song using the names and descriptions of the rain forest animals. For example,

> The slow-moving sloth's connected to the quick-fingered capuchin.
> The quick-fingered capuchin's connected to the blue hummingbird.
> The blue hummingbird's connected to the golden toad.

Continue chanting down the list.

4. Cut strips of tagboard and have each child print the name of a rain forest animal on his or her strip.

5. Ask sixteen children to stand up, holding the names of the animals, but rearranged in random order. So the song might begin, "The blue hummingbird's connected to the fluttering bat."

6. Sing through the new arrangement of animals.

Something to think about
On the next day, add to the chain by inserting the names of rain forest plants and insects.

For Science And Nature: Camouflage

What the children will learn
To recognize how camouflage aids in survival

Materials you will need
Field trip permission (if no wooded area is available nearby), parent volunteers

What to do
1. Walk to a wooded area.

2. Disperse the children in twos or threes and have them sit very quietly.

3. Ask them to watch a small patch of soil or leaves.

4. Ask them to look closely to see whatever is living there—beetles, grubs, snails, ants.

5. Ask them to disturb the area gently, by lifting leaves, moving a stick, looking on the underside of a leaf. Note how much life there is in the area, and how it is camouflaged.

6. Back in the classroom, discuss how insects and small animals use camouflage to help them survive.

Something to think about
Place WELCOME TO THE GREEN HOUSE in the science display area. Let the children try to find all the animals camouflaged in each scene.

For Writing Center: Chain Of Animals

What the children will learn
To write and sing a song about the rain forest creatures

Materials you will need
List of animals from the music and movement story s-t-r-e-t-c-h-e-r, chart paper, marker

What to do
1. Read over the list of animals compiled from WELCOME TO THE GREEN HOUSE.

2. Adapt the children's chant, "Over in the meadow," to create a chant about the rain forest. For example:

> Over in the rain forest, in their green, green home, lived an old mother sloth and her little sloth one. "Move!" said the mother. "I move," said the one. So they slowly moved for a peek at the sun.

> Over in the rain forest, in their green, green home, lived an old mother capuchin and her little capuchins two. "Swing!" said the mother. "We swing," said the two. So they swung across trees near the sky so blue.

> Over in the rain forest, in their green, green home, lived an old mother hummingbird and her hummingbirds three. "Hum!" said the mother. "We hum," said the three. So they hummed near the flowers, the orchids and a bee.

> Over in the rain forest, in their green, green home, lived an old mother lizard and her little lizards four. "Wake!" said the mother. "We wake," said the four. So they stretched and stretched on the rain forest floor.

Something to think about
Print all the songs and chants on a chart tablet. Call this the class "big book" of music.

143

References

Bunting, Eve. (1993). **SOMEDAY A TREE**. Illustrated by Ronald Himler. New York: Clarion.

Seuss, Dr. (1971). **THE LORAX**. New York: Random House.

Tresselt, Alvin. (1972, 1992). **THE GIFT OF THE TREE**. Illustrated by Henri Sorensen. New York: Lothrop, Lee and Shepard.

Yolen, Jane. (1993). **WELCOME TO THE GREEN HOUSE**. Illustrated by Laura Regan. New York: Putnam.

Zak, Monica. (1992). **SAVE MY RAINFOREST**. Illustrated by Bengt-Arne Runnerstrom. English version by Nancy Shimmel. Volcano, CA: Volcano Press.

Additional References for Trees And Rain Forests

Behn, Harry. (1949, 1992). **TREES**. Illustrated by James Endicott. New York: Henry Holt. *A gentle poem that admires trees.*

Cowcher, Helen. (1988). **RAINFOREST**. New York: Farrar, Straus and Giroux. *The story of how the news spread among the animals of the rain forest that there was a new arrival, a man with huge machines.*

Hirschi, Ron. (1991). **FOREST**. Illustrated by Barbara Bash. New York: Bantam. *By answering questions posed by the text, the reader guesses the identity of various animals found in the forest.*

Rauzon, Mark J. (1992). **JUNGLES**. New York: Doubleday. *Through photographs and dense text, the reader explores the plant and animal life, geography and future of jungles.*

Thornhill, Jan. (1991). **A TREE IN A FOREST**. Toronto, Canada: Owl. *A Young Naturalist Foundation publication, the book shows the forest during the four seasons and explores the relationships of birds, insects, animals, sights and sounds to the life cycle of the tree.*

11

DESERT LIFE

Desert Voices
This Place Is Dry
Cactus Hotel
Desert
Mojave

DESERT LIFE

DESERT VOICES

By Byrd Baylor and

Peter Parnall

Byrd Baylor and Peter Parnall collaborate on a beautiful book that describes the desert through the eyes of its inhabitants: the pack rat, jackrabbit, spadefoot toad, rattlesnake, cactus wren, desert tortoise, buzzard, lizard, coyote and human being. In lyrical prose, Byrd Baylor communicates the voices of the animals and the excitement, yet retains the sanctity of this fascinating place. Parnall's line drawings with their sparse etched-in colors focus the eye and the interest on the desert animal's world.

Read-Aloud Presentation

Ask the children to look closely at the jackrabbit and coyote on the cover of DESERT VOICES. Notice that jackrabbit is aware of coyote. Look at the title pages and note that coyote seems to be following a scent. Turn to the dedication page and observe jackrabbit scampering away, half-hidden by rocks, while coyote watches. Show the children these illustrations first, then ask them what they think the author will tell us, based on what they saw in the illustrations. Call attention to significant features: the animal, plants, terrain, time of day. The book can be enjoyed by reading straight through, or savored more gradually by reading a few descriptions at a time.

STORY STRETCHER

For Art: Drawings Highlighted With Colors

What the children will learn
To use a highlighting technique

Materials you will need
Paper, pencils, markers

What to do
1.   With a small group of children in the art area, look again at Peter Parnall's technique of highlighting aspects of his drawings.

2.   Ask the children to draw first with pencil, then use the markers to highlight only the main features of their drawings.

3.   Invite a few children to talk about what they plan to draw and what they may highlight.

Something to think about
Some children will have difficulty only highlighting main features. They need closure, and filling their whole picture with color provides that closure. Often,

younger children will highlight their pictures, show them to the teacher or to a friend, then proceed to color in the rest of the picture. As an extension, have the children create one picture with color highlights and a second picture entirely painted with color. Display the contrasting pictures side by side.

ANOTHER STORY STRETCHER

For Art: Sand In My Picture

What the children will learn
To add texture to their paintings using sand

Materials you will need
Paper, watercolor or tempera paints, newspapers, glue brushes, white glue, margarine tub, scrap paper, sand

What to do
1.   Place newspapers over table surfaces.

2.   Let the children paint their desert scenes with watercolor or tempera paints on painting paper.

3.   While the paint is still wet, show them how to let a handful of sand run gradually through their fingers onto the part of their painting that represents sand.

4.   Hold the painting up and shake off the excess sand.

5.   If you want to be more precise with the sand, allow the paintings to dry, then brush a light layer of white glue, thinned with water, onto the part of the painting that is to be sandy. Sprinkle the sand onto the painting and shake off the excess.

Something to think about
If Native Americans live in your area, visit a display of sand paintings or show photographs of them. Native American sand paintings are part of religious

ceremonies. Sands of different colors are poured onto a flat surface, and the sands are used to recreate ancient symbols.

For Classroom Library: Reading Again For Details

What the children will learn
To extend comprehension by reading details

Materials you will need
Chart tablet, marker

What to do
1. Discuss how beautifully Byrd Baylor describes the animals.

2. Let the children select one animal they would like to hear about again.

3. Read the lyrical prose. Ask the children what specifics they learned about the animal from Byrd Baylor's description.

4. Make a chart of animal names and add details alongside each one, using key words.

Something to think about
Extend the story s-t-r-e-t-c-h-e-r by identifying words or phrases that the children might not understand. For example, in the description of the pack rat, "mica chip," is used. Let the children infer the meaning of a mica chip from what they have learned from the book.

For Science And Nature: Desert Plants

What the children will learn
To associate plants with their significance in the desert landscape

Materials you will need
Cactus plants, paper, markers, books about cacti

What to do
1. Make a list of all the words that refer to plants in Byrd Baylor's descriptions of desert animals.

> berries and roots
> mesquite beans
> summer cactus fruit
> cholla cactus
> greasewood bush
> grass
> twigs
> weeds
> bush
> cactus
> stickery branch
> spines
> tender blades
> juicy cactus fruit
> straw

2. Begin a cactus collection for the class. Ask parents and grandparents to donate small cactus plants. Label the cacti.

3. Read about the care of a cactus plant. For example, some small cacti require only a tablespoon of water per month.

Something to think about
Invite a parent who is a gardener, or members of a cactus gardening society, to bring specimens to class and talk with the children about caring for these plants.

For Science And Nature: Desert Terrain

What the children will learn
To improvise a desert scene

Materials you will need
Sand table, sand, rocks, small cardboard boxes, index card, marker

What to do
1. Print a sign that reads, "Create the environment which Byrd Baylor described in DESERT VOICES."

2. Provide materials listed and let the children improvise with others they collect from around the room.

Something to think about
Photograph the children's desert terrains. Appoint a different set of sand table excavators each day of the week.

11
DESERT LIFE

THIS PLACE IS DRY

By Vicki Cobb

Illustrated by Barbara Lavallee

Intriguing facts about the Sonora Desert, its people, animals and plants invite the young reader to imagine what life must be like in this desert. Beginning with plants and their capacity to survive virtually without water, the book explores survival mechanisms in the desert—for scorpions, black widow spiders and tarantulas, among others. Desert snakes, like the coral snake and rattlesnake, are beautifully illustrated. Other animals featured are roadrunners, Gila monsters, jaguars and pack rats. The book describes the vanished Hohokam Indians and their lives as farmers and creators of beautiful baskets and pottery. The settlement of Phoenix and its dependence on water is also discussed. The final page shows a beautiful Indian woman displaying a blanket inspired by the desert.

Read-Aloud Presentation

Print the following questions on the chalkboard, then read THIS PLACE IS DRY, answering the questions as you read: Do flowers bloom in the desert? What lives to be over 150 years old and is home to a variety of birds, small animals and insects? How do animals survive temperatures of over 130 degrees? What desert bird eats snakes and lizards? Which desert bird is the fastest runner on the North American continent? After reading the book and answering the questions, announce the story s-t-r-e-t-c-h-e-r-s and let each child choose at least one for the day.

STORY STRETCHER

For Art: Displays Of Baskets, Pottery, Jewelry, Blankets

What the children will learn
To appreciate the originality and the patterns found in Native American arts and crafts

Materials you will need
Borrowed baskets, pottery, jewelry, blankets, index cards, ink pens

What to do
1. In a newsletter to parents or school colleagues, ask to borrow baskets, pottery, costume jewelry and blankets they may have collected in travels to the Southwest.

2. Ask the donors to provide as much information as possible about the item, such as place of purchase, the artist's name and whether the item replicates a traditional pattern.

3. Let the children help create a beautiful display of the art.

4. When the display is set up, invite children from other classes to come and see it.

5. Compare the designs of these objects to those pictured in THIS PLACE IS DRY.

Something to think about
If you teach in a community where parents are unlikely to have collected arts and crafts on their travels, inquire of civic groups or among your friends for display items.

STORY STRETCHER

For Mathematics: Measurements In Story

What the children will learn
To associate measurements with interesting facts

Materials you will need
Chart tablet, markers

What to do
1. In the mathematics area of the classroom, gather a few children together and read THIS PLACE IS DRY again.

2. Pause every time the author mentions a number or a measurement, and print it on the chart tablet.

3. After finishing the book, ask the children to look at the chart and explain what each measurement or number means. For example, 2 1/2 inches refers to the amount of rain for the year in Phoenix.

Something to think about
With older students, classify the numbers by what they represent. Some numbers represent time, for example, like the year 1911. Others represent distance, such as 200 miles of canals. Many represent quantities, like a quart of water.

For Science And Nature: Desert Refrigerators

What the children will learn
To create an antiquated but effective means of keeping food cool

Materials you will need
Large earthenware flower pot, coarse cloth, ice pick, can, water, bowl, fruit

What to do
1.   Invert a large earthenware flower pot so that the small end is up.

2.   Place a bowl of fruit under the flower pot.

3.   Spread a coarse, loosely woven cloth on top of the upturned flower pot.

4.   With an ice pick or a can opener, punch a small hole in a can.

5.   Place the can on top of the cloth.

6.   Pour water into the can. The water will drip out slowly onto the cloth. The cloth will hold the water and cool the air in the earthenware flower pot, keeping the bowl of fruit cool.

Something to think about
Soak earthenware pots in water and feel their coolness. Place them in the sun to dry and compare the temperature difference.

For Science And Construction: Canal System

What the children will learn
To construct a series of canals

Materials you will need
Sand table, sand, soil, plastic pipes, pitchers of water

What to do
1.   Read the passage in THIS PLACE IS DRY in which the author describes the ancient system of canals in the Phoenix area.

2.   Fill the sand table with sandy soil.

3.   Ask the children to find a way for water to go from one side of the sand table to the other. Let them experiment on their own.

4.   They can dig canals and secure the banks by wetting the soil and letting the banks harden. They can also elevate one side of the sand table so that the water drains to the lower side. They can build up one side so that it is higher in elevation than the other.

5.   On another day, add PVC pipes, or even straws, and let the children improvise.

Something to think about
Teachers often do too much thinking for children. Try posing intriguing problems and letting the children think of and test out solutions. Older children can record the solutions they try and note what works well and what does not.

For Social Studies: Phoenix Pen Pals

What the children will learn
To write letters

Materials you will need
Overhead projector, transparencies, washable ink pens, paper, pencils, large envelopes, postage

What to do
1.   Consider becoming pen pals with a class in Phoenix.

2.   Contact the local board of education. Ask for the elementary education director and find out the names of teachers in the Phoenix area who might be interested in becoming pen pals with your class. Agree to an exchange of at least three letters.

3.   Brainstorm with the children to identify questions they have about Phoenix. Write the questions on the overhead transparencies.

4.   Discuss what they would like to tell their pen pals about themselves to help the Phoenix students get to know them better.

5.   Let the children write and edit the letters for clarity and readability.

Something to think about
Writing to pen pals to seek information about their lives in the city is both a social studies and language arts activity.

CACTUS HOTEL

By Brenda Z. Guiberson

Illustrated by Megan Lloyd

The book tells the story of the life of a saguaro cactus, from its emergence as a tiny seed pod through its slow growth over two hundred years. A pack rat eating the pulpy seed pod frees the individual seeds. After twenty-five years, the cactus has grown to two feet in height. After fifty years, it is ten feet high, and after sixty, eighteen feet high. During its life cycle, the cactus is home to many desert animals and insects. Small animals burrow in the desert floor to be near the saguaro's shade and the food it shelters. When the saguaro has achieved fifty feet in height, seven long branches and eight tons of weight, it stops growing. Even after it falls to the ground, after two hundred years, it continues to provide a home for ants, a collared lizard, a ground snake and termites. Megan Lloyd's colorful illustrations invite the reader into the desert and make life inside a cactus imaginable.

Read-Aloud Presentation

Read the title of the book, CACTUS HOTEL, without showing the cover. Ask the children what they think of when they hear CACTUS HOTEL. Show the cover illustration and identify the creatures featured on its border. Begin reading the book, then ask the children to recall what they learned about the pack rat from THIS PLACE IS DRY. Continue reading, without interruption, the story of how the cactus becomes a hotel. Leaf through the book a second time, listing all the birds, small animals and insects which live in and near the saguaro cactus.

STORY STRETCHER

For Art: Lift-A-Circle Pictures

What the children will learn
To make a display of a cactus hotel

Materials you will need
Green and dark green construction paper, scissors, glue, colored pencils

What to do
1.   Ask the children to draw a large cactus on green construction paper, then cut it out.

2.   Invite them to cut small circles of darker green paper.

3.   Ask them to draw birds and small animals in their cactus hotel rooms using colored pencils.

4.   Glue the darker green circles over the animal hotel rooms in the cactus. Glue only the top of each circle so that they can be lifted to show the little creatures living inside.

Something to think about
Make a desert burrow scene instead of a cactus hotel. Let the children draw and color the desert floor and make lift-a-circle

pictures to reveal the animals in their burrows.

STORY STRETCHER

For Classroom Library: Ask And Answer

What the children will learn
To state their questions, conjecture and confirm their answers

Materials you will need
Chart tablet, paper, desert books, materials from Saguaro National Monument (if available)

What to do
1.   With the entire class or a small group of children in the library corner, make a list of questions about the cactus and desert life. Some of the questions children will probably ask are:

Will the saguaro grow where we live?
How does the saguaro keep from drying up in the hot desert?
What does the fruit of the saguaro taste like?
Do the thorns hurt the birds and animals?

2.   Have the children conjecture about the answers to these questions and write their responses on chart paper. Do not give any hints as to right or wrong conjectures.

3.   Give the children time to explore other books and materials on the desert, then return to the questions and answer them.

Something to think about
Teachers often do too much thinking for children. What we want to do is to encourage them to answer their own questions. We can recognize that the children may have enough information to begin inferring answers from it.

For Mathematics: Measuring The Age By Height

What the children will learn

To associate growth patterns and measurements

Materials you will need

Spool of string, yardsticks, masking tape, chart paper, marker

What to do

1.   Read CACTUS HOTEL and write the age and growth measurements of the cactus on chart paper.

> *10 years—4 inches tall*
> *25 years—2 feet tall*
> *50 years—10 feet tall*
> *60 years—18 feet tall*
> *150 years—50 feet tall*

2.   Help the children measure lengths of string that correspond to the heights of the saguaro in CACTUS HOTEL.

3.   Tape the lengths of string to the classroom floor.

4.   On the first day, form an outline of a saguaro on the floor of the classroom using masking tape. Make the cactus as tall as the string is long.

5.   On subsequent days, create taller and taller saguaro cactus masking tape outlines.

Something to think about

If the classroom is not large enough for the largest saguaro outlines, move into the hallway and post a sign for children passing by that explains what the cactus outline represents.

For Science And Nature: Cactus Water Supply

What the children will learn

To observe the effects of water storage

Materials you will need

Variety of small cactus plants from a nursery, measuring spoons and cups

What to do

1.   Read the printed instructions provided by the nursery concerning the watering of cactus plants.

2.   Ask the children to water some of the cactus plants exactly as directed.

3.   Give other cactus plants ten times the amount of water recommended.

4.   Water other cactus plants until the water stands in the overflow dish of the flower pot.

5.   Place the cactus plants near a window.

6.   Observe daily for changes in the three different sets of cacti.

7.   After a week, using tongs and a knife, cut open one plant from each set and compare the plant fibers.

Something to think about

Keep some of the cactus plants that were watered properly for classroom decorations. Mark on the classroom calendar which days the cactus plants should be watered and how much.

For Social Studies: Saguaro National Monument In Arizona

What the children will learn

To locate a desert and a special ecosystem

Materials you will need

United States map, large map of southern Arizona and northern Mexico (if possible), self-addressed stamped envelope

What to do

1.   Read the additional information notes at the end of CACTUS HOTEL about the saguaro cactus.

2.   Help the students find the location of the Saguaro Forest, which is identified in southern Arizona as the Saguaro National Monument.

3.   Write to the Saguaro National Monument, 3693 South Old Spanish Trail, Tucson, Arizona 85730.

4.   Inquire about any free printed materials and the price of slides that would show the desert and the Saguaro National Monument.

5.   If possible, order slides of the saguaro.

6.   Point out the need for protecting special plants, just as we protect endangered animals.

Something to think about

If you have families in your classroom who have traveled in the Southwest, they may have slides that you could borrow.

DESERT LIFE

DESERT

By Ron Hirschi

Illustrated by Barbara Bash

Through descriptive prose and thought-provoking riddles, Ron Hirschi helps the young reader explore the mysterious desert. Starting with night scenes and ending with day scenes, the book's landscape features a variety of desert animals. The last animal to explore the desert is a child. Bash's watercolor illustrations each have a small square insert which gives a visual clue as to the answer to the riddle Hirschi has posed. The book provides additional information on two pages titled "More About Your Desert Discoveries." Twelve animals are discussed in more detail. The intriguing match of text and illustration keep primary age children guessing the answers.

Read-Aloud Presentation

If this is the fourth desert book you have read aloud to the children, they already know a great deal about deserts. Ask the students each to write one discovery or intriguing fact on a small slip of paper. Collect the slips of paper and place them in a piece of desert pottery or another interesting container. Point out that the book DESERT is part of a series called "Discover My World." Pause while reading for the children to examine the inserts carefully, so that they can discover the animal featured on the next page. At the end of read-aloud time and throughout the day, remove slips of paper from the container and ask the children to read them to the class. Return the slips to the container.

STORY STRETCHER

For Art: Desert Pictures-Within-A-Picture

What the children will learn
To draw or paint landscapes as well as close-up views

Materials you will need
Sturdy drawing or painting paper, small Post-it notes or small note pads, tape, brushes, paints, crayons, markers, chalks

What to do
1. Leaf through DESERT and notice the artist's technique of illustrating both a close-up view and a distant view of the featured animal. The close-up view is inserted into the upper left-hand section of the illustration.

2. Let the children place a Post-it note or tape a small piece of paper in the upper left-hand section of their drawing or painting paper.

3. Encourage the children to paint a large desert scene.

4. Complete the desert scene by using the illustrator's technique of inserting a small picture within a picture. Ask the children to draw at least one animal on the insert and place it on their desert scene in the upper left-hand corner.

5. Display the desert scenes.

Something to think about
Consider asking younger children to make night and day desert scenes.

STORY STRETCHER

For Classroom Library: Class Desert Discoveries

What the children will learn
To categorize information

Materials you will need
Discovery slips from the read-aloud presentation, index cards, markers, tape, posterboard, boxes or baskets or large envelopes

What to do
1. Ask a small group of children to read the discovery slips and divide them into categories like:

> *reptiles*
> *birds*
> *insects*
> *spiders*
> *plants*
> *heat*
> *cacti*
> *water supply*

2. Print the name of each category on an index card. Tape the card to a box or basket or large envelope or to the table top.

3. After the children have determined the categories, ask other students to come to the library to read and categorize the discovery slips.

4. Once the children tire of sorting and classifying the information, assemble the

discovery slips onto a posterboard which can remain on display.

Something to think about
After a few days, let other children redesign the task by thinking of new categories.

For Science And Nature: Comparisons Of Animals

What the children will learn
To compare desert inhabitants on the basis of size

Materials you will need
Chalkboard and chalk, large index cards, markers or crayons, children's encyclopedia

What to do
1.   On the chalkboard, write the names of the twelve desert inhabitants mentioned in the book.

2.   Give twelve children large index cards and ask each child to draw a desert inhabitant.

3.   On the reverse side of each card, print in large letters the name of the inhabitant.

4.   Tell the children to arrange the cards according to the sizes of the inhabitants. Encourage discussion and disagreement about how to compare rattlesnakes (coiled or uncoiled), lizards and tarantulas. What the children will soon learn is that they need more information.

5.   Help the students continue their research by looking in a children's encyclopedia.

Something to think about
For older students, extend the story s-t-r-e-t-c-h-e-r by creating a food chain of desert animals.

For Writing Center: Children Make Word Searches

What the children will learn
To create and solve word searches

Materials you will need
Chalkboard, chalk, graph paper, pencils

What to do
1.   On the chalkboard, list the twelve inhabitants of the desert. Write "coyote," the first inhabitant mentioned in the book, across the top of the chalkboard, spacing out the letters.

2.   Print the second inhabitant, "owl," down the left-hand side of the board, positioning the "w" under the first "o" in coyote.

3.   Continue constructing the word search, but do not insist that each inhabitant's name be connected to the previous one.

4.   Show the children how to insert additional letters to create the word grid.

5.   Distribute graph paper and let the children make up their own word searches. Encourage them to fill in the names of all the desert inhabitants first, then camouflage them by randomly adding other letters.

6.   Photocopy the children's word searches and let them solve each other's.

Something to think about
This story s-t-r-e-t-c-h-e-r is adapted from a suggestion by teachers Robin Burke and Brenda Barnard. Also make word searches containing desert words from the other books read for this unit.

For Writing Center: Writing Riddles

What the children will learn
To write and solve riddles

Materials you will need
Chalkboard, chalk, large index cards, markers

What to do
1.   Read again Ron Hirschi's DESERT. Note how he provides clues to the identity of each desert inhabitant.

2.   Using the list of desert inhabitants from the library story s-t-r-e-t-c-h-e-r, have the children explain two or three characteristics of the inhabitant that everyone knows.

3.   Go back through the list, adding less commonly known information, such as the facts provided at the end of the book. For example, the leopard lizard is described as looking like a miniature version of Tyrannosaurus rex.

4.   Ask a small group of writers to compose riddles using these characteristics. For example: "This animal hunts at night. Can be found around desert springs. All the family wear masks. What is it?" The answer is the raccoon.

5.   After the children have investigated further about the desert inhabitants, have them compose more difficult riddles.

6.   Number the cards and provide an answer key. Hide the key under a large rock and call it the desert rock.

Something to think about
Tie the art story s-t-r-e-t-c-h-e-r and the writing story s-t-r-e-t-c-h-e-r together by having the children compose riddles for the desert inhabitants they drew for art.

MOJAVE

By Diane Siebert

Paintings by Wendell Minor

MOJAVE is a lyrical poem about the desert that evokes visual and emotional images. The poem explores geology, weather, plants, rock formations, birds, small animals, wild mustangs, ghost towns, colors, lines and sounds. The desert speaks: "I am the desert. I am free. Come walk the sweeping face of me." Siebert's poem and Minor's illustrations are fitting tributes to the beauty, majesty and mystery of the Mojave Desert.

Read-Aloud Presentation

MOJAVE makes a wonderful introduction or finale to the unit on the desert ecosystem. Read the first lines of the poem to the children, then give them a few minutes to brainstorm the topics they think the poet will mention in her book. Write the children's predictions on the board. Read MOJAVE without pausing, so as not to interfere with the beautiful lyrical poetry. At the end of the reading, ask several children for their favorite passages. Leaf through the pages and compare the children's predictions to the actual contents.

STORY STRETCHER

For Art: Painting Mountain And Desert Terrains

What the children will learn
To experiment with creating shades of color, lines and other techniques for making MOJAVE landscapes

Materials you will need
Paints (tempera, watercolors, acrylics), brushes, sturdy paper, paper towels, scraps of paper, plastic knives

What to do
1. With small groups of children in the art area, look through Minor's paintings in MOJAVE and notice the lines, shadows, sharp and jagged edges, spattered paints, fluffy clouds, wispy plants.

2. Try mixing colors to achieve the desert colors. Encourage experimentation.

3. Using the paints, plastic knives and paper towels, let the children experiment with creating lines. Cut through wet paint with the plastic knife and notice how the result looks like the edge of a giant rock. Blot wet paint with paper toweling and notice how it absorbs some color, leaving behind a wispy print that looks like a sage brush.

4. After much experimentation, encourage the children to paint a desert scene.

Something to think about
When young children are exploring the possibilities of a medium, they need many days to practice. Leave the paints out for several days to allow them to experiment.

STORY STRETCHER

For Classroom Library: Tape Recording Desert Voices

What the children will learn
To appreciate and recognize the beauty in different voices

Materials you will need
Class members or school volunteers, tape recorders, stapler

What to do
1. Recruit children from the class, school personnel, volunteers or older children to read different pages of MOJAVE.

2. Tape-record an introduction to the book, reading the title, author's name and illustrator's name, as well as directions about the sound the listener will hear when it is time to turn the page. Do not tell who the readers are.

3. Record a page-turning signal, like snapping a stapler near the tape recorder microphone.

4. At the beginning of the tape, have all the readers read the opening lines together. At the end of the tape, read the same three lines.

5. Place the listening tape in the library area of the classroom,

along with headphones, a listening station and a copy of the book.

Something to think about
If you cannot assemble all the readers at once, stop the tape recorder at each page-turning signal. Start again, taping a new person in a different location.

For Classroom Library: Word Meanings In Context

What the children will learn
To understand the meanings of new words

Materials you will need
Chart tablet, marker

What to do
1.   Read through each page of MOJAVE and let the children tell you which words are new to them, such as:

> arroyos
> stampedes
> retreat
> domes
> creosote
> limestone
> chollas
> arid
> descendants
> prickly pear
> unyielding
> craggy

2.   After each word is named, read the page on which it appears. Ask the children either to define the word, or to think of something of which it reminds them, or with which it is associated.

3.   Let interested children decide to read one of the words and practice reading the page which contains that word.

Something to think about
Children often know the meanings of words even when they cannot define them. Practice with reluctant readers, reading the more difficult passages and letting them tape-record themselves reading their rehearsed versions.

For Science And Nature: Scientific Facts Learned From Poetry

What the children will learn
To recognize that factual information can be stated in interesting, even poetic ways

Materials you will need
Chart tablet paper, markers

What to do
1.   With a small group of children, make a chart of science facts about the desert.

2.   Read each page of MOJAVE and state a scientific fact about the desert. For example, reading the first page, one fact the children might state is: "The Mojave has red sandstone hills."

3.   Continue constructing the science fact chart by writing a simple statement derived from the lyrical language of the poem.

Something to think about
Let the children rewrite their scientific facts using poetic language of their own.

For Writing Center: Walk My Environment With Me

What the children will learn
To use the skeleton of MOJAVE to write about their own environment

Materials you will need
Chalkboard, chalk, writing paper, book binding materials

What to do
1.   As you read through MOJAVE, list the main topic of each page. For example, page one is terrain; page three, an animal; etc.

2.   Each main topic is part of the poem's skeleton.

3.   Ask the children to brainstorm what they might say about the environment where they live. Read again the three lines which begin MOJAVE. Let the children think about how to rewrite the lines to apply to their environment. For example: "I am the seashore. I am free. Come walk the sandy beaches of me." Or: "I am the city. I am free. Come walk the sidewalks, parks and shops with me."

4.   Let the children write their own descriptions on each topic: terrain, animals, weather, beauty, plants, special places and sights.

5.   Tell them to reread their descriptions and underline parts that they find particularly appealing.

6.   Share the descriptions in small groups.

7.   Encourage the children to continue working on their environmental poems, without concern for rhyming.

8.   Let the children select which parts of their poems to display with the desert paintings and drawings.

Something to think about
Encourage small groups of children to work together as listening groups. One child reads and the others listen. At the end, they compliment the reader on particularly effective phrases and expressions. Some children may want to write together as writing partners. Consider binding the children's environmental poems into a class book or individual books. (See the book binding illustrations in the appendix.)

References

Baylor, Byrd, and Parnell, Peter. (1981). **DESERT VOICES**. New York: Charles Scribner's Sons.

Cobb, Vicki. (1989). **THIS PLACE IS DRY**. Illustrated by Barbara Lavallee. New York: Walker and Company.

Guiberson, Brenda Z. (1991). **CACTUS HOTEL**. Illustrated by Megan Lloyd. New York: Henry Holt.

Hirschi, Ron. (1992). **DESERT**. New York: Bantam.

Siebert, Diane. (1988). **MOJAVE**. Illustrated by Wendell Minor. New York: Harper Collins.

Additional References for Desert

Baylor, Byrd. (1975). **THE DESERT IS THEIRS**. Illustrated by Peter Parnall. New York: Charles Scribner's Sons. *A Caldecott Honor Book about the ways that the plants, animals and Desert People live together in harmony.*

Jernigan, Gisela. (1988). **ONE GREEN MESQUITE TREE**. Illustrated by E. Wesley Jernigan. Tucson: Harbinger House. *Introduces the numbers one through twenty in rhymed text and illustrations describing various plants and animals of the desert.*

Lerner, Carol. (1991). **A DESERT YEAR**. New York: Morrow Junior Books. *Organized by season, the book explores the lives of birds, reptiles, amphibians, arthropods and plants.*

Reynolds, Jan. (1991). **SAHARA: VANISHING CULTURES**. San Diego: Harcourt Brace Jovanovich. *Through photographs and text, describes the way of life of the Tuaregs, a nomadic culture that lives in the Sahara, the world's largest desert.*

Woelflein, Luise. (1993). **DESERT ANIMALS**. Illustrated by Barbara Gibson. New York: Scholastic. *A pop-up book with folding pages and interesting facts about three desert animals on each page.*

NATIVE AMERICAN STORIES

In My Mother's House
The Mud Pony
Fire Race: A Karuk Coyote Tale
Dream Wolf
Dragonfly's Tale

NATIVE AMERICAN STORIES

IN MY MOTHER'S HOUSE

By Ann Nolan Clark

Illustrated by Velino Herrera

This collection of twenty-nine poems by Ann Nolan Clark chronicles the lives of the Tewa people of New Mexico, who live in a pueblo. The stories told through the poems show a community of people working together. We gain insights into an agricultural society that uses plants for food and medicine, that respects Nature, whose religion and art is evident in the beauty of their pottery and design. First published in 1941, reissued in 1991, this Caldecott Honor Book simply and beautifully respects the people to whom it pays tribute. Although a few illustrations of horses and plows are out-of-date, the tone and tenor of the poems are not. Herrera's illustrations render people dressed for festivals and horses grazing in simple line drawings or in color.

Read-Aloud Presentation

Because there are twenty-nine poems, select a few to read aloud and others to read at intervals throughout the day or the week. The poems are grouped by categories such as home and council, the fields, farm animals, plants and wild animals. The closing poem pays tribute to the great mountains. Begin by reading "Home," "The Pueblo" and "The Council." Locate New Mexico on a map of the United States. Explain that the Tewa live in houses that are connected, much like our apartment buildings and condominiums. New Mexico is very dry, so the people must use water wisely in order to grow food.

STORY STRETCHER
For Art: Tewa Designs

What the children will learn
To make designs with black ink and to appreciate the difficulty of making symmetrical designs with paint

Materials you will need
Scrap paper, construction paper, black fine-point markers, black tempera paint, fine brushes, unglazed pottery or earthenware flower pots and acrylic paints (optional)

What to do
1. Look at the graphic designs throughout the book.

2. Read about the women making pottery and decorating it with painted black lines.

3. Ask the children to make designs on scrap paper with black fine-point markers. Once they like their designs, they can try making them on brown, white and manilla colored paper.

4. After they have experimented with the markers, encourage the children to try with the brushes.

5. Demonstrate how to load the paint onto the brush, how to roll the tip so as to create a fine line and how to pull the tip along the surface of the paper in one direction so as to leave a trail of black paint.

6. Encourage the children to replicate their fine-point marker designs in paint.

Something to think about
Paint unglazed pottery or earthenware flower pots with acrylic paints.

STORY STRETCHER
For Block Building: Pueblo And Plaza

What the children will learn
To build a pueblo community

Materials you will need
Large hollow blocks, butcher paper or large brown grocery bags, tape, crayons or markers

What to do
1. Ask several children who enjoy special projects to create a pueblo.

2. Look at the IN MY MOTHER'S HOUSE illustrations for clues as to how the pueblo and plaza should look.

3. Help the children find materials they would like to use.

4. Allow several days for the block building to take place.

5. Leave the building project up and talk about it as you read other poems and gather information about the Tewa people.

Something to think about
If you have a parent or grandparent in the class who is a mason, invite him or her to demonstrate how bricks are laid

and how plastering keeps houses cool.

For Cooking And Snack Time: A Tewa Snack From Trees

What the children will learn
To eat foods the Tewa people enjoy

Materials you will need
Apricots, plums, apples, pinon nuts (if possible)

What to do
1.   Read the poem "Trees": "Trees are good to us."

2.   Serve the fruits and the nuts whole so the children will see how the fruit looks when it is picked from the tree.

Something to think about
Plan a Tewa lunch like the one described in "Home," the opening poem. Serve tortillas, frijoles, melons, corn, peaches and red plums.

For Mathematics: Symmetrical Designs

What the children will learn
To recognize symmetry and to create symmetrical designs

Materials you will need
Photocopies of symmetrical designs, paper, charcoal, fine-point markers or pens, small hand mirrors, strings, beads

What to do
1.   Draw several symmetrical designs that represent natural phenomena. Photocopy them and give copies to the children.

2.   Demonstrate how to prove that a design is symmetrical, meaning that both sides of the design look the same. Hold a mirror up along the center of the design sideways to the paper. The

design should repeat itself in the reflection.

3.   Symmetry is an important mathematical concept. Show the children how to draw symmetrical patterns by folding a sheet of paper in half and using charcoal to draw half a pattern on one side of the fold. By closing the paper along its fold again, they create a faint image on the other side. Show them how to trace over the faint image to complete the pattern. Use fine-point markers to go over the entire charcoal pattern.

4.   Encourage the children to create symmetrical patterns with beads. Place a paper clip in the middle of a string. Show them how to create a pattern with beads on one side of the clip, then create a mirror image of the pattern with beads on the other side of the clip.

Something to think about
Make the task more interesting by having one child create a pattern and another child create the mirror image. They can also exchange beads.

For Science And Nature: Water Must Not Be Wasted

What the children will learn
To use water, not waste it

Materials you will need
Sand and water table, sand, potting soil, wooden or plastic boards, pitchers, blades of grass, small length of hose, large plastic bucket or another water table.

What to do
1.   Read about water in the five poems titled "Fields," "Arroyos," "Ditches," "Irrigation," "Spring" and "Pipeline."

2.   Set up the sand table and ask a few builders to create a landscape

with a mixture of sand and potting soil.

3.   Pose several problems for the builders to solve:

What causes arroyos?
How could the water from a flash thunderstorm be saved and used?
How can we get water from the land to the pueblo?

4.   Let the builders decide how to create an arroyo (a deep cut in the land caused by flash flooding).

5.   After they have practiced pouring a lot of water from a pitcher and washing away some of the soil, let them decide how they could channel the water that would prevent its washing away the soil.

6.   Encourage the builders to make ditches by creating small dams out of wooden or plastic boards, which can be raised to irrigate the corn field. (Let them create the corn field by sticking blades of grass in the soil.)

7.   Pose the final problem: how to get the water from the sand and water table to the pueblo previously built in the block center. Let the children discover that they can pipe it over by pouring water through the garden hose, in the same way that the Tewa connected the pipes to the spring. Perhaps they will discover that they need a holding tank for the water.

Something to think about
Discuss ways to conserve water in the classroom. Make a chart of water conservation measures.

12
NATIVE AMERICAN STORIES

THE MUD PONY

Retold by Caron Lee Cohen

Illustrated by Shonto Begay

A poor boy longs for a pony, but the only one he can afford is the pony he molded from river bank clay. When buffalo are sighted, his village moves on to the hunt, leaving the poor boy behind. Distraught, he dreams that the pony is real and that it speaks, urging the boy to trust him. When the boy awakens, he finds that the pony is real. The pony takes the boy to his family and guides the hunters to the buffalo. When the boy grows older, he is made chief, and the pony stays with him. In the end, the pony does leave, but leaves behind a wise and respected chief. Shonto Begay is Navajo, and his water-color illustrations reflect the story's magical tone. The minimal lines and watery backgrounds help create an impression of the mystical.

Read-Aloud Presentation

Explain to the children that the poems from IN MY MOTHER'S HOUSE are about real Native Americans. THE MUD PONY is a traditional Skidi Pawnee tale told for entertainment. Like other Native American stories, it is meant to teach a lesson. Do not show the cover of THE MUD PONY. Begin with the inside title page, which shows a tiny clay pony. Read the tale without pausing to discuss it. Expect that near the end of the story, when the boy becomes chief, the children may break into applause. They will become sad when the pony leaves him. Let the children share their feelings about the different parts of the story.

STORY STRETCHER
For Art: Clay Ponies

What the children will learn
To use modeling clay

Materials you will need
Modeling clay, wire, wire pliers, plastic knives

What to do
1. Let the children work with the modeling clay until it is malleable.

2. Show them how to bend and break lengths of wire using wire pliers.

3. Explain to the students why a wire frame is necessary to create a clay pony in a standing pose.

4. Cut the wire into lengths suitable for the four legs, back, neck and head.

5. Wrap clay around the wire and shape it.

6. Use the plastic knives to sculpt manes and tails into the clay.

7. Leave the ponies on display in the art center and around the classroom.

Something to think about
If your school has an art specialist, ask for help with the project.

STORY STRETCHER
For Classroom Library: In Search Of Other Child-Hero Stories

What the children will learn
To compare similar tales

Materials you will need
Chalkboard, chalk, reference books

What to do
1. Ask the children what lesson they think this story tells.

2. Read the acknowledgement page of THE MUD PONY. The author describes this story as a traditional tale of the Skidi Band of the Pawnee Indians. According to the author, "These stories exhibit the Pawnee belief that no matter how lowly one's origin, the path to honor is open through adherence to virtues such as constancy and a humble spirit."

3. With the help of the librarian, find other child-hero tales like San Souci's THE LEGEND OF SCAR FACE, and dePaola's THE LEGEND OF THE INDIAN PAINTBRUSH. Read the stories and compare what each has in common. A tribe is saved by the heroics of a poor, weak or somehow different child, whom a great spirit helps to become a tribal leader.

Something to think about
If you think this discussion is too advanced for your students, ask them to retell the story in their own words by looking at the illustrations.

For Cooking and Snack Time: Beef Jerky

What the children will learn
To understand that beef jerky is a way to preserve beef

Materials you will need
Small samples of beef jerky

What to do
1. Explain to the children that during the times that the Plains Indians hunted the buffalo, there was no refrigeration. Instead, they cured the meat by smoking it over a fire.

2. Let the children try beef jerky. If any of your students have never tasted jerky before, tell them that it is very chewy and tastes like beef.

Something to think about
Do not insist that children try the jerky if they do not want to.

For Social Studies: Where Do The Pawnee Live?

What the children will learn
To realize that Plains Indians still exist

Materials you will need
Map of the United States

What to do
1. Show the children the region of the United States commonly called the Great Plains: Kansas, Nebraska, Iowa, parts of Oklahoma, Texas, Colorado, Montana and South Dakota.

2. Read the passage of THE MUD PONY in which the boy sees the village tepees. Explain that tepees were easy to move and allowed the Pawnee to follow the buffalo herds. Explain that buffalo herds no longer roam free on the plains, and that the Pawnee live in houses, not tepees.

Something to think about
It is important to help children understand that Native American is a category that includes many different peoples with different histories. Similarly, young children should understand that today Native Americans live modern lives with modern conveniences, but many keep the old traditions alive because they are meaningful to them. If you live in a Great Plains state, investigate the Native American people who lived and continue to live in your region.

For Writing Center: Pony Poems

What the children will learn
To use descriptive language

Materials you will need
Chart tablet paper, markers, writing paper, pencils

What to do
1. Ask the children, "What would it be like to have a pony?"

2. Write down the words and phrases with which the children respond: "great," "scary," "beautiful," "like a dream," "ride him everywhere," "run and gallop everywhere," "better than a bike."

3. Ask the children to imagine themselves riding, and ask where they would go: "far into the country," "off the riding trail," "away over to the mountains," "to the camp where I went last summer."

4. Ask the children to imagine what their pony would look like, and to write their descriptions on the chart tablet: "palomino," "not too big to get on," "like Black Beauty," "wild with everyone but me," "almost like a unicorn."

5. Ask the children to write responses to the phrase, "If I had a pony...." Tell them it is okay to write in words and phrases, that they do not have to write in sentences.

6. After a few children have written their descriptions, read a few of the more lyrical and poetic.

7. Let the children who are interested revise their pony poems. Others may want to write a new story about suddenly getting a pony.

Something to think about
Encourage the children to add illustrations and place their poems and drawings on the bulletin boards.

NATIVE AMERICAN STORIES

FIRE RACE:
A KARUK COYOTE TALE

Retold by Jonathan London

Illustrated by Sylvia Long

Long ago, the animals were cold, and they had no fire to warm themselves. Wise Old Coyote proposed a plan to steal the fire guarded by the vicious Yellow Jacket sisters. The Karuk tale also involves other animals with human traits: Eagle, Cougar, Fox, Bear, Measuring Worm, Turtle and Frog. With the help of the trickster Coyote, they learn to work together. Entertaining and dramatic, FIRE RACE leaves the listener with two morals: avoid vanity and work together. Long's beautifully detailed and brightly colored illustrations convey the drama and the Karuk landscape. Decorative articles like walking sticks, baskets, pottery and blankets reveal the Karuk culture.

Read-Aloud Presentation

Cover the title of the book, then open the dust jacket so that an entire scene is revealed. Let the children identify all the animals they can see. Ask them to think up titles, based on the illustration. Write their titles on chart tablet paper or on the chalkboard. Ask the children also to predict whom they think the story's hero will be. Read FIRE RACE, pausing at the illustrations of Coyote at the door of the Yellow Jacket sisters. Show them the sisters, and see whether the children notice that the sisters are entirely yellow, without stripes. Finish the story and ask the children what they think its lessons are. What is the storyteller trying to teach us?

STORY STRETCHER

For Art: Charcoal On Yellow Designs

What the children will learn
To decorate using charcoal, an ancient method

Materials you will need
Charcoal, scrap paper, yellow construction paper, scissors

What to do
1.   Let the children experiment with charcoal—thin, thick, long and short pieces—to make drawings on scrap paper. Use the points and sides of the pieces to create designs.

2.   Cut yellow jacket shapes from yellow construction paper.

3.   Ask the children to draw designs with charcoal on the yellow jackets.

4.   Older students may prefer to use charcoal to illustrate their drawings or to make the traditional Karuk designs pictured on the baskets and blankets.

Something to think about
If you live in California, visit the Hover Collection of Karuk Baskets at the Clarke Memorial Museum in Eureka. Bring back pictures or slides of the decorative designs. Let the children create similar designs using charcoal.

ANOTHER STORY STRETCHER

For Art: Decorative Arts

What the children will learn
To use paints to decorate a walking stick

Materials you will need
Dowels or fallen limbs, acrylic paints and small brushes or permanent ink markers

What to do
1.   Look at Grandfather Coyote's decorated walking stick.

2.   If you live in a forested area, take a walk in search of fallen limbs that would make good walking sticks. Enlist the help of a craftsperson or parent volunteer to strip away the bark.

3.   Paint the dowels or stripped limbs with the acrylic paints or permanent ink markers to create decorated walking sticks.

4.   Show the children that holding the marker or paintbrush in place, while turning the walking stick, creates a more even design.

5.   Exhibit the walking sticks in the classroom. Take one down each day and call it the story stick.

Something to think about
Encourage the children to make decorative necklaces. Call attention to the necklaces that the animals in the book wear. They are made of shells because the Karuk live near the ocean.

For Classroom Library: Flannel Board Story

What the children will learn
To sequence the events in a story

Materials you will need
Flannel board, construction paper, laminating film, scissors, glue, old emery boards

What to do
1. Draw the animals from the book on construction paper.

2. Laminate the paper animals and cut them out.

3. Cut emery boards into two-inch strips.

4. Glue the emery boards onto the backs of the laminated pieces.

5. Retell the story of FIRE RACE by arranging the animals in the order of their appearance in the story.

6. Leave the flannel board pieces and the book on display in the classroom library for the children to use in retelling the story to each other at their leisure.

Something to think about
Flannel board stories are excellent tools for kinesthetic learners. Try to make at least one flannel board story per unit.

For Classroom Library: Fire Bringer Stories

What the children will learn
To compare Native American tales

Materials you will need
Chart paper and marker or chalk and chalkboard

What to do
1. Discuss the main events in FIRE RACE.

2. Read RAINBOW CROW and discuss similarities and differences between the two tales.

3. Create a Venn diagram to chart these comparisons. Make two circles that overlap in the middle. In the overlapping sections, write the similarities. In the outer sections, write the differences.

Something to think about
Locate other sources of fire bringer tales and continue the comparisons.

For Writing Center: A Different Hero

What the children will learn
To use a story skeleton to write a new tale

Materials you will need
Chart tablet paper and marker or chalk and chalkboard

What to do
1. List the names of all the animals in FIRE RACE:

Coyote
Eagle
Mountain Lion
Fox
Bear
Measuring Worm
Turtle
Frog

2. Ask the children to describe these animals.

3. Brainstorm with the students about what might happen if one of the other animals went to the Yellow Jacket sisters. How might that animal approach the sisters? Perhaps Eagle would tease the sisters into a flying contest and, while they were away, Mountain Lion would bound into their house and steal the fire. Perhaps Measuring Worm would sneak through a crack in the wall and,

while the Yellow Jackets slept, inch a bit of fire out the door to Fox, who would run as fast as he could down the mountain.

4. Encourage the children to write their different versions of the tale, thinking about how the unique characteristics of each animal determines that they will approach problems differently.

Something to think about
Read the afterword of FIRE RACE and ask the children to write an afterword for their stories, explaining that their stories are inspired by the Karuk tale of FIRE RACE.

12
NATIVE AMERICAN STORIES

DREAM WOLF
By Paul Goble

Two young children stray from their parents, who are picking berries. Lost and afraid, the children spend the night in a cave. The boy dreams that a wolf protects them. When he awakens, he finds that it is no dream. Wolf is real, and he helps them find food and leads them back to their village. The children tell of their rescue. The elders are grateful and bestow great gifts on kindly Wolf. From that day forward, there has been a close kinship between the wolf and the Wolf People. Paul Goble's award-winning illustrations are colorful, detailed, stylized and respectful of the Great Plains Indians. The last scene, which shows modern berry pickers, offers a wonderful comparison to the scenes of berry-picking Indians in traditional dress.

Read-Aloud Presentation

Show the children the cover of DREAM WOLF and ask whether this is a kindly wolf or a wolf who will harm the children. Introduce the boy as Tiblo and the girl as his younger sister Tanksi. Read DREAM WOLF. Pause at the end of the story and talk about how many Native American stories offer a moral. Let the children think about what lesson the storyteller wants us to learn. Also read the acknowledgement page of DREAM WOLF, which will help the children understand that the lesson is to respect all animal life and not to fear animals. With older students, also read and discuss the quotation from Chief Standing Bear of the Lakota, found on the title page.

STORY STRETCHER
For Art: Crayon Etching

What the children will learn
To experiment with etching

Materials you will need
Black and dark brown and dark blue tempera paint, white glue, crayons, paper, brushes, plastic knives

What to do
1. Have the children completely cover their papers with crayon marks of many different colors.

2. Mix a few drops of white liquid glue into the tempera paint. Let the children choose which colors they want to use.

3. Paint the papers completely over with tempera paints and let them dry overnight.

4. Look at the illustrations of the children lost in the mountains and inside the cave. Notice how the artist made white lines that show through very dark, almost black paint.

5. Ask the children to use their plastic knives like pencils, scraping away or etching lines into the black paint, exposing the colors beneath. The lines that they etch are like the lines that pencils make.

Something to think about
Plan to leave the materials out for several days. As children see the work of others, they will become interested.

ANOTHER STORY STRETCHER
For Art: Reflection Pictures

What the children will learn
To create a reflection print

Materials you will need
Manila or construction paper, charcoal, crayons, markers

What to do
1. Look at the illustration on the title page of DREAM WOLF, which shows the wolf howling at a full moon.

2. Show the children how to fold their papers in half by folding the paper down horizontally.

3. Above the fold, ask the children to draw with charcoal an animal or figure or pattern of their choosing.

4. Close the paper along the fold. The charcoal drawing will make a faint outline on the opposite side. With crayons or markers, color in the darker figure above the fold and create a lighter version below the fold, as if it were a reflection.

Something to think about
With younger children, make reflection pictures by soaking a piece of yarn in tempera paint. Let the children coil the yarn down onto one side of the paper, then

fold the other side over and press lightly. Open the paper to see the darker pattern and its lighter reflection.

For Cooking And Snack Time: Berries

What the children will learn
To wash and prepare berries

Materials you will need
Blueberries or other berries, fruit roll-ups

What to do
1. Serve blueberries or other berries alone or as part of a fruit snack.

2. Read the passage from DREAM WOLF in which the berry pickers gather great quantities of berries. Some berries they eat immediately, others they mash and dry in the sun to save for the winter.

3. Serve fruit roll-ups, which are similar to the mashed and dried berries.

Something to think about
If there is a berry farm nearby, take the children to pick blueberries, blackberries, raspberries or huckleberries.

For Science And Nature: Wolves In Folktales And Wolves In Reality

What the children will learn
To compare wolves in folktales and real wolves

Materials you will need
Chalkboard, chalk, index cards

What to do
1. List the ways that wolves are described in folktales and fairy tales like "Little Red Riding Hood" and DREAM WOLF.

2. Read WOLVES by Seymour Simon and list characteristics from these descriptions of real wolves.

> *Look like large dogs*
> *Close relative of dogs*
> *Loyal to their packs*
> *Adaptable to different climates*
> *Many different colors and sizes*
> *Runners with stamina*
> *Powerful jaws and canine teeth*
> *Marvelous hearing*
> *Make many different sounds—barks,*
> *growls, whines, screams, howls*

3. After reading the book, let the children talk about the interesting facts they have learned about wolves.

4. Make a display of the facts for the science center by writing them on index cards. Display DREAM WOLF and WOLVES in the science area of the classroom.

Something to think about
Read Seymour Simon's afterword about wolves and Paul Goble's acknowledgment page about wolves.

For Writing Center: Learning Logs From Folktales And Reality

What the children will learn
To recognize facts from multiple sources

Materials you will need
Journals or learning logs, pencils, colored pens

What to do
1. Construct journals or learning logs by placing lined and unlined paper into folders, or by stapling loose pages together inside a cover.

2. Look through DREAM WOLF and read the first pages that describe people making camp and picking berries.

3. Ask the children to write facts from the introduction and from the illustrations. For example, there once were so many berries that, dried and stored, they provided food for the entire winter.

4. Continue reading, letting the children decide what is fact and what is fantasy. For example, it is a fact that big horn sheep live in the mountains. It is a fact that bears are in the mountains. But the idea that wolves talk to children is fiction.

Something to think about
Ask children who are interested to write a story about a wolf who is kind to children. Encourage them to imagine a new adventure.

12
NATIVE AMERICAN STORIES

DRAGONFLY'S TALE

Retold and illustrated by

Kristina Rodanas

The Ashiwi offend the spirits of the Corn Maidens by wasting food. As punishment, their crops do not grow, and the people wander the desert in search of food. Two sleeping children, a boy and a girl, are accidently left behind when the villagers go in search of food. The boy makes his little sister a beautiful toy dragonfly from cornstalks. The dragonfly magically comes to life and flies off to find the Corn Maidens and tell them of the children's distress. When the children wake the next morning, their house is filled with beans, squash, a mound of corn reaching to the ceiling—enough to get them through the winter. In the spring, they plant corn seeds and their crops prosper. When the villagers return, there is enough for everyone. No one ever wastes food again. The bright and colorful illustrations detail the landscapes, beautiful clothing and festival dress.

Read-Aloud Presentation

Ask the children what "waste not, want not," means to them. Look at the cover of DRAGONFLY'S TALE and ask the students to describe what they see. Tell them that the two children are brother and sister. Let them look closely at the cornstalk dragonfly that the children are holding. Read DRAGONFLY'S TALE. After the scene in which the children offer food to the beggars, encourage a few students to predict what will happen next. After the scene in which the dragonfly comes to life, encourage one or two other children to predict what will happen next. At the end of the book, ask one or two children to explain the important lessons of the story.

STORY STRETCHER

For Art: Corn Husk Sculptures

What the children will learn
To make toys from corn husks

Materials you will need
Corn husks (from ears of corn or craft stores or farmers), pencils or popsicle sticks, scraps of construction paper, heavy thread or dental floss, scissors, watery tempera paint, small brushes

What to do
1. Read the description of how the little boy made the dragonfly toy for his sister. Let the children think of ways they could make a dragonfly from materials found in the classroom.

2. Make the body of the dragonfly by wrapping a moistened corn husk around a pencil or popsicle stick. Tie it in place with heavy thread or dental floss.

3. Make the wings of the dragonfly by shaping the corn husks.

4. Glue narrow strips of construction paper to the body so that they stick out like antennae.

5. Touch a small brush gently into watery tempera paint. Stroke the color onto the wings, just as the little boy did. Watch the color follow the veins of the husk.

6. Allow the dragonflies to dry over night.

7. Tie dental floss onto the dragonflies and hang them as mobiles, or let the children fly them as toys.

Something to think about
Corn husk has been used as a fiber for making toys in many cultures. (Inspired by Carol Petrash's description of Corn Husk Dolls in EARTHWAYS, 1992, from Gryphon House.)

STORY STRETCHER

For Cooking And Snack Time: Corn Meal Muffins

What the children will learn
To follow a recipe

Materials you will need
Toaster oven, corn muffin mix, muffin tin, mixing bowl, measuring cup, water, wooden spoon, vegetable oil, margarine or butter, honey, napkins, chart tablet paper, marker

What to do
1. On chart paper, print the recipe and directions for baking corn muffins from the back of the package.

2. Involve several children in the baking process by making several batches. Ask one child to read the recipe, another to measure, another to mix and another to serve.

3. Serve hot with butter or margarine and honey.

Something to think about
Consider making the recipe from scratch. If you really want children to appreciate the source of the corn meal, have them grind corn.

S T O R Y   S T R E T C H E R

For Music And Movement: Writing A Rain Chant

What the children will learn
To compose a chant expressing the need for rain

Materials you will need
Drums, chalkboard, chalk

What to do
1. Read the passage of the story in which the people danced and asked for rain.

2. Let the children think of words that sound to them like a rain chant. Talk about how sad the people felt, so their dance would be slow. One possibility would be a slow, steady beat, the children saying "rain" at each shift of the foot, with an extra beat at the end of the line.

> *Rain rain rain*
> *We need rain*
> *Corn needs rain*
> *Squash needs rain*
> *Beans need rain*
> *Sky send rain*
> *We need rain*
> *Corn needs rain*
> *Squash needs rain*
> *Beans need rain*
> *Rain rain rain*

3. Pretend that a cloud is coming across the sky. As it begins to rain, beat the drum more rapidly, turn and hop around more excitedly.

> *Rain is coming*
> *Wind is blowing*
> *Drops are falling*
> *Rain sky rain*
> *Rain here, rain now*
> *Rain for corn and squash and beans*
> *Rain rain*
> *Rain!*

Something to think about
If you live near Native American dancers who would be willing to come to your school, invite them. Ask them to allow the children to dance with them. Remember that some dances are sacred ceremonies and outsiders may not participate, but many of the dances that celebrate harvest and ask for rain can be shared.

S T O R Y   S T R E T C H E R

For Science And Nature: Corn Needs Rain

What the children will learn
To observe how water supply affects the growth of corn

Materials you will need
Seed corn, patio pots, potting soil

What to do
1. In the spring, plant seed corn in patio pots.

2. Shape the soil into hills, poke a finger into the soil, drop a seed into the hole and cover it with soil.

3. Watch for the corn to grow.

4. Water some pots with a gentle sprinkle every day. Give other plants half as much water and compare the differences in their leaves. Let one plant wither and die for lack of water.

Something to think about
It takes several months for corn to grow to harvest. Beans can be planted more easily, if you prefer a quicker crop. You might also try growing squash, another food mentioned in DRAGONFLY'S TALE.

S T O R Y   S T R E T C H E R

For Writing Center: Dragonfly Messages

What the children will learn
To apply the lesson of the DRAGONFLY TALE to their own lives

Materials you will need
Writing folders, paper, pencils

What to do
1. Ask the children to think and write about the lessons that the storyteller conveyed: "not to waste food" and "not to be given to displays of wealth."

2. Let the children think of situations to which this lesson could apply today, such as the cafeteria at school.

Something to think about
Native American storytellers do not directly state the morals to their stories. They believe that, as children hear the stories again and again from their elders, they will interpret the morals without any adult preaching. (Adapted from a discussion with Jan Peters about her students' interpretations of DRAGONFLY TALE.)

References

Clark, Ann Nolan. (1941, 1991). **IN MY MOTHER'S HOUSE**. Illustrated by Velino Herrera. New York: Penguin.

Cohen, Caron Lee. (1988). **THE MUD PONY**. Illustrated by Shonto Begay. New York: Scholastic.

Goble, Paul. (1990). **DREAM WOLF**. New York: Macmillan.

London, Jonathan. (1993). **FIRE RACE: A KARUK COYOTE TALE**. Illustrated by Sylvia Long. San Francisco: Chronicle.

Rodanas, Kristina. (1992). **DRAGONFLY'S TALE**. New York: Clarion.

Also Mentioned in this Chapter

Simon, Seymour. (1993). **WOLVES**. New York: HarperCollins.

Van Laan, Nancy. (1989). **RAINBOW CROW**. Illustrated by Beatriz Vidal. New York: Alfred A Knopf.

Additional References for Native American Stories

dePaola, Tomie. (1988). **THE LEGEND OF THE INDIAN PAINT-BRUSH**. New York: G. P. Putnam's Sons. *Little Gopher has the special gift of using paint to tell stories, and he keeps the stories of his people alive. Wherever he sticks his paintbrush into the ground, an Indian paintbrush plant grows.*

Martin, Bill, Jr. and Archambault, John. (1966, 1987). **KNOTS ON A COUNTING ROPE**. Illustrated by Ted Rand. New York: Henry Holt & Co. *A fictional story about Boy-Strength-of-Blue-Horses, an Indian boy who is blind, and his grandfather. By matching the parts of the story to the knots on a counting rope, the boy and his grandfather retell the story of the boy's birth, his first horse and the horse race.*

Ortiz, Simon. (1977, 1988). **THE PEOPLE SHALL CONTINUE**. Illustrated by Sharol Graves. San Francisco: Children's Book Press. *An epic story of Native American people from the time of the Creation to the present.*

Roth, Susan L. (1990). **THE STORY OF LIGHT**. New York: Morrow. *Inspired by a Cherokee myth which explains how the animals brought light into the world.*

San Souci, Robert. (1978). **THE LEGEND OF SCAR FACE: A BLACK-FEET INDIAN TALE**. Illustrated by Daniel San Souci. New York: Doubleday. *A retelling of a Blackfeet Indian legend in which a young brave travels to the land of the Sun to ask for the hand of his beloved.*

FOLKTALES FROM AROUND THE WORLD

Mufaro's Beautiful Daughters: An African Tale
The Princess and the Beggar: A Korean Folktale
The Story of Wali Dâd
Zomo the Rabbit: A Trickster Tale from West Africa
The Rooster Who Went to His Uncle's Wedding: A Latin American Folktale

MUFARO'S BEAUTIFUL DAUGHTERS: AN AFRICAN TALE

By John Steptoe

Inspired by an African story published in 1895, Steptoe writes about Mufaro's two beautiful daughters—Nyasha, the happy and kindly one, and Manyara, the ill-tempered and selfish one. Nyasha grows millet, yams, sunflowers and other vegetables in a well-kept garden where a little green snake keeps her company as she sings and works. When a call from the king goes throughout the land, seeking for "The Most Worthy and Beautiful Wife" to become his queen, Mufaro decides to send his daughters. Manyara, eager to get to the city first, sets off ahead of the family and servants. Along the way, she mistreats a little boy and an old woman. When Nyasha encounters them, she gives a yam to the hungry boy and sunflower seeds to the old woman. For her kindness, Nyasha is made queen, and Manyara becomes a servant in her household. The lush illustrations are characteristic of the flora and fauna of Zimbabwe.

Read-Aloud Presentation

Talk with the children about the two purposes of folktales: to entertain and to teach lessons about living. Look at the cover of MUFARO'S BEAUTIFUL DAUGHTERS: AN AFRICAN TALE and ask the children to interpret Manyara's expressions. Read the tale, pausing briefly for the children to predict what Manyara will do when she meets the hungry little boy. Pause again when Nyasha meets the little boy, and ask the children to predict what she will do. Continue reading without pausing. At the end of the story, ask the children what lesson the folktale conveys.

STORY STRETCHER

For Art: Colorful Birds And Flowers

What the children will learn
To experiment with color and perspective

Materials you will need
Tempera paints, brushes, paper

What to do
1. Look through the book at Steptoe's paintings. Call attention to the beautiful flowers and birds.

2. Notice the bright tropical colors of the birds and flowers.

3. Let the children experiment with mixing colors to achieve the bright pinks, reds, oranges, yellows and fuchsias.

4. Call attention to the ways that Steptoe uses perspective. Often the flowers and birds are placed in the foreground, near the viewer.

5. Encourage the children to use tropical colors and to situate flowers and birds in the foreground to highlight their beauty in the style of Steptoe.

Something to think about
With younger children, concentrate more on the colors and color mixing.

STORY STRETCHER

For Cooking And Snack Time: Nyasha's Baked Yams And Sunflower Seeds

What the children will learn
To prepare a healthy, natural snack

Materials you will need
Yams or sweet potatoes for baking, vegetable brushes, aluminum foil, oven, sunflower seeds, napkins, juice

What to do
1. Arrange with the school cafeteria or the center's food service to bake the yams or sweet potatoes in their ovens, or bake them in a microwave yourself.

2. Let the children help wash the yams or sweet potatoes by scrubbing them with vegetable brushes.

3. Wrap the yams in aluminum foil and bake them like other potatoes. (Do not wrap them in aluminum foil, of course, if you bake them in the microwave.)

4. Serve the baked yams as a snack. Talk with the children about the part that yams play in many meals in South Africa, the setting for MUFARO'S BEAUTIFUL DAUGHTERS. Help them remember that Nyasha gave the hungry boy a yam.

5. Cut the baked yams in half and show the children how to eat them with the skins and without the skins, just as we eat other potatoes.

6. Serve cracked sunflower seeds in twisted napkins and help the children remember that Nyasha

gave the old woman a pouch of sunflower seeds.

Something to think about
Try other yam and sweet potato recipes.

For Music And Movement: Nyasha's Gardening Songs

What the children will learn
To compose a song of work and pleasure

Materials you will need
Chart tablet, marker, auto harp (optional)

What to do
1. Read the pages of MUFARO'S BEAUTIFUL DAUGHTERS that describe how Nyasha worked in her garden growing millet, yams, sunflowers and vegetables. It was said that the plants grew better because Nyasha sang while she worked.

2. Let the children compose a gardening song. Decide what the tempo might be as she planted, chopped, weeded and watered.

3. Try softly clapping hands and snapping fingers in a rhythm of clapping on one beat, snapping on two, rocking the body back and forth, and humming until the children have the beat.

4. A beginning for Nyasha's gardening song might be:

I am Ny-ash-a
(clap snap   clap snap   clap snap
*   clap snap   clap snap)*
This is my gar-den
Here I pla-nt seeds
Here I wat-er sprouts
Here I see leaves grow
Mil-let, yams and more
Sunflowers bright as sun
Gar-den-ing is work
Gar-den-ing is fun
I am Ny-ash-a
(clap snap   clap snap   clap snap
*   clap snap   clap snap)*

Something to think about
If this rhythm and song do not appeal to you, try a more lively one. For example, adapt "Whistle While You Work" to create "Sing While You Garden." Or try adapting "Here We Go 'Round the Mulberry Bush" to create "Here We Go Down the Rows." Add other gardening phrases.

For Social Studies: Where Is Zimbabwe?

What the children will learn
To locate Zimbabwe on the continent of Africa

Materials you will need
Map of the world showing the countries and major cities of Africa

What to do
1. Help the children locate the continent of Africa.

2. Read the dedication page in MUFARO'S BEAUTIFUL DAUGHTERS, where Steptoe dedicates the book to the children of South Africa.

3. Call attention to the directions on the map: North, South, East and West.

4. Have the children find Zimbabwe.

5. Read the acknowledgement page and the back cover of the dust jacket for more information about Zimbabwe. As the children look back through the illustrations, help them to see the ways that the artist has used the archeological ruins of Zimbabwe.

Something to think about
While studying each folktale in this unit, identify its country of origin.

For Writing Center: Character Sketches

What the children will learn
To develop characters in their writing

Materials you will need
Chalkboard, chalk, writing folders, paper, pencils

What to do
1. Make two columns on the chalkboard. Label one Nyasha, the other, Manyara.

2. Ask the children to describe the main characters. For example, Nyasha was kind, but Manyara was unkind.

3. Continue the list until the children can think of no other words to describe the two sisters.

4. Find passages in MUFARO'S BEAUTIFUL DAUGHTERS and read them aloud to demonstrate for the children how the author described the two sisters by showing their relationships with others. He built their characters throughout the story.

5. Explain that some people describe MUFARO'S BEAUTIFUL DAUGHTERS as a Cinderella story. Let the children think about the parallels between the wicked stepsisters and Manyara, and the parallels between Nyasha and Cinderella.

6. Ask the children to write a story in which there is one very kind and nice person and one who is ill-tempered and mean. Encourage them to help their readers get to know the two people by showing the things they do, rather than simply telling the reader what they are like.

Something to think about
Younger children may prefer to draw the characters, talk about them and then write the character sketches.

FOLKTALES FROM AROUND THE WORLD

THE PRINCESS AND THE BEGGAR: A KOREAN FOLKTALE

Adapted and illustrated by

Anne Sibley O'Brien

The Weeping Princess is teased that because she cries so much, she ought to marry Pabo Ondal, the filthy beggar boy. When the king decides to marry the Weeping Princess to a nobleman, she refuses and instead goes in search of Pabo Ondal. With a few gold coins, the princess sets off for the mountains, where she finds Pabo Ondal and teaches him to read and write, to ride and hunt and to think like a scholar. At a festival, the king sees a wonderful horseman and wants to know who the rider is. The king hears a beautiful poem and wants to know who the poet is. Finally, it is revealed that he is Pabo Ondal, and that he was taught by the Weeping Princess, who no longer weeps. In beautiful watercolor pastels, O'Brien portrays a lush and mystical forest, a colorful city life and costumes to complement the ancient tale.

Read-Aloud Presentation

Ask the children why a princess might weep. What would a princess have to be happy about, and what might make a princess so sad that she wept almost all the time? On the chalkboard, print "The Weeping Princess," "Pabo Ondal," "King," "Queen." Read THE PRINCESS AND THE BEGGAR. At the end of the story, ask the children to talk about the significance of the queen in the story. The queen gave the Weeping Princess the gold coins after she was banished from the palace by the king.

STORY STRETCHER

For Art: Watercolors

What the children will learn

To use the watery effects of the watercolor medium

Materials you will need

Scrap paper and heavy paper suitable for watercolors, watercolor paints, brushes, small plastic bowls, paper toweling, masking tape (optional)

What to do

1. Look at the illustrations of the mountain scenes in THE PRINCESS AND THE BEGGAR. Call attention to the way that the artist portrays the mist in the mountains by making the watercolors even more watery and diffuse.

2. Let the children experiment on scraps of paper. Wash the paper over with plain water first, then dip the brush into the watercolor paint and let the color flood out over the paper.

3. With paper toweling, dry the foreground slightly.

4. Dry the brush on a paper towel, then load more paint onto it.

5. Paint the greenery and the details with the drier brush.

6. After the children have experimented, let them paint anything they choose.

Something to think about

Learning to use a medium like watercolor takes years of practice. However, simple techniques, like using drier or wetter paper, drier or wetter brushes, help the child to see the many possibilities.

ANOTHER STORY STRETCHER

For Art: Poetry Scrolls

What the children will learn

To make decorative paper for special poems

Materials you will need

Rice paper or tractor-feed computer paper, cardboard paper towel tubes or wooden dowels, tape, ribbons, colored pencils or crayons or markers

What to do

1. Look at the illustrated scene near the end of the book, which shows the judge reading Ondal's poetry scroll.

2. Show the children how to make a long scroll with rice paper or computer paper.

3. Let the children write a nature poem or copy a favorite poem about nature onto the scroll.

4. Offer the children colored pencils, crayons or markers to decorate the borders of the paper.

5. Roll the ends of the paper scroll onto empty paper towel tubes or wooden dowels. Tape the ends in place so that the tape is not visible. Use double-sided tape, if possible.

6. Roll the poem up and tie the two rollers together with a length of ribbon.

Something to think about
Invite a parent or community volunteer who knows how to write Korean characters to come to class and write the poem in Korean.

STORY STRETCHER

For Classroom Library: Storytelling With Flannel Board

What the children will learn
To sequence the events of a story

Materials you will need
Flannel board, felt pieces

What to do
1. Construct flannel board story pieces from felt: a royal carriage, crown, poetry book, bag of gold, paper and pen, horse, bow and arrow, poem scroll, mountain.

2. Ask the children to tell you the significance of each piece.

3. Demonstrate the flannel board story technique by retelling the book in your own words, using the flannel board pieces as props to recreate the sequence of the story.

4. Place the book, flannel board and story pieces in the classroom library for the children to use on their own.

Something to think about
If you do not have felt, make the pieces out of construction paper, laminate them and glue an old emery board or scrap of sandpaper onto the back of each piece, which makes them adhere easily to the flannel.

STORY STRETCHER

For Social Studies: Where Is Korea?

What the children will learn
To locate South Korea on a world map

Materials you will need
World map showing continents and countries

What to do
1. Read the dust jacket description of Anne Sibley O'Brien's childhood. She lived in South Korea for thirteen years and first heard the story of the Weeping Princess there.

2. Locate the continent of Asia and the nation of South Korea. Call attention to the other countries near Korea, such as Japan and China.

3. Help the children locate their own country and state.

Something to think about
Let the children decide whether the folktale of THE PRINCESS AND THE BEGGAR originated near the coast or in the interior. The answer is the interior, because the setting is the forest and the mountains.

STORY STRETCHER

For Writing Center: Inspired By Ondal's Poem

What the children will learn
To write a nature poem

Materials you will need
Writing folders, paper, pencils

What to do
1. Read Ondal's nature poem near the end of THE PRINCESS AND THE BEGGAR.

2. Ask the children to select something from nature that they think is very beautiful, such as a mountain stream, beautiful birds, a squirrel scampering among the trees, a sunrise reflecting on a lake.

3. Begin by asking them to write any words and phrases that occur to them to describe the beautiful scene or thing.

4. Ask the children to create in their minds a visual image of the beautiful place or thing.

5. After the children write, ask them to refine their poems and print them onto the poem scrolls they made in art.

Something to think about
Use the paper scrolls from the art activity as a way to publish the children's poems.

THE STORY OF WALI DÂD

Retold and illustrated by

Kristina Rodanas

Rodanas retells and illustrates a folktale set in India. A simple grass cutter lives in a hut and has bread and onions for dinner. Because of his simple life, Wali Dâd saves a few coins every day. When his money jar is filled, he goes to the marketplace and buys a simple gold bracelet with a beautiful pearl. It is too lovely for his humble hut, so he asks a traveling merchant to give it to a beautiful woman. The beautiful woman, the Princess of Khaistan, in appreciation, gives Wali Dâd a camel-load of fine silks. Wali Dâd sends the silks to the Prince of Nekabad, who sends twelve splendid horses to Wali Dâd in thanks. The exchange of gifts escalates until the Princess of Khaistan and the Prince of Nekabad meet. They marry, finally allowing Wali Dâd to return to his humble life. Rodanas, an elementary school art teacher, fills the book with enthralling illustrations: expressive faces, fluid and colorful silk garments, magical horses and elephants and a majestic royal caravan.

Read-Aloud Presentation

Without letting the children see the cover of the book, introduce them to Wali Dâd by reading the first page and showing the illustration of the grass cutter counting his pennies. Ask the children to predict what the humble man will buy at the marketplace. Pause again while reading the story for the children to predict what the Princess of Khaistan will do when she receives Wali Dâd's beautiful bracelet. Ask the children to predict what will happen when the Prince of Nekabad receives the camel-load of silks. Finish reading without any further interruption. Ask the children what the moral or lesson of the story is.

STORY STRETCHER

For Art: Patterns, Fabrics, Classic Shapes

What the children will learn
To observe closely and experiment with creating patterns

Materials you will need
Drawing paper, pencils, tempera paints, brushes, colored pens

What to do
1. With a small group at the art center, look through THE STORY OF WALI DÂD and notice how Rodanas creates a sense of place with the patterned silks, turbans, bejeweled elephants, curled toes of shoes and arches of doorways.

2. Ask the children to draw and color or paint, creating features that would help the person viewing their artwork to know that the setting is a magical place.

Something to think about
With younger children, consider cutting an Indian arched doorway into the top of the drawing paper.

This book is also a wonderful demonstration of perspective, offering a tool to help the children observe and appreciate the artist's technique, without expecting them to be able to paint or draw in perspective.

STORY STRETCHER

For Classroom Library: Stick Puppets From The Wali Dâd Story

What the children will learn
To sequence the story and retell it in their own words

Materials you will need
Construction paper, markers, colored pencils, scissors, laminating film, glue, tongue depressors or popsicle sticks

What to do
1. Let the children make the main characters and props needed to tell the story. Let each child choose one to make. Create horses, mules, elephants and flags until each child is busy creating a stick puppet. Major characters and props include:

> *Wali Dâd*
> *Merchant*
> *Princess of Khaistan*
> *King of Khaistan*
> *Prince of Nekabad*
> *Bracelet*
> *Silk scarf*
> *Camels with load of silks*
> *Prancing horses*
> *Mules with packs of silver*
> *Bejeweled elephants*
> *Flags*

2. Cut out the illustrations.

3. Laminate them and trim the laminating film.

4. Glue the laminated character onto a tongue depressor or popsicle stick.

5. Involve the class in retelling the story of Wali Dâd.

6. Place the stick puppets in the library for children to use in retelling the story on their own.

Something to think about
If you have a parent or someone else in the community who speaks with an Indian accent, ask the person to record THE STORY OF WALI DÂD. Place the recording at the listening station in the classroom library for the children to enjoy.

For Social Studies: Locating India

What the children will learn
To find India on a map of the world

Materials you will need
Map of the world, magnifying glasses, index cards, marker

What to do
1. Help the children find India. First locate China, because it is such a large land mass.

2. Then point out India.

3. Print the names of the Princess of Khaistan and the Prince of Nekabad on index cards.

4. Encourage the children to search on the map for the places where the Princess and the Prince might live. Because these are imaginary places, the children will find names that are similar, but not the same. The children will conclude that these are imaginary places.

Something to think about
Help children to understand that India is a real place, but Wali Dâd is an imaginary character. Read the information on the acknowledgement page about the source of this folktale, a book published in 1904 by Andrew Lang, which Rodanas used as her source.

For Special Event And Creative Dramatics: Beautiful Saris And Silks

What the children will learn
To appreciate the beauty of the garments of Hindu cultures

Materials you will need
Lightweight silks or other materials, borrowed saris

What to do
1. Invite a woman from India or another Hindu culture to demonstrate how to drape a sari.

2. If possible, ask the woman who brings the sari to leave fabrics with which the children can play in creative dramatics. If this is not possible, bring in one-yard lengths of lightweight fabric and let the children enjoy draping them like saris or wrapping them like turbans.

3. Add costume jewelry for the children to enjoy.

Something to think about
A sari is a long piece of lightweight silk wrapped around the body and draped over the shoulder, usually worn by Hindu women.

For Writing Center: Another Wali Dâd Adventure

What the children will learn
To change settings and retain characteristics

Materials you will need
Writing paper, art supplies for illustrations

What to do
1. With a small group of writers, brainstorm extensions of THE STORY OF WALI DÂD. For example, write a story about the wedding of the Princess of Khaistan and the Prince of Nekabad. Will Wali Dâd be there? How will he act? What will he do?

2. As another writing experience, some children might place Wali Dâd in our country and tell a similar story of a humble person whose unselfish act sets off an elaborate chain of events.

3. Publish and illustrate the Wali Dâd series of stories.

Something to think about
Always let the children choose whether or not they want to participate in the writing extensions of stories. Insist that everyone write every day, but allow children involved in other writing projects to continue those they design.

ZOMO THE RABBIT: A TRICKSTER TALE FROM WEST AFRICA

By Gerald McDermott

Zomo the Rabbit is clever, but he wants more. He goes to Sky God and asks how he can become wise. Sky God tells him that to earn wisdom he must carry out three impossible tasks: capture the scales of Big Fish, the milk of Wild Cow and the tooth of Leopard. Through a series of clever tricks, Zomo succeeds in each task. Sky God praises Zomo for his cleverness and offers him a gift of wisdom: that when he sees Big Fish, Wild Cow and Leopard, it would be wise to run fast. McDermott's bold and comical graphics are in bright colors on sunny yellow and orange backgrounds. The patterns in Zomo's shirt, hat and drum, as well as the plants and flowers, help the reader identify the tale's setting as West Africa.

Read-Aloud Presentation

Discuss the meaning of the word "trickster." Note that in traditional tales, the rabbit is often a trickster. Some students may think of Bugs Bunny, who is always tricking his friends in the cartoons. Ask the children to listen for the three tasks Zomo must accomplish to prove himself. Read ZOMO THE RABBIT, pausing just once in the story, when the Sky God tells Zomo the three things he must do to gain wisdom. After the reading, call attention to the fact that in many folktales, the trickster is the one who is tricked in the end.

STORY STRETCHER

For Art: Zomo's Geometric Fabric Patterns

What the children will learn
To make beautiful geometric patterns

Materials you will need
Brightly colored posterboard, pencils, scissors, glue

What to do
1.   Cut large pieces shaped like shirts from posterboard of different colors.

2.   Look closely at McDermott's illustrations of Zomo and note the beautiful geometric patterns.

3.   Encourage the children to trade scraps of posterboard until they have each collected many different colors.

4.   Ask them to cut geometric shapes from the scraps.

5.   Glue the geometric shapes onto Zomo's shirt to create a pattern.

Something to think about
Cut squares and triangles of brightly colored fabrics and glue them onto Zomo's shirt. Invite a West African who has traditional clothing to wear a shirt or another garment with the beautiful patterns.

STORY STRETCHER

For Classroom Library: Flannel Board Story Of Zomo

What the children will learn
To retell the story of ZOMO THE RABBIT

Materials you will need
Flannel board, bright construction paper, laminating film, glue, old emery boards

What to do
1.   Let the children create flannel board pieces out of construction paper upon which they have drawn with markers the following characters and props:

> *Zomo*
> *Drum*
> *Fish*
> *Fish scales*
> *Palm tree*
> *Cow*
> *Rock*
> *Tooth*
> *Sky god*

2.   Cut the children's drawings from the construction paper.

3.   Laminate the drawings to make the flannel board pieces.

4.   Cut old emery boards into small strips and glue them onto the backs of the story pieces so that they will stick to the flannel board.

5.   Let the children use their flannel board pieces to help you retell the story of ZOMO THE RABBIT.

Something to think about
Place the flannel board, story pieces and ZOMO THE RABBIT in the classroom library for the children to use in retelling the story on their own.

For Music And Movement: Drums And Stories

What the children will learn
To play drums and make rhythms that tell a story

Materials you will need
Traditional drums

What to do
1. Ask a music teacher to bring traditional drums to the class.

2. Accompanied by the beat of the drum, retell the story of ZOMO THE RABBIT.

3. Distribute drums among the class members. Teach them how to make different rhythms with their fingers, knuckles, heel of the hand, arms, even elbows.

4. After a few minutes of experimentation with creating sounds, decide how to beat the drum during different parts of the story.

5. Let the children accompany the story with their drums. Ask the music teacher to be the head drummer, and the children to follow the rhythms as you tell the story.

6. Explain that many cultures use drums for storytelling—African, Native American, Canadian, Asian.

Something to think about
Invite a West African storyteller to your class to tell a drum story.

For Social Studies: Where Is West Africa?

What the children will learn
To locate West Africa and identify the countries there

Materials you will need
World map

What to do
1. Help the children locate Africa and decide what part is considered West Africa.

2. Note the shape of Africa. Call attention to the directions on the map of West, East, North and South.

3. Read the acknowledgements in ZOMO THE RABBIT and observe that the Zomo tale originated in Hausaland, Nigeria.

4. Locate Hausaland, Nigeria, and help the children see that it is in West Africa.

5. Recall that the story of MUFARO'S BEAUTIFUL DAUGHTERS was set in Zimbabwe in South Africa.

Something to think about
Our goal for the children is not that they memorize the countries, but that they become aware of many different continents and countries and begin to explore the world map.

For Writing Center: Tricksters And Morals

What the children will learn
To give Zomo's advice

Materials you will need
Writing folders, bright collage materials

What to do
1. With a small group of writers, read the story of ZOMO THE RABBIT again.

2. Discuss what advice means. Many trickster stories have morals that are meant to give us advice.

3. Help the children think through the moral of the story of Zomo. One moral of the story is that he is not big and he is not strong, but he is very clever. Another is that tricksters often get tricked in the end. Another is to appreciate what one is, rather than wish to be something else. For example, Zomo is clever, but rather than appreciate his cleverness, he seeks to be something different.

4. Ask the children to write to ZOMO and advise him about appreciating who he is and what he can do.

Something to think about
Children often have difficulty stating morals. Ask the children also whether they think ZOMO will take their advice.

13

FOLKTALES FROM AROUND THE WORLD

A WHITEBIRD BOOK

THE ROOSTER WHO WENT TO HIS UNCLE'S WEDDING: A LATIN AMERICAN FOLKTALE

by Alma Flor Ada

Illustrated by Kathleen Kuchera

The author heard this Latin American folktale from her grandmother, a gifted storyteller in the Cuban tradition. Many versions of this tale can be found throughout the Spanish-speaking world. Rooster is dressed is his exquisite wedding finery and groomed with combed feathers and a very shiny beak. As he hurries along the path to the wedding, he spots a single golden kernel of corn floating in a puddle of mud. When he pecks the golden kernel, he gets his shiny beck dirty. He implores the velvety grass to clean his beak, but the grass refuses. He begs the woolly lamb to eat the grass, but she refuses, and on the chained story continues. This book was selected by Tomi dePaola as one of the Whitebird Books. Kuchera engraved zinc plates and painted with brilliant colors to produce the artistic prints.

Read-Aloud Presentation

Get dressed up as if you are going to a wedding. Your appearance will spark a lot of curiosity about where you might be going. Talk with the children about how you shopped for your clothes, borrowed something special and then fixed your hair. Let the children talk about when they get dressed up for church or synagogue or for parties. Have them tell how hard it is to keep from getting messy or dirty and keep everything just right while their parents get ready. Show the cover with the picture of Rooster and explain that he is also going to a wedding and that he has taken great pains with his appearance to look just right for this special occasion. Ask the children to predict what they think will happen to Rooster. Read the story and pause for the children to predict whether or not Rooster will peck the golden kernel of corn in the mud puddle. Let the children join in the repeated chain of events as Rooster tries to get his shiny beak clean. At the end, ask the children if the story reminds them of any other tales they have heard. Announce the story s-t-r-e-t-c-h-e-r-s for the book.

STORY STRETCHER

For Art: Mural With Brilliant Florescent Colors

What the children will learn
To experiment with florescent colors and layered designs

Materials you will need
Chart tablet paper, long length of brightly colored butcher paper, florescent paints or markers, brushes, table, yardstick

What to do
1. Ask a group of interested muralists to think of the main scenes of the story. List them on a chart tablet.

2. Draw a pencil line along a yardstick to divide the mural paper into scenes.

3. Divide the artists in small groups or in pairs to draw scenes on the mural paper using paint or colored makers.

Something to think about
Consider letting the children make a collage of figures by asking each child to draw one bright and exquisitely dressed wedding guest at Rooster's Uncle's wedding.

STORY STRETCHER

For Creative Dramatics: Storytelling

What the children will learn
To recall a story in sequence and tell it with expression

Materials you will need
Large index cards, markers

What to do
1. Help a group of children who want to be storytellers to recall the main events of story. List the main scenes on large index cards, one scene per card. Use a key phrase to help the children recall the scene. For example, on card one, print the words, "feathers and beak." On card two, "walking along path."

2. When the entire story is mapped out in main events and keywords, read the cards and let the children tell about that scene in their own words.

3. Invite the storytellers to tell the story to the class.

4. Have one child act as narrator and other children become the main characters, the velvety grass, the woolly lamb, the stubborn dog,

the hard stick, the clever fire, the babbling brook and the warm and wise sun.

Something to think about
Continue the storytelling on other days with other storytellers, or let those who are most interested continue by telling the story to other classes. Also, find other chained and cumulative stories to tell, such as Nonny Hogrogian's ONE FINE DAY.

STORY STRETCHER

For Music And Movement: Festive Wedding Music

What the children will learn
To recognize Latin American-inspired music from Spanish speaking cultures in your community

Materials you will need
Latin American musicians and their instruments or recordings of their music, rhythm band instruments

What to do
1. Ask a music teacher's assistance if you do not have access to Latin-American musicians or music.

2. Invite a group of musicians to your classroom. Prepare them ahead of time for the length of the program, the connections of music and folktales, and be certain they are willing to let the children examine the musical instruments closely and actually play them.

3. After the musicians have played, let small groups of children interact with them and beat the drum, strum the guitar, play the violin or other instruments. Explain to the children ahead of time that they cannot blow the horns or trumpets.

4. If you do not have access to Latin American musicians, find recordings of traditional Latin American music. Help children sense the rhythms and the beats by moving to the music. Add rhythm band instruments to the listening and moving.

5. Parents from Latin American communities might enjoy sharing the difference in music from different cultures.

Something to think about
It is important not to group all Latin American cultures together. Take advantage of the community in which you live and invite musicians who represent the Spanish speaking culture in your community. For example, in Tampa where I live, the Cuban community would be the predominant Spanish speaking culture. In New Mexico, Mexican-American musicians could be invited.

STORY STRETCHER

For Special Event: Dressed In Wedding Finery

What the children will learn
To enjoy the beauty and special feelings of weddings and celebrations

Materials you will need
Instant print camera

What to do
1. Invite a male and female friend who have been in a wedding to come to class all dressed in their wedding finery. If possible, invite people from a Spanish-speaking culture.

2. Let the wedding guests tell about their finery and how they selected the items.

3. Show pictures of the wedding.

4. Take pictures of the wedding guests.

Something to think about
Invite friends from other cultures to come to the classroom and show their wedding finery.

STORY STRETCHER

For Writing Center: A Chained Story

What the children will learn
To adapt the scaffold of the story to their own version

Materials you will need
Chart tablet paper, marker, writing folders, pencils, markers

What to do
1. After the writers have heard the story of THE ROOSTER WHO WENT TO HIS UNCLE'S WEDDING and listened to the storytellers retell the tale, they will have internalized the scaffold or outline of the story.

2. Read Tomie dePaola's "A Note About the Story" found before the title page. Emphasize that when Alma Flor Ada's grandmother told the story, she often changed the characters. For example, sometimes instead of the main character being a rooster, it was a horse, or a cow, or a goat.

3. Let the writers brainstorm some other changes in characters which the main characters might meet along the way.

4. Encourage the writers to write their own version of the story and illustrate it.

Something to think about
More experienced writers might change the plot and the setting of the story by changing what they expect from the characters. The only instruction you might keep is to ask them to write a chained story.

References

Ada, Alma Flor. (1993). **THE ROOSTER WHO WENT TO HIS UNCLE'S WEDDING: A LATIN AMERICAN FOLKTALE.** Illustrated by Kathleen Kuchera. New York: G.P. Putnam's Sons.

O'Brien, Anne Sibley. (1993). **THE PRINCESS AND THE BEGGAR: A KOREAN FOLKTALE**. New York: Scholastic.

McDermott, Gerald. (1992). **ZOMO THE RABBIT**. San Diego: Harcourt Brace Jovanovich.

Rodanas, Kristina. (1988). **THE STORY OF WALI DÂD**. New York: Lothrop, Lee & Shepard.

Steptoe, John. (1987). **MUFARO'S BEAUTIFUL DAUGHTERS: AN AFRICAN TALE**. New York: Lothrop, Lee & Shepard.

Also Mentioned in this Chapter

Hogrogian, Nonny. (1974). **ONE FINE DAY**. New York: Macmillan

Additional References for Folktales From Around the World

Anderson, Joy. (1986). **JUMA AND THE MAGIC JINN**. Illustrated by Charles Mikolaycok. New York: Lothrop, Lee & Shepard. *Juma did not believe in magic, but he longed to be some place where he would not have to study or to behave. Through a magical jinn, Juma gets his wish. The tale is from Lamu Island off the coast of Kenya.*

Gerson, Mary-Joan. (1992). **WHY THE SKY IS FAR AWAY: A NIGERIAN FOLKTALE**. Illustrated by Carla Golembe. Boston: Little, Brown and Company. *A tale of plenty and hunger that offers the moral of not wasting what we have and recycling what we can.*

Haley, Gail E. (1970). **A STORY-A STORY**. New York: Athenaeum. *Winner of the 1971 Caldecott Medal, this Anansi or spider story is about the origins of story on earth.*

Lawson, Julie. (1993). **THE DRAGON'S PEARL**. Illustrated by Paul Morin. New York: Clarion. *During a terrible drought, a cheerful, dutiful son finds a magic pearl that forever changes his life and the lives of his mother and neighbors.*

Wisniewski, David. (1992). **SUNDIATA**. New York: Clarion. *Using exquisite paper and beautiful colors, Wisniewski retells the story of Sundiata, who overcame physical handicaps, social disgrace and strong opposition to rule Mali in the thirteenth century.*

FANTASY AND FANTASTIC TALES

The True Story of the 3 Little Pigs! by A. Wolf
The Talking Eggs: A Folktale From the American South
Abuela
The Ghost-Eye Tree
Fritz and the Mess Fairy

THE TRUE STORY OF
THE 3 LITTLE PIGS!
BY A. WOLF

As told to Jon Scieszka

Illustrated by Lane Smith

Wolf tells his side of "The Three Little Pigs," beginning with a birthday party for dear Granny Wolf, a sneeze and a cup of sugar. Wolf went over to the little pig's house to borrow sugar for Granny's cake, but he had such a terrible cold that, just as the pigs were about to open the door, he sneezed a giant sneeze, which caused him to huff and puff. The great sneeze did all the damage to the little pig's straw house. Of course, the same thing happened at the next house, made of sticks. The third little pig rather rudely refused to let Wolf come into his brick house. The police came and arrested Wolf for making a commotion after the third pig said something bad about Wolf's granny. The two reporters who wrote the newspaper story about the events jazzed up the story and made him sound like a Big Bad Wolf. Smith's hilarious illustrations in sepia tones have a surreal quality that fit this fractured fairy tale.

Read-Aloud Presentation

Without referring to "The Three Little Pigs," read THE TRUE STORY OF THE 3 LITTLE PIGS! BY A. WOLF. Draw the children's attention to the cover of the book, which is printed like a newspaper. Also point out the pig reading the newspaper, holding the paper with his foot, as if the foot were a hand. At the end of the story, encourage the children to laugh about the surprises throughout. Discuss the viewpoint of this story, and observe that every story is told from a particular point of view.

STORY STRETCHER

For Art: Newspaper Artists

What the children will learn
To create a cartoon storyboard

Materials you will need
Cartoons from the newspaper, drawing paper, pencils, colored pencils, markers or crayons, scissors, glue, sheets of newspaper

What to do
1. Let the children look at the sequence of events in one of their favorite serial cartoons in the newspaper.

2. Cut the cartoon panels apart. Have the children reassemble them in the correct order.

3. Show the children how to fold a sheet of manila paper three times: one fold creates halves, two folds create fourths, and three folds, eighths.

4. Unfold the paper. Using the fold lines as guides, cut the sheet of paper into eight small rectangles.

5. Read THE TRUE STORY OF THE 3 LITTLE PIGS! BY A. WOLF and decide what are the story's eight main scenes.

6. Print a few words that signify one scene on each rectangle, like "wolf-no sugar," meaning that the wolf is baking a cake for his granny and discovers he has no sugar.

7. On the reverse side of each rectangle, the child draws and colors a picture of the scene.

8. When all the scenes are illustrated, the artist glues his or her storyboard in the correct sequence on a sheet of newspaper. Display the storyboards in the art center.

Something to think about
With younger children, form partnerships in which each child is responsible for four scenes. For larger cooperative projects, more children can work together.

STORY STRETCHER

For Classroom Library: Collecting Fractured Fairy Tales

What the children will learn
To compare and contrast the original fairy tale with the fractured or retold fairy tale

Materials you will need
A collection of fractured fairy tales, such as THE STINKY CHEESE MAN, JIM AND THE BEANSTALK, THE PAPER BAG PRINCESS

What to do
1. Pair the children into reading partnerships that will last for at least two weeks.

2. Ask the partners to read the original story, like "The Little Red Hen," and then read the fractured version, "Listen Hen," in THE STINKY CHEESE MAN.

3. Vote on the class favorites among these fractured fairy tales.

Something to think about
Connecting reading and writing through library and writing center story s-t-r-e-t-c-h-e-r-s is very natural in this unit. Whenever possible, engage children in both literacy processes.

STORY STRETCHER

For Cooking And Snack Time: An Upside-Down Birthday Cake

What the children will learn
To follow the directions for making a pineapple upside-down cake

Materials you will need
Large baking pan, vegetable oil, flour, cake mix, eggs, water or milk, powdered sugar, canned pineapple, red cherries, measuring cups, spoons, mixing bowls, oven, plates, napkins, candles

What to do
1. Because THE TRUE STORY OF THE 3 LITTLE PIGS! BY A. WOLF is an upside-down story, and because all the trouble starts when innocent Wolf just wants to make his poor granny a birthday cake, bake a pineapple upside-down cake in honor of the story.

2. Bake the cake according to the package directions. Before pouring the batter into the pan, however, arrange pineapple rings to cover the bottom of the pan and place red cherries in the center of each pineapple ring.

3. Pour the batter into the pan.

4. Bake the cake and serve it so that the side with the pineapple and cherries is on the top.

5. Add candles and sing, "Happy Birthday, Granny Wolf."

Something to think about
Remember that adding humor and frivolity to your classroom motivates children. Do not be afraid to show your comic side, but never poke fun at the children.

STORY STRETCHER

For Writing Center: Newspaper Accounts Of Other Fairy Tales

What the children will learn
To rewrite accounts as if they had appeared in the newspaper

Materials you will need
Chart tablet paper and markers or chalk and chalkboard

What to do
1. Explain to a group of writers that newspaper accounts are supposed to tell the who, what, when, where, why and how of stories.

2. Brainstorm a list of questions that the newspaper reporter might have asked Wolf, for example, "What were you doing outside Third Pig's House at two o'clock?"

3. Let the children work with their writing partners. One child asks the questions, the other writes the answers. Together they compose the newspaper story, asking and answering to create the who, what, when, where, why and how.

Something to think about
If you have access to a computer software newspaper program, lay out the children's stories and print them. Older children at the school might also create a newspaper version of the fractured fairy tales for the younger ones.

ANOTHER STORY STRETCHER

For Writing Center: Wolf's Version Of Other Fairy Tales

What the children will learn
To write from a different point of view

Materials you will need
Writing folders, paper, pencils, art supplies for illustrations (optional)

What to do
1. Let the children select other stories that they could tell from a different point of view: "Goldilocks and The Three Bears" from the Little Bear's perspective, "The Three Billy-Goats Gruff" from the troll's point of view, "The Little Red Hen" from the dog or cat's point of view.

2. Form writing partnerships and let the children brainstorm a beginning for their stories. Once the children have a beginning, they can usually continue through to the end of their stories.

Something to think about
Some young first graders may have difficulty changing point of view. Point-of-view writing is also a good exercise for writing partners across grade levels: try pairing third graders with first graders, for example.

THE TALKING EGGS: A FOLKTALE FROM THE AMERICAN SOUTH

Retold by Robert D. San Souci

Illustrated by Jerry Pinkney

THE TALKING EGGS won the Coretta Scott King Award and was a Caldecott Honor Book for 1990. Adapted from a Creole folktale, this Cinderella story is about two sisters: lazy Rose, her mother's favorite, and sweet Blanche, forced to work hard taking care of her mother and her sister. An old witch-woman takes Blanche into a magical world where even the animals have special charm. There she discovers the talking eggs, which give her gifts of clothing, finery, a buggy and pony. When Rose tries to win the same favors from the old witch-woman, her bad ways and refusal to do what the old woman tells her, leave her haunted by toads, yellow jackets and a wolf. Rose and her mother live out their lives in poverty. Pinkney's watercolor and pencil illustrations are exquisitely rendered, with enough magic of their own to draw the reader back through the story for the sheer pleasure of seeing it unfold again.

Read-Aloud Presentation

Read the full title of the book, THE TALKING EGGS: A FOLKTALE FROM THE AMERICAN SOUTH, and the acknowledgement page, which explains that this story is thought to have originated with the Creole culture. Talk about the ways that stories are told over and over, changing a bit as they are retold. Read THE TALKING EGGS and ask the children whether the story reminds them of any other they have heard. Some children may say that it reminds them of "Cinderella." Look through the illustrations with the children again, recalling what the pictures illustrate.

STORY STRETCHER
For Art: Bejeweled Eggs

What the children will learn
To decorate eggs in imaginative ways

Materials you will need
Plastic eggs, ribbons, paper, stars, glitter, plastic jewels, rubber cement, craft books, egg cartons, scissors, baskets, glue gun (optional)

What to do
1. Look at the illustrations of jeweled eggs in THE TALKING EGGS.

2. Collect plastic hosiery eggs or plastic craft eggs.

3. Place collage materials on a table and let the children decorate their eggs.

4. To display the eggs, cut sections from egg cartons and turn them upside down, creating a nest.

5. Display other eggs in baskets and use the baskets as centerpieces for the snack table.

Something to think about
Inquire at local craft stores or craft guilds for egg decorators who might display their creations at your school. Also ask the school librarian to find pictures of Faberge eggs for the children to see. Teachers concerned about the environment may wish to decorate real eggs instead of using plastic eggs.

STORY STRETCHER
For Classroom Library: THE TALKING EGGS As A Cinderella Story

What the children will learn
To compare and contrast the Creole folktale with the European tale

Materials you will need
Chart tablet paper and markers or chalk and chalkboard

What to do
1. Explain to the children that THE TALKING EGGS is sometimes described as a Southern Cinderella story.

2. Help the children recall the Cinderella story: its characters, main scenes, magic and conclusion. Write what they recall of the Cinderella story.

3. With marker or chalk of a different color, write what the children say about characters, main scenes, magic and conclusion of THE TALKING EGGS.

4. Let the children decide whether or not they think the stories have enough in common to call THE TALKING EGGS a Cinderella story.

Something to think about
First graders often do not see the similarities as sufficient to make THE TALKING EGGS a

Cinderella story. Many second graders are more open to the suggestion, and third graders often accept the idea.

For Creative Dramatics: Retelling With Props

What the children will learn
To enjoy telling a story using minimal props

Materials you will need
Hand fan, bucket, shawl, decorated egg, plain egg, basket, silk scarf, tape recorder, video camera

What to do
1. Rehearse the storytelling by letting a small group of children look through the book and retell the story in their own words.

2. Add a few props and ask one child to tell the story to the whole class, or to a small group of listeners, using the props.

3. Plan a few practice sessions of storytelling during which the children record and listen to themselves.

4. Videotape a few of the storytellers.

Something to think about
To encourage more storytellers, invite others to learn stories and videotape these children telling their stories. Assemble a library of these videotapes for use in the classroom.

For Music and Movement: Square Dance, Virginia Reel, Cakewalk

What the children will learn
To follow directions and respond rhythmically

Materials you will need
Recording of simple square dances, Virginia reel

What to do
1. Have the children listen to the music and find the beat. Clap hands, snap fingers or slap thighs.

2. With your aide or volunteer, perform some of the movements as directed by the recording.

3. Practice the movements with the children, both without the music and with the music. Do not expect young children to be able to follow complicated instructions.

4. An alternative is to do the "Hokey Pokey."

Something to think about
If you have difficulty locating dances and recordings, talk to the physical education and music teachers. They usually have these resources. Invite country line dancers to come to class and teach a few movements to the children. Because line dances do not require partners, young children often prefer them.

For Writing Center: Blanche's Life In The City

What the children will learn
To extend the story

Materials you will need
Crayons, colored pencils, pastels, markers, writing folders, paper, pencils

What to do
1. The author describes Blanche's later life as follows: "Blanche had gone to the city to live like a grand lady—though she remained as kind and generous as always."

2. Ask a small group of writers to imagine Blanche's life in the city.

3. Ask them to draw pictures showing Blanche in the city.

4. Invite the illustrators to add captions to their pictures.

5. Engage a small group of writers in combining the illustrations with dialogue and background information to tell a story.

6. Bind the story into a book. (See the instructions for book binding in the appendix.)

Something to think about
Young children often write better if they begin with a visual image and expand upon it, rather than begin by writing.

ABUELA

By Arthur Dorros

Illustrated by Elisa Kleven

Rosalba's story tells how she and her grandmother, Abuela, fly over Manhattan, a story inspired by Rosalba's imagining what it would be like if the birds from the park picked her up and flew away with her. Abuela and Rosalba do acrobatics in the sky, float near the ocean and almost touch the waves, fly along the docks to see workers unloading ships, fly past the Statue of Liberty and near the airport. They visit their neighborhood, flying down for a lemonade at Rosalba's aunt and uncle's store. When they tire, they rest on a cloud. At the end of the book, Rosalba and Abuela walk near the edge of the lake in the park, ready to imagine another adventure. Elisa Kleven's charming, witty, detailed, full-color pictures leave lots of room for lovely imagination.

Read-Aloud Presentation

Recall with the children the cover of TAR BEACH and the little girl's dream that she was flying above the city. Show the students the cover of ABUELA and notice that a little girl and her grandmother are flying over the city. Immediately, the children know that the story is imaginary. As you show the title page, note that the name is made of fabric pieces. Read ABUELA. Afterwards, invite the children to discuss what makes the relationship between Rosalba and Abuela so special.

STORY STRETCHER
For Art: Fabric Collage

What the children will learn
To make decorative nameplates

Materials you will need
Large index cards, pencil, scissors, masking tape, printed fabric scraps, white glue, colored pencils, letter patterns or stencils (optional)

What to do
1. Let the children write their names on large index cards, in cursive or in print, and show them how to make the single line into an outlined shape. Cut around the printed letters or around the entire name, if the letters are written in cursive. The result is a name pattern.

2. Tape the pattern onto a scrap of printed fabric and trace around it.

3. Cut the name out of the fabric.

4. Glue the fabric name onto another large index card.

Something to think about
Some children may prefer to write their names in cursive or print, create outline shapes and decorate the letters with colored pencils to make them look like fabric.

ANOTHER STORY STRETCHER
For Art: Scenes From Our City Or Countryside

What the children will learn
To view the world from a different perspective

Materials you will need
Variety of art supplies, markers, crayons, pastels, colored pencils, paper, acrylics, tempera paints, brushes

What to do
1. Ask the children to draw and color or paint some scenes they would see if they were flying over their city or the surrounding countryside.

2. Help the children think of a famous landmark they could fly over, like the Statue of Liberty, which Rosalba and Abuela flew over.

3. Display the children's flights of fantasy in the art and library areas of the classroom.

Something to think about
Older primary age children can create a mural of their flight over the city. Spread butcher paper over a table. With light pencil marks, divide the paper into different scenes. Let a group of mural makers decide how to divide the responsibilities.

For Classroom Library: Flying Stories

What the children will learn

To incorporate scenes from their neighborhoods into their own stories

Materials you will need

Pictures from the art story s-t-r-e-t-c-h-e-r, tape recorder

What to do

1. Gather a small group of interested children in the classroom library.

2. Review the pictures they created for the art story s-t-r-e-t-c-h-e-r.

3. Using the pictures, help the children tell their own stories of flying above their neighborhoods.

4. Tape record the children's stories. To introduce each story, record the name of the child and the name of the story before they begin telling the story.

5. Put the page and the pictures in the classroom library.

Something to think about

If some of your students come from families whose first language is Spanish, include tapes with speakers reading in English and, whenever possible, in Spanish as well.

For Cooking and Snack Time: Mangoes, Bananas, Papaya

What the children will learn

To prepare and taste fruits that are healthy snacks

Materials you will need

Mangoes, bananas, papayas, paring knives, tablespoon, spoons, small fruit bowls, napkins, orange juice

What to do

1. If possible, take a small group of children with you to the supermarket to purchase mangoes, bananas and papayas.

2. Let other children peel and slice the mangoes and papayas.

3. Show the class the large seeds from the mangoes and the little black seeds from the papayas. Use a spoon to remove the seeds.

4. Slice the fruit and serve it in fruit bowls.

Something to think about

Also show the tiny black specks in the banana to the children, explaining that they are also seeds, but are so small that we eat them. We cannot eat mango or papaya seeds.

For Writing Center: Incorporating Spanish Phrases Into Stories

What the children will learn

To understand the meaning of Spanish phrases and use them in their writing

Materials you will need

Chart tablet paper, markers, writing folders, paper, pencils

What to do

1. With a small group of writers, some who know Spanish and others who do not, look back through ABUELA and list all the Spanish words and phrases.

2. Using clues from the text, decide what each word or phrase means. For example, while Rosalba and Abuela are flying near the bus stop, they wave to the people and say, "Buenos dias." The people wave back and say, "Good morning." The reader then knows the meaning of "Buenos dias."

3. After all the Spanish phrases are copied from ABUELA and translated into English by the children, leave the charts in the writing center area.

4. Ask the children to incorporate at least one Spanish word or phrase into the next story they write.

5. When the writers read their stories in class, call attention to the Spanish words.

Something to think about

Invite a specialist in English as a Second Language (ESOL) to your class and learn ways that you and your students can support ESOL students as they learn English.

FANTASY AND
FANTASTIC TALES

THE GHOST-EYE TREE

By Bill Martin, Jr.

and John Archambault

Illustrated by Ted Rand

A young boy is sent to the edge of town to bring back a bucket of milk from Mr. Cowlander's barn. On this dark and windy autumn night, the boy and his sister must pass the scary ghost-eye tree beside the path. The tale unfolds with a touch of fright and more than a little suspense. The story is also about sibling rivalry and a brave sister who pretends not to be scared. To add to the charm and mystery, the little boy wears a hat that is too big and keeps blowing away. Ted Rand's deep navy backgrounds, black silhouettes, gray shadows and reflected lights make this scary tale even more frightening.

Read-Aloud Presentation

A perfect Halloween book, or simply a good book for autumn or a wintry day, THE GHOST-EYE TREE offers a little fright, even if the events are imaginary. So the children may join in with you at the appropriate pause in the story, teach them this phrase: "There's nothing here but an old oak tree." Darken the room and read the book in a suspenseful whisper, with dramatic emphasis.

STORY STRETCHER

For Art: Shadows Of Scary Trees

What the children will learn
To create night scenes

Materials you will need
Construction paper (dark blue, black and yellow), pencils, scissors, glue

What to do
1. Call attention to the tiny eyes, far up in the ghost-eye tree, in Ted Rand's cover illustration.

2. Ask the children who are interested to draw a scary tree, one which would frighten them if they were walking at night, without looking at Ted Rand's illustrations.

3. Have the children sketch their scary trees on black construction paper, cut them out and glue them onto the dark blue paper.

4. Let the children add a yellow moon peeping through the bough of the tree.

Something to think about
If you live in an area where Spanish moss grows, invite the children to imagine that as the oak limbs blow, the Spanish moss blows, making the tree look even more like a ghost. Add moss to the limbs of the tree.

STORY STRETCHER

For Classroom Library: Sound Effect Stories

What the children will learn
To make sound effects with their voices and objects

Materials you will need
Metal bucket, dry leaves, broom, branch with dry leaves, old shoes, tape recorder, cassette tape, microphone

What to do
1. Ask the children what sound effects they would add to a tape recording of THE GHOST-EYE TREE to make it more scary. For example, they could make the sound of the wind blowing with their voices. They could make the sound of dry leaves blowing by pushing dry leaves across a concrete floor with a broom. They could make a scary scratch by scratching a limb on a tabletop, or make footstep sounds by walking shoes across a tabletop.

2. Let the children experiment with tape recording these sounds.

3. Send the sound effects people off to a quiet area in the hallway or to an office to practice.

4. Select a director who will orchestrate the readers and the sound effects technicians.

5. Let several children read the story with expression, and the sound effect technicians record the sounds.

6. Play the tape of THE GHOST-EYE TREE and let listeners guess how the special sounds where made.

Something to think about
Encourage children to add sounds to the stories they write themselves.

For Creative Dramatics: Reader's Theater

What the children will learn
To read with expression

Materials you will need
Multiple copies of the book, large index cards and markers

What to do
1. With a small group of readers, decide upon a few phrases that the whole class could read, on cue, which would add to the drama of the story. They might, for example, decide upon the following phrases:

> "Oooo. . . I dreaded to go . . .
> I dreaded the tree . . . ."
> "'Fraidy cat!'"
> "There's nothing to dread in an old oak tree."
> "I'm tough! Real tough."
> "You look stupid."

2. Each child writes the phrases on a large index card in the order one through five.

3. Read the narrator's part of the story, and assign a boy reader and a girl reader to read the dialogue between the little boy and his big sister.

4. Hold up one or more fingers to indicate which phrase the chorus of children should read aloud.

5. Rehearse the choral reading with the two readers.

6. Rehearse the choral reading with just the chorus.

Something to think about
Tape-record the choral reading and place it in the classroom library.

For Creative Dramatics: A Magic Hat Makes The Story Go On

What the children will learn
To listen and compose parts of a story while following a story line

Materials you will need
Old hat

What to do
1. Tell the children that this is the hat from THE GHOST-EYE TREE. It is a magic story hat. Whenever you wear it, you feel a story coming on.

2. Whenever you place the hat on someone's head, it becomes magic. The story keeps on going, even though you are no longer wearing the hat.

3. Begin a story about the hat. Tell whose hat it was, and how you came to have the hat, then stop at a dramatic point. Place the hat on a child's head and encourage him or her to add a little to the story.

4. Place the hat on another child's head and let that child add to the story.

5. Continue adding to the story until everyone has contributed at least a sentence or two.

6. Return the hat to your head and end the story by saying, "And that is how I came to own this magic story hat."

Something to think about
Many teachers reading this story s-t-r-e-t-c-h-e-r are probably worried about head lice being transferred from one child to another. If this is a concern, wear the magic story hat yourself and tap children on the shoulder when it is their turn to add to the story.

For Writing Center: Scary Stories

What the children will learn
To set the mood by using descriptive language

Materials you will need
paper, pens, pens or pencils

What to do
1. Read THE GHOST-EYE TREE again and identify ways that the authors create a sense of suspense and fear.

2. The authors set the stage for fright with their description of the dark and windy night and phrases like "Oooo . . . " and "fraidy cat."

3. Invite the children to think of ways they might describe a night to let their readers know immediately that this will be a scary tale.

4. When the children have finished their scary stories, let them use the editing group process to edit and redraft.

5. Make a class book of scary stories for Halloween, or bind each child's story and place it in the class library.

Something to think about
One of the best ways for children to improve their writing is to notice how other writers write. We want to encourage children to try story forms, expressions and descriptive language that they learn from great writers. As they internalize an approach to writing, they will go on and invent their own variations.

14
FANTASY AND
FANTASTIC TALES

FRITZ AND THE
MESS FAIRY

By Rosemary Wells

Fritz is so messy that everyone can see where he has been by the mess he leaves behind. The entire family is upset with Fritz. He is reprimanded and strictly instructed to clean up his messy ways. Then one night, his science project goes awry in an unexpected way, and Fritz creates a Mess Fairy. The Mess Fairy makes an even bigger mess than Fritz does. She drinks lemonade out of twenty-three different glasses, mixes up game pieces, squeezes all the toothpaste out of the tube. Fritz thinks of a creative solution to get rid of the Mess Fairy. He cleans up the entire house while his parents sleep and cooks them breakfast. The last scene shows Fritz surrounded by a kitchen of messy dishes as he serves the family breakfast and calls himself the new Fritz. Every child, parent and teacher will identify with Fritz. The comic fantasy offers a wonderful association with those dreaded words, "Clean up this mess."

Read-Aloud Presentation

Show the cover of FRITZ AND THE MESS FAIRY. Ask the children to predict what the pink, pig-like fairy will do for Fritz. They will guess that she cleans up after him. Read FRITZ AND THE MESS FAIRY, pausing when the Mess Fairy appears to let the children predict again what she will do for Fritz. After reading the book, let the children talk about some of the more unusual things they have found while cleaning up their rooms.

STORY STRETCHER

For Art: After And Before Pictures

What the children will learn
To depict the same place in two different ways

Materials you will need
Manila paper or white construction paper, stapler, crayons or markers, scraps of construction paper

What to do
1. Ask the children to draw pictures of their rooms after they have cleaned them, when everything is in place and neat as a pin.

2. Ask the children to draw a second picture that shows their rooms after a visit from the Mess Fairy.

3. Cut strips of construction paper about an inch wide and as long as the side of their pictures.

4. Staple the after and before pictures together.

5. Fold the construction paper strip in half. Place the top half along the left side of the stapled pictures and fold the bottom half beneath the pictures. Staple the reinforcing strip in place.

6. Let the children show each other their "after" pictures, then turn the page to be surprised by how messy their rooms were before they cleaned up.

Something to think about
If your children's families have cameras and money for film and film processing, ask the children to take pictures of their rooms at home before and after they clean. Make a bulletin board with the photographs.

STORY STRETCHER

For Cooking and Snack Time: Fritz's Buttermilk Pancakes

What the children will learn
To prepare buttermilk pancakes

Materials you will need
Posterboard, marker, pancake mix, margarine, syrup, milk, eggs, vegetable oil, electric skillet, mixing bowl with pouring spout, wooden spoon, measuring cups, spatula, plates, forks

What to do
1. Print the recipe and directions for mixing buttermilk pancakes on a large posterboard.

2. Assign duties to the children: measurers and mixers, cookers and flippers, servers.

3. Let groups of children make a batch of pancakes. Serve them for a snack with a pat of margarine, syrup and milk.

Something to think about
On another day, serve Fritz's father's favorite breakfast, bran muffins and oranges.

For Mathematics: Inventory Of Found Items

What the children will learn
To sort and categorize materials

Materials you will need
Large table, plastic storage bins, cardboard storage boxes, plastic crates, clipboard, pencil

What to do
1. Ask a group of children to collect everything around the room that is not properly stored.

2. Place the items, large and small, onto the sorting table.

3. Inventory the materials by naming, counting and, if necessary, describing them. Write this list on a clipboard.

4. Sort and categorize the materials.

5. Let the inventory takers decide on storage solutions.

6. Leave one large box for lost and found items.

Something to think about
Keep track of the amount of waste paper for one week. Pour waste paper into a large box each day rather than letting the custodian remove it. At the end of the week, weigh the paper. Ask older primary age students to calculate equivalent weights. For example, our waste paper weighs as much as ten library books, one hundred erasers, twenty ropes and five balls, and so forth.

For Special Project: Cleaning Up After The Mess Fairy In Our Classroom

What the children will learn
To work together to make our room clean and neat

Materials you will need
Chalkboard and chalk, wastebaskets, brooms, mops, sponges, dish pans or buckets, cardboard storage boxes, index cards, marker, magnetic clips

What to do
1. Ask the children to look around the classroom and explain what needs to be done to make it cleaner and neater.

2. Write each job on the chalkboard.

3. Print each child's name on an index card and draw it from an empty wastebasket.

4. With a magnetic clip, place each child's index card beside a job listed on the chalkboard.

5. After all the jobs are completed, celebrate by making buttermilk pancakes for a snack.

Something to think about
Cleaning up a room gives children a sense of pride. Avoid harsh cleaning supplies. Gentle soap and water are usually enough. Ask the custodian to write the children a thank you note for cleaning up the room so well.

For Writing Center: The Mess Fairy Comes To My House

What the children will learn
To change the setting and characters while retaining the outline or skeleton of a story

Materials you will need
Writing folders, pencils, art supplies for illustrations (optional)

What to do
1. Invite the entire class to write stories using their own names and the Mess Fairy, for example, "Christina and the Mess Fairy" or "Damien and the Mess Fairy."

2. This variation of FRITZ AND THE MESS FAIRY is sure to be a popular topic for writing. Plan on several days for the children to write and edit their stories.

3. Share the stories in small groups or with the entire class.

Something to think about
Invite the custodian to hear the "Mess Fairy Stories."

References

Dorros, Arthur. (1991). **ABUELA**. Illustrated by Elisa Kleven. New York: Dutton.

Martin, Bill, Jr. and Archambault, John. (1985). **THE GHOST EYE TREE**. Illustrated by Ted Rand. New York: Holt, Rinehart and Winston.

San Souci, Robert D. (1989). **THE TALKING EGGS**. Illustrated by Jerry Pinkney. New York: Dial.

Scieszka, Jon. (1989). **THE TRUE STORY OF THE 3 LITTLE PIGS! BY A. WOLF**. Illustrated by Lane Smith. New York: Penguin.

Wells, Rosemary. (1991). **FRITZ AND THE MESS FAIRY**. New York: Penguin.

Also Mentioned in this Chapter

Briggs, Raymond. (1970). **JIM AND THE BEANSTALK**. New York: Coward-McCann.

Ringgold, Faith. (1991). **TAR BEACH**. New York: Crown Publishers.

Additional References for Fantasy And Fantastic Tales

Katz, Avner. (1993). **TORTOISE SOLVES A PROBLEM**. New York: Willa Perlman Books, HarperCollins. *In the days before tortoises had shells, one talented young tortoise sets out to design the perfect house for his fellow crawlers.*

Munsch, Robert N. (1980). **THE PAPER BAG PRINCESS**. Illustrated by Michael Martchenko. Toronto: Annick. *A princess rescues her prince from a dragon, but in the end, leaves her inconsiderate prince because he doesn't like her paper bag outfit.*

Scieszka, Jon and Smith, Lane. (1992). **THE STINKY CHEESE MAN AND OTHER FAIRY STUPID TALES**. New York: Viking. *Madcap revisions of familiar fairy tales.*

Wiesner, David. (1991). **TUESDAY**. New York: Clarion. *Winner of the Caldecott Medal, Wiesner's story is about frogs rising on their lily pads, floating through the air, and exploring nearby houses while their inhabitants sleep.*

Wood, Audrey. (1985). **KING BIDGOOD'S IN THE BATHTUB**. Illustrated by Don Wood. San Diego: Harcourt Brace Jovanovich. *Despite pleas from his court, a fun-loving king refuses to get out of his bathtub and rule the kingdom.*

POETRY

Emily

Talking Like the Rain: A Read-to-me Book of Poems

Brown Angels: An Album of Pictures and Verse

Secret Places

If You're Not Here Please Raise Your Hand: Poems About School

Emily
by Michael Bedard · pictures by Barbara Cooney

EMILY

By Michael Bedard

Illustrated by Barbara Cooney

The story is told by the child who lives across the street from the poet, Emily Dickinson, a mysterious recluse. Emily lives with her sister in the big yellow house in Amherst, Massachusetts, and she has not been seen outside the house in twenty years. One day an invitation arrives, asking the little girl's mother to come to the yellow house and play the piano. With the written invitation, comes pressed flowers. When her mother goes to play the piano, the child wanders up-stairs and meets the mysterious poet. The child brings the poet a gift of lily bulbs, and Emily gives the child a poem written on a scrap of paper. Barbara Cooney's illustrations portray the sparse but col-orful life of a New England period home, and set the mood for a fleeting connec-tion between a child and a poet.

Read-Aloud Presentation

For background, read the afterword. Decide whether to read it to the children before beginning the story or afterwards. Talk about what a recluse is, and why some people shelter themselves from others. Read EMILY without pausing. At the end, invite the children to comment on the "special feelings" pages of the book. Leaf through the pages and pause at the scene on the staircase landing, where the child gives Emily a lily bulb and Emily gives the child a four-line poem. End the read-aloud presentation by reading Emily Dickinson's poem again and letting the children comment, if they choose.

STORY STRETCHER
For Art: A Light In A Window

What the children will learn
To use a technique for viewing the world through a window

Materials you will need
Drawing paper, rulers, colored pencils, acrylic paints, crayons, markers

What to do
1. Look through Barbara Cooney's illustrations in EMILY and notice the different ways that the windows of the little girl's house and the windows of Emily Dickinson's house are pictured, as if the reader were looking outwards through the windows.

2. Ask the children to move their papers to a vertical position.

3. With a ruler, ask the children to draw a large rectangle on the paper.

4. The children may choose to draw anything they like, looking though their "window." Some will draw the little girl looking across at the big yellow house. Others might draw the view from their windows at home or the view from the classroom window.

Something to think about
Show a few Andrew Wyeth prints, which often portray a scene through a window.

STORY STRETCHER
For Cooking And Snack Time: Emily Dickinson's Gingerbread

What the children will learn
To follow a recipe and bake gingerbread

Materials you will need
Chart paper, marker, oven, baking pan, spatula, wooden spoon, sifter, mixing bowl, measuring cups and spoons, flour, baking soda, ginger, cinnamon, salt, shortening, sugar, egg, molasses, boiling water, plates, milk, napkins

What to do
1. Print the recipe for old-fashioned gingerbread on a chart. Call it Emily Dickinson's gingerbread.

   1 1/2 cups of flour
   1 teaspoon baking soda
   1 teaspoon ginger
   1 teaspoon cinnamon
   1/2 teaspoon salt
   1/2 cup margarine
   1/2 cup sugar
   1 beaten egg
   1/2 cup molasses
   2/3 cup boiling water

2. Sift the dry ingredients together in one mixing bowl.

3. Blend the molasses, egg and margarine together in a second mixing bowl. Add the boiling water.

4. Gradually add the dry ingredients to the moist ingredients, blending until the dry ingredients are mixed in, then adding more.

5. Pour into an 8" x 8" x 2" greased baking pan.

6. Bake at 375 degrees for 25 minutes, or until the gingerbread springs back at the touch.

7. Cool 10 minutes before removing from the pan.

8. Serve hot with cold milk.

Something to think about
Keep all the recipe charts and make a class big book of recipes. With younger children, use a mix instead of this recipe.

STORY STRETCHER

For Music And Movement: The Piano And Reviving Music

What the children will learn
To enjoy hearing and playing a piano

Materials you will need
Piano

What to do
1. If you are a musician, choose music that seems to fit the period of the story. A Brahms lullaby might be a good choice, since the story refers to the mother playing songs at night.

2. Explain that Emily invited the child's mother to play the piano because the poet needed music to revive her spirits during the dreary winter days.

3. Ask the pianist to select music that celebrates spring or otherwise lifts the spirits.

4. Invite older child musicians to play for the class. If a piano cannot be moved into your classroom, station the piano in the foyer or reception area so that the children will hear music as they arrive at school or as they go to lunch.

5. Let one of your students sit on the bench beside the pianist to experience the music at close range. The children can take turns sitting on the bench during different songs.

Something to think about
Pianos are becoming rare in classrooms; even some music classrooms have replaced pianos with electronic keyboards. Provide the children who seem most interested with additional time to play the piano, assisted by an adult or older child.

STORY STRETCHER

For Science And Nature: Pressing Flowers

What the children will learn
To follow directions for removing moisture from flowers

Materials you will need
Old telephone books or other heavy books, wax paper, scissors, iron, plain note paper or heavy white construction paper, flowers

What to do
1. Find flower buds and flowers that are beginning to open, either on outdoor or indoor plants.

2. Pick the flowers and place them between the pages of a heavy telephone book. Leave them for a week. If the telephone books in your community are thin, stack heavy books on top of the phone books. The porous pages of telephone books easily absorb the moisture from the flowers.

3. Remove the flowers and place them on a sheet of plain note paper or a plain note card. Heavy white construction paper will also work.

4. Cut sheets of wax paper large enough to cover the dried petals.

5. Using a warm iron, press a sheet of wax paper over the flower.

6. Gently remove the iron and leave the paper flat while the wax paper cools.

Something to think about
Gardeners must "dead-head" plants to keep them blooming. If you have a public garden, park or commercial building nearby with many plants, invite the gardening service to help with this story s-t-r-e-t-c-h-e-r. If not, ask a neighborhood florist or parents who have many plants to provide the flowers.

STORY STRETCHER

For Social Studies: Another Time And Place

What the children will learn
To recognize visual clues to earlier time periods

Materials you will need
Chalkboard, chalk

What to do
1. With a small group of children, leaf through the pages of EMILY and note all the visual clues that tell the reader that the story takes place in another era.

2. On the chalkboard, list what the children observe. The poet is wearing a long white dress. The children's winter clothes are old-fashioned. There are horses drawing wagons and sleighs, but no cars. The child wears high-buttoned shoes.

3. After the list is complete, write a comparison list of the things we would observe if EMILY were set in the present.

Something to think about
The children might enjoy writing about the visit to the big yellow house as if it had happened in the present. Read more of Emily Dickinson's poetry. Observe that her poetry was written a long time ago, but that good poetry, like good stories, is timeless.

TALKING LIKE THE RAIN: A READ-TO-ME BOOK OF POEMS

Selected by X. J. Kennedy and

Dorothy M. Kennedy

Illustrated by Jane Dyer

More than a hundred poems have been selected that will engage and entertain children. Poems by famous contemporary poets and famous poets from other eras are pressed between the pages of this large book, with its cheerful yellow string bookmark. The poets include Giovanni, Prelutsky, Merriam, Livingston, Ruskin, Viorst, Moore, Hughes, Rossetti, Lear, Frost, Stevenson, Dickinson. The poems are organized by topics: play, families, just for fun, birds, bugs and beasts, rhymes and songs, magic and wonder, wind and weather, calendars and clocks. The book's title is taken from the book OUT OF AFRICA, whose heroine speaks to the laborers in Swahili verse, verse described as "speaking like the rain." Jane Dyer's exquisite watercolor illustrations frolic on every page beside the poems, a wonderful accompaniment to and extension of the poetry.

Read-Aloud Presentation

If you have already read EMILY to the class, read the two poems by Emily Dickinson in TALKING LIKE THE RAIN: "Letter to Bee" and "Yellow Man, Purple Man." Look through the poetry anthology and select other poets whose works your students enjoy. Show the children that the book is organized by topics, and read poems from topic areas that you think will most interest the children, like "Getting Dirty" from the "Play" section, or "A Peanut Sat on a Railroad Track" from the "Just for Fun" section. End the session by reading a poem the children can remember easily, like one of the "Rhymes and Songs." During the week, print a poem each day on the chart tablet. Try for variety in topics, forms and poets.

STORY STRETCHER

For Art: Different Media For Different Moods

What the children will learn
To select a medium and use it to express different moods in poetry

Materials you will need
Variety of paints, papers, brushes, markers, crayons, colored pencils and chalks, scissors, construction paper, glue, large index cards, pencils or pens

What to do
1. Look through Jane Dyer's illustrations for TALKING LIKE THE RAIN. Note how she decorates the pages with flower poems in beautiful pastels, in contrast to the black skyscraper silhouettes that accompany poems about the city at night. Look at other poems and their illustrations, such as the animals dressed in funny costumes for "One Year,"

the snowflake-filled sky for "Snowman Sniffles," "The Purple Cow."

2. Ask the children to choose a favorite poem and illustrate it using any medium or combined media of their choice.

3. Display the children's illustrations. Ask them to print the poem which inspired the art on a large index card and post it near the illustration.

Something to think about
Teachers often worry that if they ask children to illustrate the poems, they will simply try to copy the illustrator's work. Our experience is that if we ask the children to create their own ways to show the poem, they will devise something original. We should also remember that our greatest artists, like our children, are inspired by the work of others.

STORY STRETCHER

For Classroom Library: Read-Aloud Poets On Tape

What the children will learn
To read poems with expression and attend to punctuation

Materials you will need
Tape recorder

What to do
1. Ask the children to tape their favorite poems from TALKING LIKE THE RAIN.

2. Rehearse the poetry reading, helping the children notice how the way a poem is punctuated and laid out on the page, actually tells the reader how to read the poem.

3. At the beginning of each reading, invite the read-aloud poet to introduce the poem by reading its title, explaining that the poem is found in TALKING LIKE THE RAIN and giving the page number.

4. At the end of each poem, let the read-aloud poets add any comments they would like to offer: what they like about the poem, other poems of which it reminds them, other poems by the same poet. The poet may also read a poem that he or she has written.

Something to think about
Teach the slowest readers to read with expression and tape-record their poems first.

For Mathematics: Poetry Can Be Numbered

What the children will learn
To construct a numerical representation of a poem

Materials you will need
Chart tablet and marker or chalkboard and chalk

What to do
1. On chart tablet paper or on a chalkboard, print a poem with a definite syllabic pattern, such as William Allingham's "A Swing Song."

2. Let the children count the syllables in each line by numbering the syllables under the words. For example, the first line, "Swing, swing," would be numbered 1, 2.

3. Continue numbering to the end of the poem and notice that the 1, 2 pattern repeats once, followed by the pattern of 1, 2, 3, 4, 5, 6, 7, 8. Each verse repeats this entire pattern twice.

4. Other poems in which it is easy to locate syllabic patterns are gathered in the "Rhymes and Songs" section of TALKING LIKE THE RAIN.

Something to think about
As another mathematics exercise, let the children vote for their favorite poets and make a graph showing their choices.

For Music And Movement: I Got Rhythm

What the children will learn
To sing, dance and move to poems that are also songs and chants

Materials you will need
Rhythm band instruments (tambourines, drums, sticks, triangles, castanets)

What to do
1. Read poems that are also songs, and then sing them.

2. Read "I Went Downtown," then snap fingers and clap out the rhythm.

3. Sing "Dickery Dean" to a jump rope rhyme. Ask children who jump rope to perform the poem as a jump rope chant.

4. Add the rhythm band instruments to both "I Went Downtown" and "Dickery Dean."

5. End by reading and then singing "Paper of Pins" or "Hush, Little Baby," commonly known as "Poppa's Gonna Buy You A Mockingbird."

Something to think about
Try adding rhythm to other poems not in the "Rhymes and Songs" section, like "Billy Batter."

For Science And Nature: Weather Poems

What the children will learn
To observe the weather and compare observations

Materials you will need
Calendar

What to do
1. Mark each day on the calendar by recording the weather.

2. Record the temperature for each day and a general description.

3. Read the poem "Weather" to introduce this activity.

4. Select a poem to read each day that expresses the weather on that day: "Who Has Seen the Wind," "The Wind Has Such a Rainy Sound," "Springtime," "Summer Shower," "Snowman Sniffles," "First Snowflake," "Cynthia in the Snow," "Winter Morning," "In the Fog."

5. Find other weather poems that express weather conditions. Check other anthologies. Choose Bill Martin, Jr. and John Archambault's LISTEN TO THE RAIN.

Something to think about
Help older children keep a weather log comparing the local newspaper's weather reports with the observations made by the class. Send to the local newspaper or television station a poem written by the class about the weather, about being a meteorologist, about the woes of predicting weather.

BROWN ANGELS: AN ALBUM OF PICTURES AND VERSE

By Walter Dean Myers

Described as "born in the dusty corner of an antique shop where the old photographs are kept," Walter Dean Myers has collected pictures of African-American children from around the turn of the century and written verses to express what he imagines them to be thinking and feeling. The sepia-toned photographs express a range of emotions, but children's smiles shine from many. Most are posed, but a few are candid. All are frozen in time, waiting for the reader to discover them. The sensitivity of the photographs, the layout of the poems, the content, and the effective use of the space on each page contribute to the collection's charm and depth. The artists are the long-forgotten photographers, and the man who discovered their work and created the layout and verse for this imaginative collection—Walter Dean Myers.

Read-Aloud Presentation

Look at the cover of BROWN ANGELS and ask the children whether they think this book is about today or long ago. Direct the children's attention to about ten photographs (which you have selected and marked beforehand) and invite the children to look closely and comment. Many will say that their grandparents have old photographs like these. Call attention to the fact that all the pictures are of children. Read a few of the poems, like "Friendship," "Love That Boy," "They" and "Blossoms," which contains the reference to "brown angels" that serves as the book's title. Read the foreword, in which Walter Dean Myers tells about his search for photographs in antique stores.

STORY STRETCHER

For Art: Display Of Old Photographs

What the children will learn
To compare old and new photographs

Materials you will need
Photo albums, old and new photographs

What to do
1. Place a beautiful album of wedding photographs or some other happy occasion in the art area.

2. Show the children the lighting, colors, clarity and other features of the photographs.

3. Bring in an album of old photographs, or use the pictures from BROWN ANGELS to compare lighting, color, shadows and backgrounds with the newer album.

4. Look closely at the candid shots in BROWN ANGELS and discuss what the photographs tell us about the children's lives.

Something to think about
Let the children take black-and-white photographs of themselves and compare them with the color photographs.

STORY STRETCHER

For Creative Dramatics: Dressing Old-Fashioned

What the children will learn
To dramatize another time and place

Materials you will need
High-top shoes, long cotton dresses, overalls, straw hats, fancy hats, knickers, ties, lacy shirts, mirrors

What to do
1. Ask parents to donate any old clothing that would help the children get a sense of another time.

2. Collect the clothes and let the children sort them.

3. Place a long mirror in the area and invite the children to play dress up.

Something to think about
Children naturally play, and the type of clothing will inspire period play.

STORY STRETCHER

For Social Studies: Grandparents And Great-Grandparents Bring Photographs

What the children will learn
To understand that the people in these old pictures actually lived

Materials you will need
Invitations

What to do

1. Write to several grandparents and great-grandparents of your students, inviting them to class. Tell them about the class having read BROWN ANGELS. Ask them to bring old photographs and photo albums.

2. If several grandparents accept, have them all come on the same day. Divide the children among the grandparents and let them share their photographs with the children.

3. Encourage the grandparents to think of at least one funny story and one poignant story about the people in their pictures.

Something to think about
Show the grandparents and great-grandparents the book that inspired their visit, BROWN ANGELS.

STORY STRETCHER

For Special Project: Toys Of Another Era

What the children will learn
To understand more about children's lives in the past through their toys

Materials you will need
Antique toys, modern toys

What to do

1. Look through the photographs in BROWN ANGELS and note all the old-fashioned toys: the goat wagon, tricycle, dolls, ceramic figures, umbrellas, baskets and batons.

2. Contact an antique dealer or a children's museum. Invite the toy specialist to bring antique toys for the children to see.

3. Make a display of the antique toys.

4. Let the children bring in a few of their own modern toys to add to the display.

5. If possible, leave antique toys out for the children to play with.

Something to think about
Survey parents and grandparents from your school to find out who has an interest in old dolls and toys. Many would be very happy to come to class to explain their hobby and the significance of the toys.

STORY STRETCHER

For Writing Center: Letters To A Child In Another Time

What the children will learn
To write imaginatively

Materials you will need
Stationery, pencils

What to do

1. Ask children who are interested to select children from BROWN ANGELS whom they would like to meet, and with whom they would like to have a conversation.

2. Think up a list of questions that they would like to ask the child in the photograph. For example, "If I could meet you, I would like to know if those high-topped shoes hurt your feet, if you ever have arguments with your sister who is frowning in the picture. I would like to know where you got the doll with the white face, and if you have any dolls with brown faces."

3. After the children brainstorm "If I could meet you" questions, invite them to write a letter to the child.

Something to think about
Let older children pretend that they receive responses to their letters. How would the child in the picture reply?

199

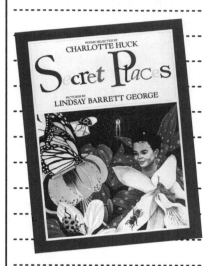

SECRET PLACES

Poems selected by Charlotte Huck

Illustrated by Lindsay Barrett George

As the author notes in the book's fore-word, "All of us have secret places, joyful places that we love intensely." This book offers a tribute to those special places. Nineteen poems invite the reader to visit secret places, including Watson's "Hiding Place," McCord's "This is My Rock," Baylor's "From Your Own Best Secret Place," Coatsworth's "The Maple" and Fisher's "Autumn Leaves." Lindsay Barrett George's bright illustrations are large enough for a whole class to see easily, and the oversized book is wide enough for two friends to hold open on their laps.

Read-Aloud Presentation

Ask the children if there is a place where they like to go and hide in order to dream, to be alone, to avoid the commotion of too many people or too much noise. Tell the students about a secret place that you enjoyed as a child. Show the cover of SECRET PLACES and ask whether the cover portrays an actual or an imaginary place. Select a few poems to read. A good poem with which to begin is Watson's "Hiding Place." (Its illustration serves as the cover illustration as well.) A good poem with which to continue is Fisher's "The Hideout." End the poetry reading with "The Box" by Myra Cohn Livingston. Read the introduction, in which Charlotte Huck observes that some secret places are special containers or boxes where we hide our keepsakes, things that remind us of something or someone special.

S T O R Y   S T R E T C H E R

For Art: Decorative Boxes

What the children will learn
To decorate boxes

Materials you will need
Small sturdy boxes, collage materials (fabrics, colored foil, ribbon, glitter, tiny shells, gift wrap, stickers), scissors, glue, stapler, masking tape

What to do
1.   Ask the children to choose a box that they like, such as a gift box, a round oatmeal box or any sturdy box that closes well.

2.   Reinforce any box hinges, like those on cereal boxes, with masking tape to ensure that they do not tear easily.

3.   Let the children decorate their boxes in any way that they choose.

Encourage them to share their ideas with each other.

Something to think about
If you know of a craftsperson who specializes in decorative boxes, invite him or her to demonstrate this craft to the class.

S T O R Y   S T R E T C H E R

For Classroom Library: Books Are Hiding Places

What the children will learn
To think of reading as a way to hide in another place and time

Materials you will need
Chart paper, marker

What to do
1.   Talk with the children about reading a story and imagining that you live inside the story. When you read CHARLOTTE'S WEB, for example, you imagine that you are there on the farm. You are hidden, so no one talks directly to you, but you see and hear everything.

2.   Let the children talk about books that made them feel so much a part of the story that it was as if they were hidden there in a secret place. Referring to MIRETTE ON THE HIGH WIRE, one child said, "I watched Mirette. I was hiding and saw her when she walked the high wire."

3.   Write on the board all the hiding places in books that the children talk about. Add to the list throughout the week. Whenever you read aloud, or the children read, ask them to add any stories that make them feel as if they were inside the story, hidden in a secret place.

Something to think about
Read ROXABOXEN by Alice McLearan and invite the children

to imagine the secret place in the desert.

For Music And Movement: Hiding Places In Our Room

What the children will learn
To enjoy the excitement of being found

Materials you will need
None needed

What to do
1.   Let the children play hide and seek in the room and on the playground.

2.   Switch off the lights and close your eyes so that you cannot see where the children hide.

3.   When all the notice has quieted, switch on the lights and look for the children.

4.   Allow the children to divide into groups of six: three hide and three seek. Let the remaining children give hints to the seekers, but without pointing or telling exactly where the children are hidden.

Something to think about
Create more suspense by playing mysterious music and having the seekers tiptoe.

For Science And Nature: Natural Objects To Treasure

What the children will learn
To describe the properties of a natural object and its appeal as a thing of beauty or significance

Materials you will need
Shells, acorns, pressed flowers, rocks, quartz, fossils, feathers, butterflies, bark, tablecloth or sheet, scissors, marker, small index cards

What to do
1.   Set up a display table in the science learning center and cover it with a plain sheet or tablecloth. Ask the children to bring in natural objects that they treasure.

2.   Cut index cards in half. Fold the halves in half to make the cards stand up.

3.   Ask each child to print his or her name and the name of the donated object on the card, for example, "Blue jay feather from Brian."

4.   Arrange the natural objects in a visually pleasing display.

5.   Give the children informal free time to talk with each other about the significance of their natural finds.

Something to think about
Consider planning a formal sharing time. Let the children decide ahead of time what questions they would like to have answered: Where did you find the object? How long have you had it? Did someone give it to you? Where do you keep it? Why is it special to you? Listing questions helps children who hesitate to speak understand what is expected, and children who ramble have guidelines.

For Writing Center: My Special Place

What the children will learn
To communicate with others in descriptive ways

Materials you will need
Writing paper, pencils, art supplies for illustrations (optional)

What to do
1.   Ask children who visit the writing center to talk with you or with their friends about places that feel special to them.

2.   After they have talked, some may want to draw the places.

3.   Encourage everyone to write about their special place. Tell the children that they do not have to write in complete sentences. Point out that poets often use phrases instead of sentences.

4.   Suggest to the writers that they jot down phrases that come to mind when they think of their special place.

5.   Let each writer write about that special place in his or her own way, as a poem, a story, a collection of descriptive words.

6.   Share the writing among the writers. Let those who are interested continue writing and editing their pieces.

7.   Plan a "Secret Places" read-aloud with the children reading their writing.

Something to think about
Publish a class book of writing about "Secret Places." Let children who did not want to write, create the illustrations or help with the layout and binding. As an alternative, include some of the children's favorite poems from SECRET PLACES.

15
POETRY

IF YOU'RE NOT HERE
PLEASE RAISE
YOUR HAND:
POEMS ABOUT SCHOOL

By Kalli Dakos

Illustrated by G. Brian Karas

Humorous poems are the young child's favorite poetry, and there is a lot to laugh about in this collection of thirty-eight poems about school. Some favorites among children include "Math is Brewing and I'm in Trouble," "I Brought a Worm," "Substitute Teacher," "It's Inside My Sister's Lunch," "Hiding in the Bathroom" and "Budging Line-Ups." While most of the poems are funny, there are a few very serious ones, including "The Cry Guy," "J.T. Never Will be Ten" and "A Lifetime in Third Grade." Karas illustrates the book with comically twisted, child-like black-and-white drawings for each poem.

Read-Aloud Presentation

Begin by reading the title poem "If You're Not Here Please Raise Your Hand." Practice reading while yawning like the sleepy teacher who is trying to wake up. Read the dust jacket of the book, which explains that the poet is a teacher. Another good poem to read is "They Don't Do Math in Texas." In addition to reading from the book during read-aloud time, schedule several poems throughout the day. Select poems to match the time of day. Read "Hiding in the Bathroom" before or after the children go to the bathroom. Read "It's Inside My Sister's Lunch," before you collect money for books or pictures or a special event. Read "Caleb's Desk is a Mess" before clean-up time.

STORY STRETCHER

For Art: The Poems Remind Me

What the children will learn
To illustrate poems

Materials you will need
Paper, crayons, colored pencils

What to do
1. Tell the children that people have described poetry as pictures that dance in our heads. Ask the children to draw and color the pictures that dance in their heads when they hear a poem read.

2. Since Karas creates sparse illustrations, the children will think of more elaborate pictures.

3. Bind the illustrations into a book or place them in a large scrapbook.

4. Place the book of illustrations in the library area of the classroom.

Something to think about
Let the children choose which poems they want to illustrate.

STORY STRETCHER

For Classroom Library: Poems On Tape

What the children will learn
To read with expression

Materials you will need
Tape recorder, tape

What to do
1. Let readers who did not participate in creative dramatics read poems on tape.

2. Rehearse to help the children read the poems with expression.

3. Introduce the tape and each poem by telling the listener the appropriate page number in IF YOU'RE NOT HERE PLEASE RAISE YOUR HAND, so that listeners may read with the tape, if they wish.

4. Group the poems about teachers, such as "Substitute," "The Mighty Eye," "Dancing on a Rainbow" and "A Teacher's Lament." Other groupings might include homework, being sick or embarrassed, exaggerated tales.

5. End the tape by reading "I'm in Another Dimension" yourself, substituting your name for Ms. Digby's.

Something to think about
Select a narrator to read the dust jacket information about the poet, Kalli Dakos.

ANOTHER STORY STRETCHER

For Classroom Library: Other Funny Poets

What the children will learn
To begin recognizing poets by their works

Materials you will need
Children's favorite poetry books, slips of paper, pencils, fishbowl or glass salad bowl

What to do

1.   Display all the poetry books from this unit, along with books by the children's other favorite poets like Bill Martin, Jr., Jack Prelutsky, Shel Silverstein, Diane Siebert, Karla Kuskin.

2.   Ask each child to write on a slip of paper the title and first line of a favorite poem. On the opposite side of the paper, write the title of the book where the poem can be found.

3.   Invite other children to draw slips from the fishbowl and guess who the poet is, or think of other lines from the same poem.

Something to think about

Do not make this story s-t-r-e-t-c-h-e-r a competition, but keep it an opportunity for the children to see how many poems they enjoy. Some poems will also be liked by other children, and some are individual favorites. With older children, try categorizing the poems by type, such as free verse, acrostic, ballad, blank verse, chant, cinquain, concrete, couplet, list poem. See THE TEACHERS & WRITERS HANDBOOK OF POETIC FORMS for additional poetry forms.

STORY STRETCHER

For Creative Dramatics: Humor Comes to Life

What the children will learn
To dramatize funny events

Materials you will need
Dress-up clothes, props from the classroom

What to do

1.   Let the children select poems that they want to dramatize.

2.   Try various approaches. Some may want to pantomime while you read the poem. Others may want to recite a short poem and act it out. Small groups of children might want to work together.

Something to think about
Involve as many children as possible, but do not insist that everyone perform. Costumes that somewhat disguise the players often help children become more relaxed and freer in their actions.

STORY STRETCHER

For Writing Center: Diary Of Funny Times At School

What the children will learn
To tell, write and share funny stories that encourage laughing at ourselves

Materials you will need
Writing paper, pencils, art supplies for illustrations

What to do

1.   Encourage the children to remember something funny that happened to them. Talk about how important it is to learn to laugh at ourselves.

2.   After the children have remembered a few events, ask individual storytellers to write their stories. Let others work as partners.

3.   Encourage older children to write the story as a narrative and rewrite it as a poem.

4.   Plan on several sharing sessions and compliment the children on learning to laugh at funny things that happen to them.

5.   Provide art supplies for illustrations. Children always want to illustrate funny stories and poems.

Something to think about
Avoid making jokes at the expense of others.

References

Bedard, Michael. (1992). **EMILY**. Illustrated by Barbara Cooney. New York: Doubleday.

Dakos, Kalli. (1990). **IF YOU'RE NOT HERE PLEASE RAISE YOUR HAND: POEMS ABOUT SCHOOL**. Illustrated by G. Brian Karas. New York: Macmillan.

Huck, Charlotte. (1993). **SECRET PLACES**. New York: Greenwillow.

Kennedy, X.J. and Kennedy, Dorothy. (1992). **TALKING LIKE THE RAIN: A READ-TO-ME BOOK OF POEMS**. Illustrated by Jane Dyer. Boston: Little Brown.

Myers, Walter Dean. (1993). **BROWN ANGELS**. New York: Harper Collins.

Also Mentioned in this Chapter

Martin, Bill, Jr., and Archambault, John. (1988). **LISTEN TO THE RAIN**. Illustrated by John Endicott. New York: Henry Holt.

McLerran, Alice. (1991). **ROXABOXEN**. Illustrated by Barbara Cooney. New York: Lothrop, Lee & Shepard.

Padgett, Ron. (Ed.) (1987). **THE TEACHERS & WRITERS HAND-BOOK OF POETIC FORMS**. New York: Teachers & Writers Collaborative.

White E.B. (1952).**CHARLOTTE'S WEB**. Illustrated by Garth Williams. New York: Harper and Row.

Additional References for Poetry

Aylesworth, Jim. (1992). **THE CAT AND THE FIDDLE AND MORE**. Illustrated by Richard Hull. New York: Athenaeum. *Presents twelve variations on the traditional rhyme "Hey Diddle Diddle."*

Grimes, Nikki. (1978). **SOMETHING ON MY MIND**. Illustrated by Tom Feelings. New York: Dial Puffins. *Prose poems about the universal concerns of growing up, as well as the problems and struggles of African Americans.*

Luenn, Nancy. (1992). **MOTHER EARTH**. Illustrated by Neil Waldman. New York: Athenaeum. *The earth celebrates the birth of a new baby.*

Schwartz, Alvin. (1992). **AND THE GREEN GRASS GREW ALL AROUND, FOLK POETRY FOR EVERYONE**. Illustrated by Sue Truesdell. New York: HarperCollins. *Poems, chants, rhythms, rhymes, funny sayings and folk poetry about people, food, school, teases and taunts, wishes and warning, love and marriage, and much more.*

Yolen, Jane. (1991). **BIRD WATCH**. Illustrated by Ted Lewin. New York: Philomel. *A collection of seventeen poems describing a variety of birds and their activities.*

AUTHOR STUDY
ELOISE GREENFIELD

She Come Bringing Me That Little Baby Girl
First Pink Light
Grandpa's Face
Night on Neighborhood Street
Daydreamers

SHE COME BRINGING ME THAT LITTLE BABY GIRL

By Eloise Greenfield

Illustrated by John Steptoe

Kevin wanted a little brother, but his mother brought home a baby girl. In this story of sibling rivalry and the disruption of a boy's life by his baby sister, Kevin adjusts to the new arrival with the help of two loving parents. Telling the story in the boy's voice, Greenfield successfully captures the language and the emotional struggle of adjustment and, finally, acceptance of a new sibling. Kevin even grows to like the idea of being the big brother. Steptoe, illustrator of two Caldecott Honor Books, draws layers of lines and colors around the characters, an unusual technique for highlighting.

Read-Aloud Presentation

To begin the author study of Eloise Greenfield, show the children all the books you plan to read and point out that there are still more in the classroom library. Tell the children about Ms. Greenfield: the award-winning author of more than twenty best-selling books for children. Her stories speak to children in a very special way because she has the rare genius of remembering what it is like to be a child. She is a teacher, a mother, and a grandmother. Ms. Greenfield writes poetry and fiction. She lives in Washington, D.C., where she often teaches creative writing to children. If there are children in your classroom with new babies at home, ask them to talk about the day their sisters or brothers came home from the hospital. Show the cover of SHE COME BRINGING ME THAT LITTLE BABY GIRL and introduce Kevin, who is waiting for his mother to arrive from the hospital. Pause during the reading to discuss how Kevin felt when the neighbors brought presents for the baby, not for him. After reading the story, let anyone who has a baby brother or sister respond to the book.

STORY STRETCHER

For Art: Outlining Experiments

What the children will learn
To explore Steptoe's highlighting technique

Materials you will need
Drawing paper, markers or crayons

What to do

1. With a small group of children in the art center, look through John Steptoe's illustrations and note how he outlines the figures with several colors.

2. Begin by drawing lines. Let the children hold three markers or crayons in their fists and draw parallel lines on the paper.

3. Encourage the children to experiment with the triple lines as a border or as a baseline for their drawings.

4. Using Steptoe's technique of outlining in different colors, ask the children who seem interested to draw people or objects or a house.

Something to think about
Steptoe's technique is a graphic artist's approach. Children might also try layering lines to write their names.

STORY STRETCHER

For Classroom Library: Read-Along And Lullabies

What the children will learn
To listen to a tape and turn pages on cue

Materials you will need
Tape recorder, audiocassette tape, glass, fork, large index card, fine-point marker

What to do

1. Tape-record yourself reading SHE COME BRINGING ME THAT LITTLE BABY GIRL. Record an introduction in which you explain to the children that the sound they hear (gently tap the glass with the fork) is the page-turning signal.

2. Pause in the story at the passage in which Kevin holds the baby, and ask a few children to

sing the lullaby you have taught the class.

3. Print the words to the lullaby on an index card and insert it into the book.

4. Place the tape recording and the book in the classroom library.

Something to think about
Books that deal with sensitive issues are especially good for the listening station, because they allow a child who has a special need to revisit a story, to do so without having to ask for it to be read aloud.

STORY STRETCHER

For Music And Movement: Lullabies

What the children will learn
To sing favorite lullabies

Materials you will need
Chart tablet paper, marker

What to do
1. Choose a traditional lullaby like "Lullaby and Good Night," or a folk lullaby like "Hush, Little Baby."

2. Print the words on chart tablet paper.

3. Teach the children the words and lyrics by echo reading.

4. When the baby comes to visit, let the children sing the lullaby. (See the special project story s-t-r-e-t-c-h-e-r).

Something to think about
Ask a child who has a baby sister or brother to sing a lullaby that their family sings. (Also see the lullabies in SINGING BEE! A COLLECTION OF FAVORITE CHILDREN'S SONGS).

STORY STRETCHER

For Special Project: Inviting A New Baby To Class

What the children will learn
To hold a baby properly

Materials you will need
None needed

What to do
1. Invite a family who has a new baby to bring the baby to class.

2. If the family has a child in your classroom, let the brother or sister introduce the baby to the class and explain how he or she helps take care of the baby.

3. Seat all the children. Let those who are interested hold the baby while the mother or father sits beside them.

4. Discuss why it is important to support the baby's head.

5. Encourage the parents to talk about the ways that this baby is like the older brother or sister was as an infant.

Something to think about
Always respect the baby's needs.

STORY STRETCHER

For Writing Center: Advice To Big Sisters And Big Brothers

What the children will learn
To consider what it must be like to have a new baby in the family

Materials you will need
Writing paper, writing folders, pencils, art supplies for illustrations (optional)

What to do
1. When Kevin allows his two friends to see his baby sister, in SHE COME BRINGING ME THAT LITTLE BABY GIRL, he stays close by to make sure they hold the baby properly.

2. Ask the children who have baby brothers or sisters to tell what they have learned about taking care of babies.

3. Help them extend the list beyond simple statements about how to hold the baby, to include shopping for the baby, the attention the baby needs and their feelings about the baby.

Something to think about
Extend the activity by asking children who have toddlers as siblings to give advice about how to live with two-year-olds and their special needs.

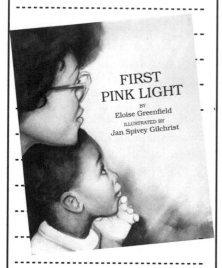

FIRST PINK LIGHT

By Eloise Greenfield

Illustrated by Jan Spivey Gilchrist

Tyree misses his father, who has been away for a month taking care of Grandmother. He hides in a cardboard box to await his father's return home. The sensitive mother eventually gives in to Tyree's pleas to stay up and wait for his father. She makes him comfortable in a hiding place from which to wait and surprise Daddy. Eventually, Tyree falls asleep and misses the first pink light of dawn when Daddy gets home. Greenfield lets the reader experience the touching moment of a father carrying a sleepy child off to bed. Jan Spivey Gilchrist's pastels and gauche capture the dawn and match the other moments in the text with sensitivity.

Read-Aloud Presentation

Ask the children to recall trying to stay awake to wait for one of their parents to return. Ask the children how long they were able to stay awake. Also inquire if anyone has ever seen the dawn. Talk about a beautiful sunrise you have seen and the glow in the sky from the first pink light. Read FIRST PINK LIGHT without pausing to break the mood. At the end of the story, ask the children to yawn and stretch and imagine a sleepy time, being held lovingly by a parent.

STORY STRETCHER

For Art: Sunrise

What the children will learn
To explore the possibilities of watercolors

Materials you will need
Watercolor paper or heavy construction paper, watercolors, brushes, masking tape, sponges, margarine tubs with water

What to do
1. Tape the watercolor paper to a tabletop or flat tray. Tape it all around the edges so that it will not crinkle when wet.

2. Show the children the sunrise and the special pink and blue lights on the cover and at the end of the book.

3. Let the children experiment with sunrises and sunsets, using dry brush and wet brush techniques with the watercolors.

Something to think about
If you have beautiful pictures of sunrises or sunsets, post them in the art center as an inspiration to the children.

ANOTHER STORY STRETCHER

For Art: Silhouettes And Sunrises

What the children will learn
To apply dark paints over dry watercolor paintings

Materials you will need
Watercolor sunrise or sunset scenes, watercolor paints, paper, brushes, water in margarine tubs, paper toweling

What to do
1. Look at the last illustration in FIRST PINK LIGHT and note the way that Jan Spivey Gilchrist shows that it is still dark, but the sun is about to rise. She has painted the houses, fences and trees in the foreground, all black, on paper washed in pink, blue and gray.

2. Ask the children to experiment by adding the silhouette of something from their neighborhood to a sunrise watercolor.

3. Put a drop of water into the block of black watercolor paint and apply it with a dry brush.

Something to think about
It is important to let the children decide whether or not they want to experiment with the art medium in this way, or would prefer to choose their own course.

STORY STRETCHER

For Music And Movement: Hiding Places

What the children will learn
To listen for musical and verbal cues

Materials you will need
Audiotape or compact disc of soft music, one large cardboard box

What to do

1. Try to capture the thrill of surprise, as well as the gentleness of soft music, by playing a game of hide and seek.

2. Let one child be "it," the seeker, and hide inside a large cardboard box, just like Tyree did in FIRST PINK LIGHT.

3. Once the child is hidden in the box, play the soft music and let everyone else tiptoe into hiding places.

4. Stop the music and let the child who is the seeker begin looking for those in hiding.

5. After a few minutes, while some children are not yet found, let them jump out and yell, "Surprise."

6. Select one of the children not found to be the next "seeker."

Something to think about
Enjoy the soft music at another time of day, when the children need a break or need to relax.

STORY STRETCHER

For Science And Nature: When Is Sunrise?

What the children will learn
To associate the time of day with sunrise and seasons

Materials you will need
Daily newspaper, calendar

What to do

1. Explain that sunrise occurs at a different time each day, earlier during the long days of summer and later during the short days of winter. Many young children will not know this.

2. Look in the daily newspaper and show the children where the times of sunrise and sunset are printed. Assign children to check the times of sunrise and sunset for the week.

3. Print the times on the calendar. Let the children decide whether the days are getting longer or shorter.

4. If you teach third graders, some of your students will be able to add and subtract the times.

Something to think about
Select a few children to watch different television stations for the weather and nightly news. The meteorologist usually reports on the times of sunrise and sunset for the next day. Ask the children to write the times on a slip of paper and bring it to class.

STORY STRETCHER

For Writing Center: Waiting Stories

What the children will learn
To recall and write about a time when it was difficult to wait

Materials you will need
Writing paper, writing folders, pencils, art supplies for illustrations

What to do

1. With a small group of writers, recall Tyree's waiting for his father.

2. Let the children discuss times when it was difficult for them to wait.

3. Encourage them to draw a scene from that experience, and then to write the story that surrounds the scene.

4. Set up listening groups in which the children listen to each other's writing, then ask questions of the writers like: "When did this happen?" "Who was waiting with you?" "Tell me more about the part where . . . " The group's questions and requests to "tell me more" help the children understand how to edit the story so

as to make it more interesting to the audience.

Something to think about
Waiting stories are part of every child's life. Encourage the writers to write more than one waiting story, or ask a group of writers to let you bind their stories into a published book about waiting.

209

AUTHOR STUDY
ELOISE GREENFIELD

GRANDPA'S FACE

By Eloise Greenfield

Illustrated by Floyd Cooper

Tamika and her grandfather have a special relationship. They enjoy their talk-walks in the park and neighborhood. He tells stories and sings to her. She loves looking at his gentle face. Tamika is startled one day when suddenly Grandpa's face is angry. He is rehearsing for a play, and the mean face she sees makes Tamika fearful. She fears that she does not know her grandfather, and that someday he might look that way at her. After several family misunderstandings, Tamika and Grandpa go for a talk-walk, and he gently reassures her of his love. Floyd Cooper's wonderful pastels fill each page with scenes from this city family whose warmth and closeness radiate from the page.

Read-Aloud Presentation

Ask that a few children talk about their grandparents. If you have children whose grandparents live with them, encourage those children to begin the sharing. Introduce GRANDPA'S FACE by showing the cover of the book and asking the children to think about the special feelings between this granddaughter and her grandfather. Read the book, pausing on the page where Grandpa's face looks mean, and ask the children to guess why he might be angry. At the end of the book, explain how sometimes children think their parents or grandparents are upset with them, when really the adults are worried about something else.

STORY STRETCHER
For Art: Pastels

What the children will learn
To experiment with shadowing and overlays of color

Materials you will need
Drawing paper, pastel chalks, sponges, plastic margarine tubs, hair spray (optional)

What to do
1.   Place GRANDPA'S FACE in the art area. Encourage the children to look more closely at the ways that Floyd Cooper layers pastel colors over each other to create new colors.

2.   Call attention to the use of gray and dark brown pastels to create shadows and folds in clothing.

3.   After the children have experimented with the pastels, dampen the paper and let them apply the pastels again, noting the differences between the dry and wet techniques.

Something to think about
To keep the pastel chalk drawings from flaking, lightly spray them with a non-aerosol hair spray.

STORY STRETCHER
For Classroom Library: Grandparents Reading And Storytelling

What the children will learn
To enjoy stories with positive images of grandparents

Materials you will need
Collection of books that include grandparents

What to do
1.   Survey the children to find out how many have grandparents living in the community.

2.   Invite the grandparents to come to class and read to the children or tell favorite childhood stories.

3.   Invite grandparents who are not available during school hours to make a cassette tape of themselves telling stories or reading. Place the tapes at the listening station in the classroom library.

Something to think about
Consider grandparents as possible volunteers to listen to children read. Contact your local association of "Foster Grandparents" for volunteers.

STORY STRETCHER
For Creative Dramatics: Costumes And Make-Up

What the children will learn
To pretend to be actors

Materials you will need
Variety of costumes or dress-up clothes, full-length mirrors, instant print camera (optional)

What to do

1. Collect an array of outgrown Halloween costumes.

2. Place the costumes in the creative dramatics area and let the children's imaginations take charge.

3. Take pictures of the improvisational actors in their costumes.

Something to think about

Consider asking children to dress up as their favorite storybook characters. If you have families with limited income, provide as many costumes as possible.

For Special Project: Attending A Play

What the children will learn

To understand that the actors are just pretending

Materials you will need

Theater group

What to do

1. Survey the neighborhood for a theater group that performs plays for children.

2. Invite them to the school to perform one-act plays. Rather than have the entire school watch a play at once, divide the students into smaller groups.

3. If any of the actors is a senior citizen, ask him or her to talk to the class about pretending and learning lines for a role in a play.

Something to think about

Invite senior citizens who are actors to come to the school. Their visit will remind the children of Tamika's story and how her Grandpa was an actor in a community theater.

For Writing Center: Grandparents

What the children will learn

To express their feelings in writing

Materials you will need

Writing paper, writing folders, art supplies for illustrations (optional)

What to do

1. Remind a small group at the writing center about the special relationship between Tamika and Grandpa.

2. Spend a few minutes discussing what the two of them do together, then let the children talk about special moments with their own grandparents.

3. Ask the children to write about a special time with their grandparents or with another older relative.

Something to think about

In our highly mobile society, some children do not know their grandparents well. If a child prefers, let him or her write about someone else's grandparents from the neighborhood.

AUTHOR STUDY
ELOISE GREENFIELD

NIGHT ON NEIGHBORHOOD STREET

By Eloise Greenfield

Illustrated by Jan Spivey Gilchrist

In this book of poetry about the nights in a city neighborhood, Greenfield's writing pulses with authenticity and sensitivity. The poet lets the reader experience the neighborhood—its children, families, friends and feelings—through the eyes of a child. The emotional range is true to the child and to the comfort of being loved in a family, the enjoyment of play, the conquering of fear and the victory of accomplishment, at least in one's dreams. Sadly, the picture is incomplete without one poem about the dangers of these streets, "The Seller." Jan Spivey Gilchrist's illustrations are realistic and loving, harsh and soft, expressive and illusive. They equal the poetry in strength and poignancy.

Read-Aloud Presentation

Look at the cover of NIGHT ON NEIGHBORHOOD STREET, then read the poem which it illustrates, "Buddy's Dream." Explain that although this book is a collection of poems, it tells the story of a neighborhood. Read the first four or five poems at one sitting. We found that "Neighborhood Street," "Little Boy Blues," "Goodnight Juma," "New Baby Poem I," "New Baby Poem II," "The Seller" and "Fambly Time" work well together for the first day's reading. The "Fambly Time" poem ends on a more positive note than the grim "The Seller." After reading the remaining poems on another day, leaf through the illustrations and let the children describe the feelings conveyed by each poem.

STORY STRETCHER

For Art: Night Pictures

What the children will learn
To use a variety of colors and techniques to create night scenes

Materials you will need
Construction paper (blue, dark brown, black), pastel chalks

What to do
1. With a small group of children in the art area, look at Jan Spivey Gilchrist's illustrations, noting how she creates colored backgrounds and layers pastels on top of the backgrounds.
2. Help children experiment with possibilities and notice shadows.

Something to think about
It is not important that the children make a representational drawing or painting of a night scene. The goal is rather that they notice and experiment with possibilities. Some children might enjoy painting or drawing a dream

scene, like the illustration of "Buddy's Dream." Of course, they would illustrate their own dreams.

STORY STRETCHER

For Classroom Library: Reading Poetry With Expression

What the children will learn
To use their voices to read with expression

Materials you will need
Chart tablet paper, marker

What to do
1. Select one of the more rhythmic poems like "Buddy's Dream" or "Lawanda's Walk" or "Goodnight, Juma."
2. Print the poem on chart tablet paper and teach the children to read it, paying attention to the lines and punctuation.

Something to think about
Let individual children choose their favorite poems, print them on index cards and display them in the classroom library area.

STORY STRETCHER

For Cooking And Snack Time: Banana Nut Bread

What the children will learn
To follow a recipe

Materials you will need
Chart tablet paper, marker, flour, salt, sugar, eggs, bananas, pecans, shortening, measuring cups, measuring spoons, mixing bowl, wooden spoon, loaf pan, oven, milk or apple juice, napkins, hand mixer (optional)

What to do
1. Print the recipe for banana nut bread on a chart tablet. If you use a prepackaged mix instead, print the steps for mixing, baking and serving.

2. Recipe for banana nut bread:

1 3/4 cups self-rising flour
1/4 teaspoon salt
1/4 cup shortening
2/3 cup sugar
2 eggs
1 cup+ mashed ripe bananas
  (2 or 3 bananas)
a few shelled pecans

Cream the shortening and sugar in a mixing bowl with a wooden spoon. Add the eggs, one at a time. Beat well. Stir the flour and salt together and add to the wet ingredients, alternating with small amounts of banana. Beat until smooth. Pour into a greased loaf pan. Bake in a 350 degree oven for one hour.

3. Serve hot with cold milk or cool with apple juice.

Something to think about
Divide the class into thirds and make at least three recipes.

STORY STRETCHER

For Music And Movement: Sidewalk Games

What the children will learn
To follow movement directions given by their peers and indicated by the rhymes and rhythms of the games

Materials you will need
Sidewalk chalk, jump ropes

What to do
1. Look through the illustrations in NIGHT ON NEIGHBORHOOD STREET and find the children's games alluded to in the illustrations or the poems, including hopscotch, jump rope and circle games.

2. Let the children work with partners to demonstrate a street game of their choosing.

3. Participate with the children in the games and teach them a jump rope rhyme from your childhood.

Something to think about
To make a mathematics game out of hopscotch, ask the children to write multiplication or counting by two's or five's.

ANOTHER STORY STRETCHER

For Music And Movement: Trumpet

What the children will learn
To enjoy trumpet music

Materials you will need
Musician and trumpet, rhythm band instruments

What to do
1. Read the two poems again in which Tonya's mother plays the trumpet: "When Tonya's Friends Come to Spend the Night" and "Night on Neighborhood Street."

2. Invite a musician who plays the trumpet in a school band to come to the classroom and play songs for the children. If the musician knows a blues song, ask her or him to play it, too.

3. Although the children will all want to play the trumpet, they cannot because to do so would spread germs. Instead, after the musician's concert, distribute the rhythm band instruments and let the children accompany the trumpet player in a march.

Something to think about
Ask the school's music teacher or a music shop owner to bring in a variety of brass instruments for the children to hear and enjoy. Inviting child musicians helps the children begin to envision themselves as musicians.

DAYDREAMERS

By Eloise Greenfield

Illustrated by Tom Feelings

A wonderfully warm poem that admires and celebrates daydreaming. Its carefully crafted language describes what others see when daydreaming happens. The book-length poem flows across the pages like a gentle and beautiful stream. Tom Feelings's illustrations in pen, pencil and ink look like charcoal across spattered backgrounds. The single subject drawings of young children exquisitely render African-American children daydreaming. Each mood and stance in the drawings matches the wonder of a mind caught in the state of daydreaming.

Read-Aloud Presentation

Collect a number of Eloise Greenfield's poetry books: HONEY, I LOVE; NIGHT ON NEIGHBORHOOD STREET; NATHANIEL TALKING. Before the read-aloud session, give the three books to three children and ask each to select one poem to read. Before the children read their selections, explain that these books are collections of poetry. The children chose from among many different poems. After the children read, ask at least two students to tell what they do when they daydream. Have one child show the class how he or she sits or stands while "just daydreaming." Then read DAYDREAMERS without pausing. After the reading, go back through the book and let the children admire Tom Feelings's sketches.

STORY STRETCHER

For Art: Self-Portrait Of Daydreaming

What the children will learn
To draw a self-portrait

Materials you will need
Selection of papers, various art media (paints, crayons, chalks, charcoal, colored pencils, markers)

What to do
1. Let the children talk about their favorite daydreaming poses. Where are they sitting or standing? What are they daydreaming about? How do their eyes and bodies look?
2. Ask the children to show the group their daydreaming poses.
3. Let the children choose among an array of art materials to decide which to use for their daydreaming self-portrait.

Something to think about
Invariably, some children will make balloons above their heads to show what they are daydreaming. Do not suggest it ahead of time, but enjoy it when it occurs.

ANOTHER STORY STRETCHER

For Art: Spatter Painting

What the children will learn
To add interest and texture to drawings or paintings by spattering

Materials you will need
Drawing paper, tempera paints, toothbrushes, margarine tubs

What to do
1. Look through Tom Feelings's illustrations for DAYDREAMERS and note the spatter painting.
2. Demonstrate how to create spatter painting by dipping a toothbrush into thick tempera paint, then running one's thumb or finger across the brush. It spatters the paint onto the paper.
3. Let the children experiment with this technique on scrap paper, then spatter-paint a picture, then spatter-paint a background for a picture.

Something to think about
Most children will want to spatter-paint and sketch over the paint. It is difficult for young children to spatter-paint over a finished sketch. They often put on too much paint and ruin their sketch.

STORY STRETCHER

For Classroom Library: Poetry Connections

What the children will learn
To select their favorite Eloise Greenfield poems

Materials you will need
HONEY, I LOVE; NATHANIEL
TALKING; NIGHT ON
NEIGHBORHOOD STREET;
DAYDREAMERS; index cards

What to do

1. Place the four poetry books by Eloise Greenfield in the classroom library.

2. Ask the children to select a favorite poem and copy the poem onto an index card.

3. Make a display of the poems and see whether there are class favorites.

4. After the bulletin board display is taken down, ask the children to take their poems home and read them to their parents.

Something to think about
First graders will find the copying task too difficult. If you have reading buddies—older children who come and read to the first graders—ask them to copy the poems for the young children.

STORY STRETCHER

For Music And Movement: Daydreaming And Poetry Poses

What the children will learn
To control their bodies

Materials you will need
Mirror

What to do

1. Ask the children to think of themselves daydreaming. What do they look like?

2. Encourage the children to try daydreaming poses in front of the mirror.

3. After the children have practiced a few daydreaming poses, look through the illustrations in the book and encourage them to mimic what they see.

4. Ask the children to move in ways that words in the poem suggest. Eloise Greenfield uses terms, for example, like "double dutch," "crisscrossing," "hopscotch," "glide," "roller skate," "bump" and "promenade."

5. After the children have imitated these poses and movements, read the poem again. Ask them to close their eyes and feel the sensations they experienced as they moved.

Something to think about
With younger children, use the mirror mostly as a tool for rehearsing the movements and the daydreaming poses.

STORY STRETCHER

For Writing Center: Daydreaming

What the children will learn
To write about their daydreams

Materials you will need
Writing paper, writing folders, pencils, art supplies for illustrations (optional)

What to do

1. With a small group of writers in the writing center or library area, read Eloise Greenfield's DAYDREAMERS again, looking more closely at Tom Feelings's expressive artwork.

2. Let the children talk about what they daydream, when they daydream, where they daydream and how daydreaming makes them feel.

3. Ask the children to write about themselves daydreaming.

4. Plan a sharing time for the children to read what they have written. Let the children choose whether or not they will read their daydreaming pieces to the whole class. Some pieces may feel too

private to share with a large group. Let the children decide.

Something to think about
Pair this story s-t-r-e-t-c-h-e-r with the art self-portraits to create a display of art and writing.

References

Greenfield, Eloise. (1981). **DAYDREAMERS**. Illustrated by Tom Feelings. New York: Dial.

Greenfield, Eloise. (1976, 1991). **FIRST PINK LIGHT**. Illustrated by Jan Spivey Gilchrist. New York: Black Butterfly Children's Books.

Greenfield, Eloise. (1988). **GRANDPA'S FACE**. Illustrated by Floyd Cooper. New York: Philomel Books.

Greenfield, Eloise. (1991). **NIGHT ON NEIGHBORHOOD STREET**. Illustrated by Jan Spivey Gilchrist. New York: Penguin.

Greenfield, Eloise. (1974). **SHE COME BRINGING ME THAT LITTLE BABY GIRL**. Illustrated by John Steptoe. New York: HarperCollins.

Also Mentioned in this Chapter

Hart, Jane (Ed.) (1982). **SINGING BEE! A COLLECTION OF FAVORITE CHILDREN'S SONGS**. Illustrated by Anita Lobel. New York: Lothrop, Lee & Shepard.

Additional References for Author Study—Eloise Greenfield

Greenfield, Eloise. (1978). **HONEY, I LOVE**. Illustrated by Diane and Leo Dillon. New York: Harper and Row. *A collection of fifteen poems that celebrate a child's emotions and self-confidence.*

Greenfield, Eloise. (1988). **NATHANIEL TALKING**. Illustrated by Jan Spivey Gilchrist. New York: Black Butterfly Books. *A nine-year-old thinks in raps, poems and chants and questions his life and times in his city neighborhood.*

Greenfield, Eloise. (1988). **UNDER THE SUNDAY TREE**. Illustrated by Amos Ferguson. New York: Harper and Row. *A collection of poems and paintings that evoke life in the Bahamas.*

Greenfield, Eloise. (1933). **WILLIAM AND THE GOOD OLD DAYS**. Illustrated by Jan Spivey Gilchrist. New York: HarperCollins. *William longs for the good old days when his grandmother could see and people came to visit her in her restaurant.*

Little, Lessie Jones, and Greenfield, Eloise. (1978). **I CAN DO IT MYSELF**. Illustrated by Carole Byard. New York: Thomas Y. Crowell. *Donny is determined to buy his mother's birthday present all by himself, but he meets a scary dog on the way home.*

AUTHOR STUDY
BILL PEET

The Wump World
Chester the Worldly Pig
Hubert's Hair-Raising Adventure
Kermit the Hermit
Merle the High Flying Squirrel

AUTHOR STUDY
BILL PEET

THE WUMP WORLD
By Bill Peet

In an imaginary world of grassy meadows and beautiful streams, the Wumps live simple lives until they are invaded by strange machines and people from the planet of Pollutus. The fable of the Wumps parallels our own world in obvious ways. Many children feel that their safe worlds are shattered by monsters beyond their control. Adults long for the security of a simpler life, for freedom from all that pollutes our planet, and from the powerful who plant their flags in our space. Deceptively simple and remarkably close to reality, the Wump World offers hope for the future in the image of the little green plant pushing its way through the city pavement. The expressive cartoon faces that Bill Peet gives the Wumps are so full of feeling that readers young and old will empathize with them.

Read-Aloud Presentation

Show the cover of THE WUMP WORLD, which portrays the Wumps grazing in a lovely green meadow. Turn to the pages that show the Wumps living underground. Ask the children to think about what might have driven them there. Read THE WUMP WORLD without pausing for discussion. Let the children share any responses that they have. Older students may comment upon how much the Wump World is like the Earth, filled with smog in the cities, polluted rivers in the country and dying trees in the forest. At the end, recall activities that the class did during the neighborhood unit, including ways that they cleaned up their world. Show the last page and comment about our need for many green plants to clean our air.

STORY STRETCHER

For Art: Before And After Pictures

What the children will learn
To imagine two worlds

Materials you will need
Heavy paper, markers, colored pencils, pastel chalks

What to do
1.   Fold a large sheet of drawing paper in half.

2.   On one side of the fold, ask the children to draw the Wump World before the Pollutus People arrived. On the other side, draw what the Wump World looked like after they arrived. As an alternative, ask the children to draw a polluted area of our world on one side, and what it would like if it were cleaned up on the other.

Something to think about
If you have photographs of a littered or polluted area that the children helped clean up, make these photographs the centerpiece of a bulletin board display of the children's "Before and After Pictures."

STORY STRETCHER

For Music And Movement: The Wump World Song

What the children will learn
To sing and chant

Materials you will need
Chart tablet paper, marker

What to do
1.   Write the words to this "Wump World" song on chart paper.

> *We are the Wumps, and this is our world*
> *Clean and green.*
> *We are the Wumps, and someone's flying in*
> *Metal and mean.*
> *We are the Wumps, and now we are below*
> *Rumble and roar.*
> *We are the Wumps, and there's no air to breathe*
> *Huffing and puffing.*
> *We are the Wumps, shhh! It's quiet above*
> *What's happening?*
> *We are the Wumps, and we come out to*
> *Deserted streets.*
> *We are the Wumps running, looking for the*
> *Green, ahhh, green.*
> *We are the Wumps, and our World is*
> *Clean and green.*
> *Wumps, we are the Wumps,*
> *Welcome to our world (Raines, 1993).*

2.   Divide the class into singers and chanters. The singers sing the first line of the couplet in a sing-song melody. The chanters "rap" the short line.

3.   Let some children dramatize the scenes in the song by imagining how the Wumps might act.

Something to think about
If you feel that you either cannot sing the song, or you cannot think of a melody, ask the children to perform the song as a poem with two voices.

For Science And Nature: Green For Clean

What the children will learn
To plant green plants to create a healthier indoor and outdoor environment

Materials you will need
Plants, shrubs, trees, shovels

What to do
1. With the school principal or the center director, plan a special green space for the foyer, reception area or school grounds.

2. Invite a local nursery to donate plants or collect plants from parents or grandparents.

3. Discuss with the children how plants help to remove pollutants from the air.

4. Involve your class in planning for the care of the plants. Learn the names of the plants and how much light and water each requires.

5. Assign each child some responsibility for the plants. Let small groups of children work together for a week, then teach the next team what is required.

Something to think about
Younger children will not understand how plants take in carbon dioxide and release oxygen. Teach them the slogan "Green means clean," which reminds us that plants give us clean air to breathe.

For Social Studies: Designing A Wump World Flag

What the children will learn
To design a flag to represent a clean, unpolluted environment

Materials you will need
Yardsticks, colored construction paper, scissors, stapler, old white pillowcases (optional), scraps of fabric (optional), sewing machine (optional)

What to do
1. Look at the flag that the People from Pollutus plant on the hill near the Wump meadow.

2. Ask the children to design a flag that would represent the Wump World, where everything is natural and green and clean.

3. Invite the children to design their construction paper flags and staple them onto yardsticks.

Something to think about
As an alternative, cut old pillowcases in half and stitch scraps of fabric onto the cases to create the flags.

For Writing Center: Writing A Letter About Clean Air

What the children will learn
To express their concerns about the quality of the air and water

Materials you will need
Telephone book with listings of state and local government agencies, stationery, large envelope, postage

What to do
1. Locate the names and addresses of the air and water quality officials for your city, county or state by looking in the telephone book.

2. Call the telephone numbers listed to obtain the name of the agency head.

3. Let the children compose their own letters, expressing in their own words their worries about having clean air to breathe and clean water to drink.

4. If your children have participated in any project to clean up the environment, ask them to mention the project in the letter, so that the officials will know that they are doing something about their concerns.

5. Photocopy the children's letters and send the copies to a local newspaper.

Something to think about
When you write to the air and water quality officials, ask for free brochures written for children and families.

AUTHOR STUDY
BILL PEET

CHESTER THE
WORLDLY PIG

By Bill Peet

Chester wants a different life for himself than most pigs have, who end up being sent to market. Inspired by a circus poster, Chester decides to become a performer. He escapes from the farm and finds a circus. When the ringmaster places Chester in a cage with ferocious tigers, Chester faints. He is demoted to playing Rosco the Clown's baby. Chester escapes, only to find himself trapped in the woods, chased by a hungry bear, then caught by three hungry tramps. Escaping again, Chester goes to a farm, where the farmer fattens him up for market. However, a showman buys Chester, and much to Chester's surprise, the spotlight is suddenly upon him, as the announcer calls Chester's black spots a miracle, for they mimic a map of the world. Bill Peet has succeeded in creating another great adventure tale of narrow escapes, dreams of fame and fortune and real life surprises. The cartoon sketches are as comical as the dilemmas that poor Chester faces.

Read-Aloud Presentation

Show the children the cover of CHESTER THE WORLDLY PIG and ask them to tell whether the story is true or fictional. The cover shows a pig balancing on his snout on top of a fence post, a clear indication that the story is pure fiction. After reading CHESTER, show the illustration in BILL PEET: AN AUTOBIOGRAPHY of the author, as a boy, going to work on his grandfather's farm. Read about Bill Peet's life on the farm and his imaginative thinking about the animals.

S T O R Y   S T R E T C H E R

For Art: Circus Posters

What the children will learn
To decorate circus posters

Materials you will need
Tempera paints in primary colors, brushes, paper, masking tape

What to do
1. Look at the circus poster in Bill Peet's illustration of Chester's barn wall. Call attention to the ornate gold scrolls, fancy lettering and primary colors.
2. Ask the children to make a circus poster announcing themselves or Chester as circus stars.

Something to think about
Post a circus poster from a real circus on the bulletin board and encourage the children to consider the ways that the artist tells the viewer that this is a circus poster.

S T O R Y   S T R E T C H E R

For Classroom Library: A Tape Of Chester's Adventure

What the children will learn
To read with expression

Materials you will need
Tape recorder with good microphone, audio cassette tape, quiet place, stapler

What to do
1. Ask the readers to read CHESTER THE WORLDLY PIG, playing the roles of the narrator, Chester, the first farmer, five circus performers, three tramps, the second farmer and the Miracle Showman.
2. Select one student to be the orchestrator, whose role is to cue the other readers.
3. Rehearse the reading.
4. Record the reading once. Listen to the recording and let the children decide whether they want to record it a second time in order to improve the expression in their voices.
5. Be sure to record an introduction which explains that the sound of a stapler stapling is the signal to turn the page.

Something to think about
CHESTER THE WORLDLY PIG makes an excellent listening tape book because it is an adventure story. Plan to record the book again with different readers. Third graders could make a tape for first or second graders to listen to.

S T O R Y   S T R E T C H E R

For Music And Movement: Chester's Balancing Act

What the children will learn
To stand on their heads

Materials you will need
Pillows, mats or soft flooring, tumbling coach, masking tape

What to do
1. Invite a tumbling coach to the class to teach the children how to stand on their heads by first balancing against a wall.

2. If the children are too inexperienced, or lack sufficient body control, have them practice balancing on one foot in a stork pose.

3. Ask the tumbling coach to suggest other activities that help with balance, such as balance beam exercises.

4. Help young children learn how to balance by taping a six-foot strip of masking tape to the floor. Encourage the children to practice walking on it. If you place the tape near the door, many children will walk the "balance beam" while entering or leaving the room.

Something to think about
Children usually find standing on their heads much easier than adults do. Teachers can always try, however.

STORY STRETCHER

For Social Studies: Chester Is A World Map?

What the children will learn
To locate the continents on a map and on Chester

Materials you will need
Globe or map of the world

What to do
1. Look again at the illustrations of Chester in the Miracle Show.

2. Locate all the continents that Bill Peet mentions: North America, South America, Australia, Europe, Asia and Africa. Try to locate even the tiny island of Borneo.

3. Find the same continents on a world map.

Something to think about
The children will want to look back through the book and see whether they can find the continents on Chester when he was just a little pig.

STORY STRETCHER

For Writing Center: Chester Returns In Triumph

What the children will learn
To imagine another adventure

Materials you will need
Writing paper, pencils, art supplies for illustrations (optional)

What to do
1. Ask a small group of writers to imagine the next stop on Chester's tour with the Miracle Show. Where might he go next?

2. For example, he might return to the farm where he was born. All the circus performers might come to see him in the Miracle Show. The three tramps might see Chester's special wagon pass by.

3. Younger children might imagine what Chester would do if he came to their town, to their school, to their neighborhood, to their homes.

Something to think about
Older children might enjoy having Chester meet other famous pigs like Wilbur from CHARLOTTE'S WEB or Porky Pig or "The Three Little Pigs."

HUBERT'S HAIR-RAISING ADVENTURE

By Bill Peet

Hubert the Lion is proud of his elegant mane. Unfortunately, a spark flies into his mane and sets it on fire. He jumps into the river to cool his burning head, and when he runs out again, he is bald. Poor Hubert hides in a hollow tree, but the gossipy Hornbill tells all the jungle animals. When Giraffe, Gnu, Rhino, Zebra, Leopard, Hyena and Elephant come to see Hubert, they think of many different ways to grow hair on his bald head. Elephant remembers a magic cure of crocodile tears and volunteers to collect them, but the result is unexpected. In a rhyming ballad of vanity gone awry, Bill Peet's humor and gentle chiding give human traits to cartoon animals and let us laugh at one more Peet fable with a lesson to tell.

Read-Aloud Presentation

Tell the children that you are going to read another Bill Peet story. Ask them to tell you what they think the story will be like, because they know Bill Peet as a writer. They are likely to respond that the story will be funny, or that it will have animals as main characters, or that it will have a surprise ending. Do not show the cover of HUBERT'S HAIR-RAISING ADVENTURE, because it gives away the story's punch line. Instead, introduce Hubert by turning to the first page. Tell the children that this is haughty Hubert with his beautiful mane. Read the book without stopping. At the end, let the children look through the illustrations and identify those that strike them as the funniest. Many will enjoy the sight of Elephant sitting on the log trying to remember the magic potion.

STORY STRETCHER

For Art: Funny Mural

What the children will learn
To cooperate to tell a story through visuals

Materials you will need
Large table, butcher paper, marker, yardstick, tempera paints, brushes

What to do
1. Ask four or five children to paint a mural of HUBERT'S HAIR-RAISING ADVENTURE.

2. Have them decide on the main scenes that they want to paint to tell the story.

3. Ask them to make their own funny animals rather than try to copy Bill Peet's.

4. Using a yardstick, draw a line on the butcher paper to divide it into scenes.

5. Allow the muralists to work throughout the week on the painting.

Something to think about
Consider making a roller screen of the story. Cut the butcher paper in half and roll it onto cardboard paper towel tubes. Mark off the paper to create scenes. Roll out the paper to expose one scene, and ask the children to draw it. Roll on to the next scene, and so forth.

STORY STRETCHER

For Classroom Library: Hubert's Flannel Board Story

What the children will learn
To retell the story of HUBERT'S HAIR-RAISING ADVENTURE using a flannel board and story pieces

Materials you will need
Flannel board, felt or construction paper, scissors, laminating film or clear contact paper, glue, sandpaper

What to do
1. Sketch the animals, the hollow tree and a rock onto construction paper. Make four Huberts: one with a bald head, one with an elegant mane, one with a tangled mane and one with a square mane.

2. Cut the figures out and either laminate them or sandwich them between two layers of clear contact paper. Trim off the excess film or paper.

3. Glue a small strip of sandpaper to the back of each figure.

4. Tell HUBERT'S HAIR-RAISING ADVENTURE using the flannel board and the figures.

5. Place the flannel board, the story pieces and a copy of the book in the classroom library.

Something to think about
Find a convenient way to store the flannel board story. Some teachers use large plastic storage bags with zip-lock tops. They write the name of the story on a strip of masking tape placed below the zip-lock.

For Music And Movement: Balancing A Bucket Of Tears

What the children will learn
To walk carrying a bucket of water without spilling it

Materials you will need
Plastic buckets, water, paper cups (optional)

What to do
1. Let the children pretend to be Elephant, holding their arms out straight and clasping their hands to imitate a trunk.

2. Give the children buckets of water and invite them to try walking from one spot on the playground to another without spilling any water. Hurry them along by saying that poor Hubert is waiting for his magic hair cure, or that Crocodile is trying to decide whether to chase after Elephant and take back the bucket of tears.

3. If the buckets are too difficult for young children to manage, let them try walking with their arms straight out, hands clasped around a large paper cup filled with water.

Something to think about
Enjoy the fun and the messiness. Let parents know ahead of time so that the children wear clothes that no one will mind their getting wet.

For Social Studies: Hair Stylist Visit

What the children will learn
To appreciate the special training and skill required to cut hair

Materials you will need
None needed

What to do
1. Invite a parent who is a hair stylist, or your hair stylist or barber, to come to your classroom and cut your hair.

2. Ask the hair stylist to talk about his or her training, likes and dislikes about the work.

3. Encourage the stylist to name all the special instruments used: scissors, clippers, trimmers, dryers, shampoos and conditioners.

4. Call the area of the classroom where the hair stylist works, HUBERT'S HAIR SALON.

Something to think about
Explain that our community helpers are people who provide services to us, and that hair stylists and barbers provide an important service to the community.

For Writing Center: Adventures For Hubert's Jungle Neighbors

What the children will learn
To write based on thinking about animal traits

Materials you will need
Writing paper, pencils, writing folders, chalkboard, chalk, art supplies for illustrations (optional)

What to do
1. Write the names of the animals in the book on the board—Elephant, Giraffe, Gnu, Hyena, Leopard, Rhino, Zebra.

2. Remind the children that Hubert the Lion was proud of his elegant mane. Let the children wonder what the other animals would be proud of. For example, Elephant was proud of his trunk and his enormous ears. Giraffe was proud of his long neck. Gnu was proud of his horns. Hyena was proud of his laugh. Leopard was proud of his spots. Rhino was proud of his horn. Zebra was proud of his stripes.

3. Let the children brainstorm possible dilemmas these animals might find themselves in if something were to happen to them, as it did to Hubert.

4. Ask writing partners to think of a story that is parallel to Bill Peet's. The only things that must remain the same are that the characters be animals and that a magic cure occur.

Something to think about
Let the children who are interested edit their stories to improve them, then publish them in bound books. (See the appendix for a method of binding books.)

KERMIT THE HERMIT
By Bill Peet

Kermit is a greedy hermit crab who lives a lonely life on a rock in Monterey Bay. One day on the beach Kermit encounters a dog, who picks him up like a bone and buries him. A boy rescues Kermit and drops him safely into the sea. The grateful Kermit thinks up a scheme to reward his rescuer. A foiled attempt lands Kermit on a sunken ship at the bottom of the ocean where he discovers gold. With one coin in each claw, he struggles to make it to the surface. Kermit hopes that someday his rescuer will come, and Kermit can give him the stash of gold. Pelican helps Kermit find the boy who saved his life, flying with Kermit to the boy's house, a red shack on the edge of town. Kermit drops the gold coins down the chimney. Another fable of a small creature triumphing against great odds, and a kind deed rewarded, KERMIT THE HERMIT is another Bill Peet treasure.

Read-Aloud Presentation

Introduce the children to KERMIT THE HERMIT and ask them to assess how Kermit feels, based on his expression. Pause in the story after the dog buries Kermit to ask the children to predict what might happen next. When Kermit is chased by the blue shark, pause again to let the children predict what will happen to Kermit. After Kermit finds the treasure, ask the children what they think he will do with the gold. After finishing the story, ask the children what parts surprised them.

STORY STRETCHER

For Art: Kermit's Watery Home

What the children will learn
To use watercolors effectively

Materials you will need
Watercolors, paper, brushes, masking tape, paper toweling

What to do
1.   Let the children experiment with watercolors.

2.   Demonstrate how to "dry load" a brush, by applying a dry brush to wet paint, and how to "wet load" a brush, by applying a wet brush to dry paint.

3.   Show the children how to dab the paper towel gently onto the paper to remove some of the water.

4.   Use masking tape to tape the edges of the watercolor paper onto a tabletop. This helps prevent the paper's buckling when it is wet.

5.   Encourage the children to create an ocean picture associated with the Kermit story.

Something to think about
Watercolors are not easy to control, but are excellent for children because they yield so many surprises, and because children enjoy their watery effect for ocean scenes.

STORY STRETCHER

For Classroom Library: Story Retelling

What the children will learn
To retell a favorite Bill Peet story

Materials you will need
None needed

What to do
1.   Gather a small group of interested children in the classroom library.

2.   Let volunteers tell their favorite Bill Peet stories in their own words. Be sure that someone tells the story of KERMIT THE HERMIT.

3.   Encourage the storytellers to review the main events of each Bill Peet story by looking through the illustrations, but not reading the story again. This will help the storytellers use their own words to retell the story.

Something to think about
Applaud, laugh and enjoy every child's special way of telling the story. Compliment each child about something you truly enjoyed in the way she or he told the story.

STORY STRETCHER

For Mathematics: What Will You Buy With Your Treasure?

What the children will learn
To learn the cost of items they want

Materials you will need
Catalogs (from toy stores, book distributors, clothing stores), fake gold and silver coins, calculators

What to do
1.   Read the end of KERMIT THE HERMIT, which shows how Kermit's gold coins helped the poor boy's family.

2. The family was able to buy toys, books and clothes for their children.

3. Display fake gold and silver coins and let the children decide how much they are worth.

4. Give each child working at the mathematics center some coins and some catalogs.

5. Let them look up toys, books and clothes that they would like to purchase for their families and add the prices on the calculators.

6. When all the purchases are totaled, let the children determine whether they have enough money and what they will leave off their lists or add.

Something to think about
It is important to focus on giving to one's family, rather than on being greedy like Kermit was at the beginning of the story.

STORY STRETCHER

For Special Project: Trading A Treasure

What the children will learn
To price and barter

Materials you will need
Children's treasures, harmonica, old baseball cards, seashells

What to do
1. Ask the children what treasure or special thing they have that they might like to trade. Bring in items from your home like an old harmonica, baseball cards, seashells. Ask if anyone has anything in his or her desk that they would like to trade for one of your treasures.

2. When a child offers a special eraser or another treasure, reject the first offer and ask whether she has anything else to go with it. Eventually make a trade, all the

while talking about how valuable your treasure is.

3. Ask the children to bring in their treasures for a barter day. Ask them to make sure that their parents are willing for them to trade the item they bring in to barter.

4. Set up the "Bartering for Treasures" event.

5. After the bartering session, let the children talk about the trades they made that they really enjoyed.

Something to think about
Write a letter to the parents of young children, asking them to help their child select items for the treasure bartering.

STORY STRETCHER

For Science And Nature: What Are Real Hermit Crabs Like?

What the children will learn
To distinguish reality and fantasy

Materials you will need
Chalkboard, chalk

What to do
1. Read Megan McDonald's IS THIS A HOUSE FOR HERMIT CRAB? from the unit on oceans again.

2. Let the children compare the real hermit crab with the fictitious character Kermit.

3. Draw a Venn diagram (two large overlapping circles) and ask the children to decide what is the same and what is different. Label the first circle "KERMIT" and the second, "hermit crab." Where the circles overlap, let the children note what is the same in both stories. For example, Kermit lives in the ocean, on rocks and on the beach. So do real hermit crabs. Write this information in the area where the circles overlap.

Something to think about
Some science teachers frown on bringing fiction into science studies, but children seem quite capable of telling the difference between reality and fiction.

17
AUTHOR STUDY
BILL PEET

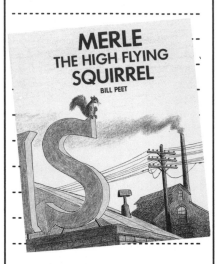

MERLE
THE HIGH FLYING
SQUIRREL
BILL PEET

MERLE THE HIGH FLYING SQUIRREL

By Bill Peet

Bill Peet, master storyteller, tells about the adventure of a compelling character, Merle the Squirrel, who longs to escape the city that scares him and find the mighty redwoods. Merle sets out across country by way of the telephone wires. But the wires seem endless, and Merle is disheartened. When he tries to rescue a boy's kite from the telephone wires, a storm comes along and blows kite and squirrel far into the country. Just as they are about to settle to earth, a huge whirl-wind hurtles kite and squirrel further west into the desert. Picked up by a cross wind, Merle continues his journey into the mountains. When the kite finally lands, in a tree in the Far West, Merle thinks he sees the ocean, but it is only the fog that envelops the tree. Merle falls asleep and awakes to discover that he is sitting on top of a gigantic redwood. In Bill Peet's cartoon hijinks, the small conquer their fears.

Read-Aloud Presentation

Bill Peet is an excellent choice for an author study because he is so popular with children of primary school age. Collect all the Bill Peet books studied in this unit and others from the school or public library. In preparation for studying Bill Peet as an author and illustrator, read BILL PEET: AN AUTOBIOGRAPHY, one of the Caldecott Honor Books for 1990. Select an incident or two from the book to share with the children each day. For example, the first day you might tell them that when Bill Peet was a child, he would draw when he was supposed to be listening to the teacher. Read about Bill Peet's horrible experience with an art teacher who made the students draw what she wanted them to draw. Talk about the five main titles and the characters in each book: MERLE THE HIGH FLYING SQUIRREL, THE WUMP WORLD, CHESTER THE WORLDLY PIG, HUBERT'S HAIR-RAISING ADVENTURE, and KERMIT THE HERMIT. Bill Peet made them all famous: a squirrel, a pig, a lion, a crab and, of course, the wumps. Read MERLE THE HIGH FLYING SQUIRREL, pausing for the children to guess how Merle could escape his fearful life in the city.

STORY STRETCHER

For Classroom Library: Squirrel's Feelings

What the children will learn
To characterize MERLE THE SQUIRREL

Materials you will need
Chalkboard, chalk, drawing paper, pencils

What to do
1.   Ask the children to describe MERLE THE HIGH FLYING SQUIRREL at the beginning of the story, at the stops along the way, and at the end of the story.

2.   List on the board all the ways they describe Merle: frightened, tired of being scared, trying to be brave, tired and discouraged, kind, surprised, adventurous, disappointed, exhausted, safe.

3.   Fold a sheet of drawing paper three times, then unfold it to produce eight rectangles.

4.   Ask the children to think of eight ways to describe the character of Merle.

Something to think about
The classroom library is an excellent place to reinforce the reading and writing connection. Children can revisit a book the teacher has read by going back into the text and thinking about a character they enjoy.

STORY STRETCHER

For Science And Nature: Safety Tips On Flying Kites

What the children will learn
To state safety rules and observe them when flying a kite

Materials you will need
Chart tablet paper, marker

What to do
1.   Read the part of the story again in which Merle the Squirrel rescues a kite tangled in telephone wires.

2.   Invite the children to look at the picture and talk about what they would do if their kite became tangled in telephone wires.

3.   Make a chart with two columns. At the top of the chart, write "Kite-Flying Safety."

4. In one column, ask the children to list "Do's":

Do fly kites where there are no wires.
Do leave a kite if it gets tangled.

5. In the second column, list "Do Not's":

Do not pull on a kite tangled in wires.
Do not get a ladder to climb up to wires.
Do not touch wires with a long pole, stick or branch.

Something to think about
Ask the neighborhood utility company to suggest safe locations in your neighborhood for flying kites. Remember that young children love to hold a kite close and to let it drift behind them while they hold the long string in their hands.

STORY STRETCHER

For Social Studies: Where's Merle?

What the children will learn
To identify different parts of the country by the terrain that Merle crosses

Materials you will need
Picture books (about countryside or farms, desert, mountains), map of the United States, push pins, red yarn

What to do
1. Attach a map of the United States to the classroom wall.

2. Locate your school on the map and mark its location with a push pin.

3. Use another push pin to mark the location of the nearest large city. Tell the children that Merle lived in a large city like the one you have marked.

4. Look at MERLE THE HIGH FLYING SQUIRREL and identify the first place that the kite took Merle—to the farms and

countryside. Identify a similar region near your school and mark it on the map with a push pin. Connect the push pins with red yarn.

5. Find the next place that Merle touched down, a desert region with thistles, tumbleweeds and rocks. Mark the location with a push pin and connect it to the strand of red yarn.

6. Keep looking through the book to identify the places Merle flies over. If he appears to be above the Rocky Mountains, mark a spot in the mountains with a push pin and connect the yarn.

7. Find Merle's last location in the Far West among the giant redwoods. Place a push pin in northern California to show where Merle made his home.

Something to think about
Bill Peet did not give us exact locations, but the story offers hints. Encourage children who have lived in or visited these parts of the country to bring in slides or postcards to show the places that Merle's journey takes him.

STORY STRETCHER

For Special Project: Merle's Kite

What the children will learn
To construct and decorate a kite

Materials you will need
Strips of balsa wood, butcher paper, tempera paints, paintbrushes, crayons or markers, stapler, masking tape, string, fabric or crepe paper streamers

What to do
1. Make a cross of balsa wood about two feet by three feet. To hold the arms in place, staple them together at the intersection of the strips or bind them with tape.

2. Cut butcher paper about two inches longer and wider than the balsa wood frame.

3. Let the children decorate their kites by painting or coloring them.

4. Fold the edges of the butcher paper several times to strengthen them and to fit the paper to the balsa wood frame.

5. Attach the paper to the tips of the balsa wood frame by stapling it in place. Tape over the staples to ensure that they do not come loose.

6. Make a tail for the kite with lightweight fabric or crepe paper streamers.

7. Attach the tail to the bottom of the balsa wood frame.

8. Staple one end of the kite string to the intersection of the balsa wood frame. Wrap masking tape over the staple and around the intersection until it seems firmly attached.

Something to think about
Invite a craftsperson who specializes in kites to bring several different kinds to class.

STORY STRETCHER

For Writing Center: Great Escapes

What the children will learn
To write an adventure story

Materials you will need
Art supplies for illustrations, writing paper, folders

What to do
1. Talk with the children about Bill Peet's illustrations. He drew pictures first and then thought of stories to go with his pictures. Tell them that many children create stories the same way. They draw something, and it reminds them of something else, and so their story begins.

2. Ask the children to draw Merle or a character of their own creation.

3. Ask them to find a partner and then begin creating an adventure for their characters to have.

4. After they feel that they have the beginning of a good story, ask them to start writing or drawing, in whichever order they prefer.

5. If the children need guidance, brainstorm ideas for appealing adventure stories: Merle makes friends in the redwoods, Merle flies over our town, Merle decides he prefer city life after all, more of Merle's friends take kite trips, kite trips to. . .

Something to think about
Always allow children to choose their own topics. However, many will be inspired by the books they read.

References

Peet, Bill. (1965). **CHESTER THE WORLDLY PIG**. Boston: Houghton Mifflin.

Peet, Bill. (1957, 1986). **HUBERT'S HAIR-RAISING ADVENTURE**. Boston: Houghton Mifflin.

Peet, Bill. (1965). **KERMIT THE HERMIT**. Boston: Houghton Mifflin.

Peet, Bill. (1974). **MERLE THE HIGH FLYING SQUIRREL**. Boston: Houghton Mifflin.

Peet, Bill. (1970). **THE WUMP WORLD**. Boston: Houghton Mifflin.

Also Mentioned in this Chapter

McDonald, Megan. (1990). **IS THIS A HOUSE FOR HERMIT CRAB?** Illustrated by S. D. Schindler. New York: Orchard.

Additional References for Author Study—Bill Peet

Peet, Bill. (1977). **BIG BAD BRUCE**. Boston: Houghton Mifflin. *When the mean bully bear meets a witch, she turns him into a little Bruce Bear, who is still mean and pesky.*

Peet, Bill. (1989). **BILL PEET: AN AUTOBIOGRAPHY**. Boston: Houghton Mifflin. *With illustrations, humor, satire and irony, Peet draws and writes about his life as a child, as a young Disney illustrator and as an author of children's books.*

Peet, Bill. (1971). **THE CABOOSE WHO GOT LOOSE**. Boston: Houghton Mifflin. *The story of Katy, who wanted to live in the open spaces instead of in a noisy train yard.*

Peet, Bill. (1966). **FAREWELL TO SHADY GLADE**. Boston: Houghton Mifflin. *Ahead of his time, Peet looks at urban sprawl through the eyes of the displaced animals whose homeland is lost.*

Peet, Bill. (1970, 1982). **THE WHINGDINGDILLY**. Boston: Houghton Mifflin. *Scamp is unhappy with his life as a dog and, in the story, is chnaged into an even more unhappy creature. "Be yourself" is the theme of the story.*

FAMOUS CHARACTERS IN A SERIES

George and Martha Rise and Shine

Amelia Bedelia

Nate the Great Goes Undercover

Bunnicula: A Rabbit-Tale of Mystery

Encyclopedia Brown's Book of Strange But True Crimes

FAMOUS CHARACTERS IN A SERIES

GEORGE AND MARTHA RISE AND SHINE

By James Marshall

George and Martha are hippos who happen also to be best friends. James Marshall has written three George and Martha books, each containing five humorous stories. In GEORGE AND MARTHA RISE AND SHINE, the two friends tease and then forgive each other. They decide that telling fibs is dangerous, have a silly misadventure with fleas, appreciate Martha's talent as a saxophonist, go to a scary movie and discover the potential for hurt feelings when Martha is excluded from George's secret club. Each episode provokes laughter and relief that the friendship survives their antics. James Marshall's cartoon renditions of the hippos are as famous as their friendship. The sparse line drawings are overlaid with lime, bright yellow, tangerine and, of course, the gray of hippos.

Read-Aloud Presentation

Collect all the George and Martha books you can find. Show the children the covers and see whether they recognize the series. If any children have read any of the George and Martha books, ask them to tell the others something about George and Martha. Write their descriptions on the chalkboard or on chart paper. Children often describe George and Martha as hippos who are friends. Engage the children in a discussion of what friends do together. Read at least two stories from GEORGE AND MARTHA RISE AND SHINE. After reading, invite the children to add to the description of George and Martha. Use the term "characterization": ask how they would characterize George and Martha. During other read-aloud sessions, complete the book and continue adding to the characterizations.

STORY STRETCHER

For Art: Make A George And Martha Fan Club Poster

What the children will learn
To interpret a friendship visually

Materials you will need
Variety of art materials, posterboard, markers, poster paints, construction paper, glue, crepe paper streamers

What to do
1.   Decorate the art area or another area of the classroom with crepe paper streamers.

2.   When the children ask about the streamers, announce that

this area of the classroom is the George and Martha Fan Club.

3.   Ask them to make posters of their favorite George and Martha stories from any of the books.

Something to think about
Allow children to work together if they choose. Find two of the newest class members or the least popular children and work with them to make the first poster. Brainstorm ideas for materials and scenes for the poster to help them succeed in working together.

STORY STRETCHER

For Classroom Library: Books And Videos

What the children will learn
To create a catalog system for books and videos

Materials you will need
Index cards, markers, paper, pencils, storage space, videos from writing story s-t-r-e-t-c-h-e-r

What to do
1.   After the children have written and performed several "Reading Rainbow" book reports, talk about the importance of cataloguing their reports so that they can easily be located.

2.   Let interested children brainstorm ways to organize the display and cataloguing of the videos.

3.   After the students have devised their system, have them explain it to the class and ask for ideas to improve it.

4.   After the class members have used the system for a while, again ask the inventors to solicit suggestions from their classmates for changes to improve the system.

Something to think about
Although it would be easier for the teacher to organize a simple card catalog for books and videos, encouraging the children to think about how to organize the materials, and to try out their ideas, promotes higher levels of

thinking. Having the inventors solicit suggestions from the class for improving their system, avoids criticism and promotes listening and critical thinking.

For Cooking And Snack Time: George And Martha, Friends' Picnic

What the children will learn
To prepare foods that their friends will like

Materials you will need
Picnic supplies (coolers, picnic baskets, serving dishes and utensils), sandwiches, juices, fruits

What to do
1.   Survey the children to learn their favorite sandwiches for picnics.

2.   Take notes on everyone's choices.

3.   Encourage children from different cultures to talk about picnic foods that their families like.

4.   Select the top three sandwich choices from among the children's favorites.

5.   Ask the cafeteria manager to provide the bread, sandwich fillings and condiments to make the sandwiches.

6.   Have three or four children prepare sandwiches for another group.

7.   Let the children serve each other at the picnic.

Something to think about
If time does not allow for a picnic, have a George and Martha popcorn party and watch a videotape of a favorite picture book character.

For Mathematics: George And Martha Surveys

What the children will learn
To collect, analyze, display and interpret data that answers questions

Materials you will need
Note pads, pencils, chalkboard and chalk or markers and chart paper

What to do
1.   Either form the entire class into pairs of "data collectors" or draw names from a hat to select a small group of data collectors.

2.   Work with the groups to decide what questions they want answered.

3.   Conduct a variety of surveys inspired by George and Martha by asking class members questions like, "What is your favorite story from GEORGE AND MARTHA RISE AND SHINE?" or "What is your favorite story from all the George and Martha books?"

4.   Survey the children to determine their favorite picnic foods for the George and Martha class picnic. (See the Cooking and Snack Time story s-t-r-e-t-c-h-e-r).

5.   Ask the children to write their questions at the top of a survey sheet. List all the children's names down the left margin of the paper. Write their answers on the line beside their names.

6.   Give the raw data to a group of data analysts. Let them decide how to collapse the answers and create a graph or some other display of the results.

7.   Create the display.

Something to think about
Consider having older reading buddies from other classrooms become mathematics buddies.

Experienced data collectors, analysts and interpreters can help younger ones. Older and younger students can compare their answers and data displays to see if third graders have different preferences than first or second graders.

For Writing Center: Producing A Video Of A George And Martha Story

What the children will learn
To script, read and film a short book report

Materials you will need
Paper and pencils or computers and word processing program, video camera, videotape, television or monitor

What to do
1.   Videotape a child's report from the public television program "Reading Rainbow."

2.   Show the videotape to the children.

3.   Invite interested children to write and produce their own video book reports.

4.   Divide these class members into script writers, readers, film makers and set producers. Ask the children to work as teams.

5.   After the videotaping is completed, schedule one video book report per day.

Something to think about
If you do not have video equipment, ask parent volunteers to loan a camera to the class. Show the videos at parent meetings to demonstrate how a developmentally appropriate language and reading program works: by involving children in reading, writing, listening and speaking in ways that are meaningful to them.

AMELIA BEDELIA

By Peggy Parish

Illustrated by Fritz Siebel

Peggy Parish's AMELIA BEDELIA series is a favorite among beginning readers. This book is one of many uproariously funny AMELIA BEDELIA stories. Amelia Bedelia is a housekeeper who takes all instructions literally. She follows exactly the written instructions left for her. For example, the homeowner leaves a note for Amelia saying, "Draw the drapes," obviously meaning for Amelia to close the drapes, but Amelia takes out pen and paper and draws a picture of the drapes. There are eight misinterpreted instructions that leave the children laughing. When the homeowner returns, the only reason that Amelia Bedelia in not fired on the spot is her wonderful lemon meringue pie. Fritz Siebel's colorful line drawings expressively and humorously depict the story.

Read-Aloud Presentation

Discuss a time when you misinterpreted directions. For example, if you asked someone, "Turn left?" and the person replied, "Right," you can interpret their response in two ways: it can mean either the direction "right," or the condition of being correct or "right." Show the children the cover of AMELIA BEDELIA and discuss how Amelia Bedelia continually misinterprets directions. Read AMELIA BEDELIA and list all her misinterpretations. Determine which ones the children thought were the funniest.

STORY STRETCHER
For Art: Contrasting Meanings

What the children will learn
To represent different interpretations of a statement

Materials you will need
Construction or manila paper, markers, crayons, paints, brushes

What to do
1. With a small group of interested children in the art center, look through AMELIA BEDELIA and list all the instructions she misinterprets.

2. Discuss what Mrs. Rogers's instructions mean, and how Amelia Bedelia interprets them.

3. Ask the children to fold a sheet of paper in half vertically, then draw a vertical line down the middle of the page along the fold.

4. On one side of the line, ask the children to draw or paint what Mrs. Rogers meant, and on the other side of the line, what Amelia Bedelia did.

5. Display the Amelia Bedelia drawings in the art center or in the library area of the classroom.

Something to think about
Whenever possible, give children a choice of media. Choices promote more creative expression.

STORY STRETCHER
For Cooking And Snack Time: Amelia Bedelia's Lemon Meringue Pies

What the children will learn
To distinguish lemon flavors

Materials you will need
Lemon meringue pie, lemon cheesecake, lemon tarts, lemon pudding, lemon yogurt, lemons, paring knives, forks, spoons, plates, glasses, milk, water, napkins

What to do
1. Plan a lemon-tasting party for snack time. Find out from the children whether any of their parents or grandparents bake lemon meringue pies.

2. Ask families to bring in lemon desserts or ask cafeteria workers to plan with you for a lemon-tasting party.

3. Begin the party by having the children roll lemons. Show them how to place lemons on a table and, with one palm over the other, press down while rolling.

4. Slice the lemons and let the children taste them.

5. Bring out the array of lemon-flavored foods and invite the children to taste them. Call the lemon meringue pie an Amelia Bedelia pie.

Something to think about
If possible, ask a parent who bakes lemon meringue pies as a specialty to bake the pie in class. Have small groups of "pastry chefs" assist the parent.

For Creative Dramatics: Amelia Bedelia's Follies

What the children will learn
To pantomime and interpret nonverbal clues

Materials you will need
Chart paper, markers

What to do
1. With a small group of interested children, list all the ways that Amelia Bedelia misinterpreted instructions.

2. Let each child choose an Amelia Bedelia phrase to pantomime.

3. Conduct a brief rehearsal of the children pantomiming their phrases.

4. At the next class group time, invite the creative dramatics students to pantomime the Amelia Bedelia phrases, and ask the audience to guess what phrase the actor is dramatizing.

Something to think about
After reading other AMELIA BEDELIA books, ask the children to pantomime her antics. Also pantomime phrases from the writing story s-t-r-e-t-c-h-e-r described below.

For Mathematics: Amelia Bedelia's Measurement Mischief

What the children will learn
To associate meaning with measurement terms

Materials you will need
Rulers, measuring tapes, yardsticks, construction paper, scissors, tape or glue, markers or crayons

What to do
1. Talk with the children about how Amelia Bedelia always mixes things up. Ask a few children to recall incidents from one or two favorite Amelia Bedelia stories.

2. Hold up a yardstick. Ask the children what it is, then encourage them to imagine what Amelia Bedelia would probably think if someone said "yardstick" to her. She might think they meant to go outside into the yard and pick up a stick.

3. Brainstorm other measurement terms like ruler, foot, hands, yard.

4. Invite the children to think up funny interpretations that Amelia Bedelia might make.

5. Let the children draw or illustrate these for a mathematics display. For example, draw a human foot and use it to measure the size of the classroom. Draw a king or queen (a "ruler") and measure the size of a table.

6. Help the children recognize that measurement terms have evolved from the literal interpretations. Explain, for example, that people used to measure the size of a room by stepping one foot in front of the other foot, and from this practice emerged the standard measurement and the term, foot.

Something to think about
Try comparisons of size: comparing standard rulers and yardsticks, for example, to the children's feet, hands and arms.

For Writing Center: Other Misadventures For Amelia Bedelia

What the children will learn
To write phrases that could lead to Amelia Bedelia adventures

Materials you will need
Chalkboard and chalk or chart tablet and marker

What to do
1. With children working at the writing center, brainstorm a list of phrases that Amelia Bedelia might misinterpret.

2. On the chalkboard or chart, list all the phrases the children come up with. Examples could be, "use a little elbow grease," "letting the cat out of the bag," "bite your tongue," "an order of fries on the side," "watering the dog," "the fork in the road," etc.

3. Have children decide which ones they would like to include in an Amelia Bedelia adventure.

4. After the children have written their Amelia Bedelia stories, hold a special Amelia Bedelia day for the writers to read their works.

Something to think about
After reading an Amelia Bedelia book aloud, let three or four children share their Amelia Bedelia writings during meetings of the entire class. Extend this study with older children by working on homonyms.

NATE THE GREAT
GOES UNDERCOVER

By Marjorie Weinman Sharmat

Illustrated by Marc Simont

Nate the Great takes on his first nighttime case. Characters who figure in the case are Sludge, Nate's dog, who loves pancakes; Oliver, his pesky neighbor; Rosamond and her cats; Esmeralda, a girl who lives down the street and provides good clues; and a mysterious someone or something who turns over the garbage cans at night. The young sleuth assembles the clues, eliminates the possibilities, is thrown off by events and ultimately, solves the mystery. Along the way, Nate the Great encounters smells that are not mysterious—like a skunk. Marc Simont alternates black-and-white charcoal drawings with illustrations to which a bit of color is added. His illustrations make Nate the Great memorable.

Read-Aloud Presentation

Ask the children if they have ever found their garbage cans overturned at night. Invite them to think about how they might solve the mystery of who or what overturned their garbage cans. Show the children the cover of the book and ask them to predict what the story is about. Read NATE THE GREAT GOES UNDERCOVER.

STORY STRETCHER

For Art: Night Scenes In Nate The Great's Neighborhood

What the children will learn
To make crayon etchings

Materials you will need
Heavy construction paper or manila paper, crayons, black or dark navy tempera paints, liquid detergent, plastic margarine tubs, plastic knives

What to do
1. Pour black or dark navy tempera paint into margarine tubs. Mix a drop of liquid detergent into the paint.

2. Invite the children to cover their construction paper entirely with many different colors of crayon.

3. Paint over the entire sheet of construction paper with the paint. Lay the painted papers flat and allow them to dry overnight.

4. Show the children how to use the edge of a plastic knife to "etch" or scratch shapes into the paint.

Something to think about
The liquid detergent in the tempera paint allows the paint to adhere to the waxy crayons.

STORY STRETCHER

For Classroom Library: Encyclopedia Reports About Night Animals

What the children will learn
To read about the night animals mentioned in NATE THE GREAT

Materials you will need
Set of encyclopedias or picture dictionaries, chalkboard and chalk or chart tablet and markers, writing paper, pencils

What to do
1. Ask the students to recall all the night animals that Nate the Great read about when he was at the library. Make a list on the chalkboard or chart tablet.

2. Reread the section of the book in which Nate goes to the library.

3. Briefly read to the children from the encyclopedia about the birds that go out at night.

4. Look up and read about cats, rats, bats, mice, shrews, skunks, raccoons, opossums and moles.

5. Ask the children to describe the animals briefly. List their descriptions on the chalkboard or chart tablet. Use key words and phrases.

6. Invite the children to decide whether or not Nate the Great should be suspicious of each animal.

Something to think about
Some children may be able to read from pictionaries or children's encyclopedias and write their own descriptions.

STORY STRETCHER

For Cooking And Snack Time: Mystery Pancakes

What the children will learn
To read and follow recipe directions

Materials you will need

Mixing bowl with a pouring spout, pancake mix, milk, eggs, vegetable oil, wooden spoon, tablespoon, electric skillet, spatula, plates, butter or margarine, syrup, variety of fresh or canned fruits, cartons of milk

What to do

1. Divide the children into teams of four or five.

2. Let the children decide who will be recipe reader, mixer-pourer, pancake turner, server-mystery maker.

3. Review each person's responsibilities. The recipe reader reads the recipe from the pancake mix box, prepares the electric skillet and sets out the ingredients. The mixer-pourer measures and mixes the batter, then pours the mixture onto the hot electric skillet. The pancake turner watches the pancakes until small bubbles begin to form, then flips the pancake. The server-mystery maker places a pancake on the plate, spoons on fruit, then places another pancake on top, thus making a mystery pancake.

4 The children eat and enjoy their mystery pancakes with servings of cold milk.

Something to think about

Older children can prepare pancake batter by adding fruit to the mixture.

For Special Project: Follow The Clues Mystery Treasure Hunt

What the children will learn

To read and follow instructions

Materials you will need

Index cards, pencils, recycled envelopes, notepaper, box of pancake mix, encyclopedia, badge maker, marker, badges,

What to do

1. Organize a Nate the Great Treasure Hunt . Have teams of four or five detectives take turns reading and following the clues.

2. Write clues on index cards and seal them inside old business envelopes. Distribute the envelopes and props from Nate the Great stories throughout the school.

3. Print "Clue #1" on the first envelope. It reads: "Go to the office and ask everyone working there if he or she knows Nate the Great. You will know when you ask the right person because he or she will give you something found in the Nate the Great story."

4. When the detectives ask the right person, he or she will give the detective team the note marked "Clue #2." which reads: "Go to the cafeteria and find the person who has the next clue."

5. Have the mystery cafeteria worker give the detectives a pancake mix box or a copy of a pancake recipe and an envelope marked "Clue #3" which reads: "Go to the library and find the next clue."

6. At the library, the next clue is hidden in the encyclopedia under N for Nate the Great. The librarian may give clues, including: "Remember where Nate looked in the library to help solve the mystery."

7. When the detectives go to the N in the encyclopedia, they will find directions that tell them to go to the workroom in the library for their last clue.

8. In the workroom, ask a parent volunteer to help the children make a "Nate the Great" badge using the school badge maker.

9. When their badges are made, the detectives put them on and return to the classroom. Warn the detectives not to tell anyone else about their clues and how they solved the mystery.

Something to think about

First graders will probably need an adult to help them along. Ask for parent volunteers.

For Writing Center: Another Nate The Great Mystery

What the children will learn

To write a story in a sequence and leave clues for the reader

Materials you will need

Writing paper, pencils, folders

What to do

1. Have the writers recall a mystery that happened in their home. Perhaps someone lost a watch or car keys or lunch money.

2. Ask the children to write the end of the story—the discovery of the lost object. Explain that mystery writers often know the beginning of a story (the mystery) and the ending of a story (the solution). To write their story, they must construct clues for the middle of the story.

3. Let the children write the middle of the story, containing the clues needed to solve the mystery.

4. Encourage the children to illustrate their stories and bind them into a collection of class mysteries. (See the appendix for instructions on a simple way to bind books.

Something to think about

As an alternative, read only the beginning and the ending of another Nate the Great mystery. Let the children write the middle of the story.

18

FAMOUS CHARACTERS
IN A SERIES

BUNNICULA:
A RABBIT-TALE
OF MYSTERY

By Deborah and James Howe

Illustrated by Alan Daniel

Harold, the dog, and Chester, the cat, are joined by a vampire bunny named Bunnicula in the Monroe household. Harold tells the story of BUNNICULA. Chester and Harold have a hard time figuring out the personality and strange behavior of the bunny the Monroe family brings home. The bunny is named Bunnicula, a combination of bunny and of Dracula, the movie that the Monroes were watching when they discovered the bunny left inside the movie theater. Chester, the cat, considers this a strange turn of events. Chester is well-read, and he knows about strange events. Chester assumes that Bunnicula is a rabbit Dracula because he sucks the juices right out of the vegetables, turning tomatoes, carrots, lettuce and zucchini white. This comedy-mystery keeps the reader in stitches and asking for more adventures from the trio of pets.

Read-Aloud Presentation

There are nine chapters in this short book of ninety-eight pages. If possible, read at least three chapters per session. After each set of three chapters, let the children predict what Harold and Chester will do. Let them discuss the double mystery in BUNNICULA: the mystery of the vegetables turning white and the mystery of why Bunnicula is sick. After reading the entire book, show the children other stories about Bunnicula and his pals, as well as other James Howe mysteries.

S T O R Y   S T R E T C H E R
For Classroom Library: Mystery Read-In

What the children will learn
To enjoy reading mysteries

Materials you will need
Variety of James Howe books, tape recording of mystery music, tape player

What to do
1. Distribute copies of other James Howe books and let the interested critics read and compare the stories.

2. Plan a James Howe read-in.

3. Gather copies of James Howe books.

4. Schedule a week of D.E.A.R. time with Howe books. (D.E.A.R. means "Drop Everything and Read.")

5. Plan fifteen minutes of D.E.A.R. time when there will be no interruption.

6. Tape-record "mystery" music.

7. At the scheduled time for D.E.A.R., dim the lights and play the "mystery" music as a signal

for all the children to collect their mysteries and begin reading.

8. Everyone reads silently for fifteen to twenty minutes. End the reading session by playing the music again.

Something to think about
If you do not have enough Howe books, allow the children to read any mystery of their choosing.

S T O R Y   S T R E T C H E R
For Cooking And Snack Time: Bunnicula's Salad

What the children will learn
To prepare a nutritious salad

Materials you will need
Tomatoes, lettuce, carrots, zucchini, knives, vegetable peelers, salad bowl, serving bowl, large salad tongs or large salad fork and spoon, cutting board, napkins, forks, salad dressing (optional)

What to do
1. Ask for volunteers to prepare a Bunnicula salad for the class.

2. Recall with the students all the vegetables that Bunnicula turned white.

3. Ask the salad chefs to wash their hands thoroughly with soap and water.

4. Show the salad chefs how to core a head of lettuce and to tear the leaves with their fingers. Let them prepare a large salad bowl full of greens.

5. Demonstrate how to use a vegetable peeler for carrots. Peel some of the zucchini and leave others green. Tell the children that the white peeled zucchini are Bunnicula's.

6. Show the children how to slice tomatoes into quarters or sixths.

7. Have the children come to the snack table and serve themselves

using the large salad tongs or salad fork and spoon.

Something to think about
Discuss how both rabbits and humans need to eat vegetables to have a healthy diet.

For Creative Dramatics: Convincing Others Without Words

What the children will learn
To use nonverbal expressions

Materials you will need
Mirrors

What to do
1.   Recall with the children Chester and Harold's attempts to communicate with the Monroe family, even though they could not talk to them. Chester, the cat, tied a towel around his neck and pretended to be a vampire in a cap. Harold tried to tell the Monroes that Bunnicula was sick.

2.   Ask for three volunteers to pretend to be Chester, Harold and Bunnicula.

3.   Ask the improvisers to act out a scene from the book without saying any words.

4.   Let three members of the audience interpret what the actors are communicating.

5.   Allow other interested children to role-play the characters, but ask them to perform other scenes from the book.

Something to think about
Creative dramatics story s-t-r-e-t-c-h-e-r-s that you want to share with the entire class can be scheduled at a group meeting time later in the day.

For Science And Nature: Caring For A Rabbit As A Pet

What the children will learn
To find out about the care of rabbits

Materials you will need
Posterboard, marker

What to do
1.   Contact a pet store owner, a rabbit breeder or someone who has a pet rabbit.

2.   Find out what breed of rabbit Bunnicula is, by showing the person the illustration from BUNNICULA.

3.   Ask him or her to bring a rabbit to the classroom.

4.   Before the visit, construct a K-W-L chart. Divide the posterboard into three columns. At the top of the first column, print a large K, which stands for what we "know" from reading BUNNICULA and from our experiences with rabbits. At the top of the second column, print a large W, which means "what we want to know." At the top of the third column, print a large L, which represents "what we learned."

5.   Before the visit, fill the K column by having the children tell what they already "know" about rabbits. Continue by asking the children what questions they "want to know" the answers to. Write their questions in the second column.

6.   During the visit, let the children ask the questions from the K-W-L chart as well as others that occur to them.

7.   After the visit, complete the K-W-L chart.

Something to think about
If possible, keep a rabbit as a classroom pet for a week.

For Writing Center: Harold, Chester and Bunnicula Character Sketches

What the children will learn
To describe characters in ways that make them memorable

Materials you will need
Tape recorder, audio tape, chalkboard, chalk, paper, pens

What to do
1.   With a small group of children interested in a writing project, discuss the three main characters in BUNNICULA.

2.   Elicit adjectives and descriptive phrases about the characters in the book.

3.   Ask the children to choose at least one character and write a character sketch. Set up the writing activity by saying, "Pretend you are telling your best friend about the characters in this book. What would you say to describe the characters so that she or he would know them even before reading the book?"

4.   After the children have written their character sketches, have them tape-record the sketches, without mentioning the character's name.

5.   Place the tapes at the listening station in the classroom library for other children to hear and to guess the names of the characters.

Something to think about
Ask older students to write characterizations of characters from other mystery stories.

ENCYCLOPEDIA BROWN'S BOOK OF STRANGE BUT TRUE CRIMES

By Donald J. Sobel and Rose Sobel

Illustrated by John Zielinski

The combination of humor and mystery is irresistible to third graders who are Encyclopedia Brown fans. ENCYCLO-PEDIA BROWN'S BOOK OF STRANGE BUT TRUE CRIMES is a scrapbook of the child-sleuth's newspaper clippings of wacky but true crimes. The highlights include a burglar who has to be rescued by the police after he gets caught in a window, safecrackers who set the money on fire while blow-torching a safe, an elephant who snatches a purse at the zoo, and a bridegroom who gets arrested to avoid his wedding. Third grade sleuths will especially enjoy solving "the case of the two-headed toothbrush," but they will laugh at the absurdity of all the stories in Encyclopedia Brown's scrapbook of wacky crimes. The small interior line drawings on every third or fourth page are by John Zielinski.

Read-Aloud Presentation

Display a large collection of ENCYCLOPEDIA BROWN MYSTERIES. No doubt some children will already know this famous character. If reading to second graders, discuss the meaning of mysteries. If reading to children unfamiliar with Encyclopedia Brown, read one of the famous early mysteries. Ask the children to talk about things they or their family members clip from newspapers. Show the cover of ENCYCLOPEDIA BROWN'S BOOK OF STRANGE BUT TRUE CRIMES. Call attention to the cover of the book, which shows children looking at Encyclopedia Brown's scrapbook. Read a few of the very humorous stories, like those about the elephant purse-snatcher or the cactus thieves. Read at least two wacky stories that involve money.

STORY STRETCHER

For Art: Encyclopedia Brown's Scrapbook Bulletin Board

What the children will learn
To illustrate the strange but true crimes

Materials you will need
Fine-point markers, old newspaper, used business envelopes, staples, stapler, white construction paper, copying paper, scrapbook, scissors

What to do
1. Ask children who come to the art center to select a few of the wacky stories they enjoyed from the book.

2. Show them how to fold a sheet of construction paper in half vertically, then draw a vertical line down the middle of the page along the fold.

3. Unfold the paper. To the left of the line, have the students retell the wacky story in their own words.

4. To the right of the line, ask them to illustrate the strange but true crime.

5. Photocopy the children's illustrations and rewrites of the stories.

6. Cut along the vertical line and separate the stories from the illustrations.

7. Cover a bulletin board with old newspaper.

8. Make a heading for the bulletin board that reads, "Solve the mystery." Print these directions on a sheet of drawing paper and staple them to the bulletin board: "Match the wacky illustrations to the strange but true crimes."

9. Staple the wacky stories onto the newspaper columns on the bulletin board.

10. Below each of the stories, staple a recycled business envelope with the back side of the envelope facing out to form a pocket.

11. Stack and shuffle the children's illustrations.

12. Invite mystery solvers to look through the illustrations and read through the wacky stories, then place the correct illustration into the envelope pocket of the matching story.

13. Place the photocopies of the children's illustrations and stories into a scrapbook. Title the page: "ENCYCLOPEDIA BROWN'S SOLUTIONS."

14. Invite the mystery solvers to double-check their bulletin board solutions by looking at the scrapbook.

Something to think about
If you can obtain a software program for formatting student newspapers, have the children create their illustrations and story retellings on the computer.

S T O R Y S T R E T C H E R
For Classroom Library: Mystery In A Mystery File

What the children will learn
To locate information by the table of contents and other clues

Materials you will need
Pens or pencils, ten file folders and ten dividers, marker, plastic file bin or tray

What to do
1. Construct a filing system by placing the file folders and dividers into a plastic file bin, tray or tub.

2. On the first divider, print the title of the first chapter of the book. Continue printing the titles of each chapter on the dividers.

3. Select one wacky story from each chapter.

4. Print the story on the inside of a folder.

5. Shuffle the ten folders.

6. Have the children read the stories printed on the inside of the folders and decide in which chapters the stories probably appeared.

7. Ask the children to place the file folders behind the appropriate dividers. For example, if the story selected was the one about the elephant who snatched a woman's purse at the zoo, then the reader would place that file folder behind the divider marked, "Wacky crimes."

8. After all the folders are sorted, the file folder sleuth checks his or her answers by looking up the case in the book.

Something to think about
Extend the story s-t-r-e-t-c-h-e-r by choosing new stories from each chapter.

S T O R Y S T R E T C H E R
For Cooking And Snack Time: Snack Sleuths

What the children will learn
To recognize fruits by their smells, textures and tastes

Materials you will need
Variety of fruits (apples, bananas, peaches, plums, grapes, pears, oranges, grapefruits, lemons), knives, serving bowls, napkins, spoons, paper bags, blindfold

What to do
1. Place several different fruits in a paper grocery bag.

2. Ask the children to close their eyes, or blindfold them.

3. Direct the blindfolded child to reach into the bag, feel the fruit and remove the fruit that he or she wants to eat.

4. Be sure that the children wash those fruits that are eaten with the skin or peel.

Something to think about
With older children, have a group of snack preparers wash the fruit and make a fruit salad.

S T O R Y S T R E T C H E R
For Mathematics: Money Mysteries

What the children will learn
To arrange stories involving money in order based on the amount of money mentioned

Materials you will need
Three or four paperback copies of the book, paper and pencil and markers or computer and printer, small Post-it notes or index cards, file folders

What to do
1. Observe that many crimes in ENCYCLOPEDIA BROWN'S BOOK OF STRANGE BUT TRUE CRIMES involve money. Invite the students to recall the stories about money that they heard during the read-aloud time.

2. Place Post-it notes on the pages of the book where the money stories appear.

3. Ask the children to print, on the Post-it note, the amount of money mentioned in the story and the page number.

4. After they have finished reading the book and located all the money mysteries, each reader should take his or her Post-it notes and arrange them in order from the lowest amount mentioned to the highest amount.

Something to think about
Let the children tell or read a story about money. Ask the file folder sleuths to look at their Post-it notes and tell on what page the story appears.

S T O R Y S T R E T C H E R
For Writing Center: Wacky Stories, Truth Or Fiction?

What the children will learn
To interpret meaning from drawings and words and to recall stories they have read

Materials you will need
Photocopies of the illustrations, paper, pencils, large index cards, small index cards, marker, push pins, bulletin board

What to do

1. Photocopy the illustrations from the book.

2. Distribute one illustration to a pair of students.

3. Ask the writers to recall the story that went with the illustration and rewrite it in their own words. These stories become the "true wacky stories."

4. Using the same illustrations, let the writers compose a fictional story to go with the drawings. These stories become the "fictional wacky stories."

5. Ask the students to print each story on a large index card.

6. After the index cards are prepared, have the children pin them onto the bulletin board.

7. Make truth and fiction cards by printing "Truth" on a few small index cards and "Fiction" on others.

8. Ask other students to read the stories pinned to the bulletin board and decide whether they are truth or fiction. Once they have decided, they pin the small "Truth" or "Fiction" index cards to the story.

9. Place a solution book or key nearby so that the students can check their "Truth" or "Fiction" assessments.

Something to think about

Invite new pairs of writers to rewrite the stories in their own words and to invent more fictional ones.

References

Howe, Deborah, and Howe, James. (1979). **BUNNICULA: A RABBIT-TALE OF MYSTERY**. Illustrated by Alan Daniel. New York: Avon Camelot.

Marshall, James. (1976). **GEORGE AND MARTHA RISE AND SHINE**. Boston: Houghton Mifflin.

Parish, Peggy. (1963, 1992). **AMELIA BEDELIA**. Illustrated by Fritz Siebel. New York: HarperCollins.

Sharmat, Marjorie Weinman. (1974). **NATE THE GREAT GOES UNDERCOVER**. Illustrated by Marc Simont. New York: Coward-McCann.

Sobel, Donald J., and Sobel, Rose. (1991). **ENCYCLOPEDIA BROWN'S BOOK OF STRANGE BUT TRUE CRIMES**. Illustrated by John Zielinski. New York: Scholastic.

Additional References for Famous Characters In A Series

Howe, James. (1982). **HOWLIDAY INN**. Illustrated by Lynn Munsinger. New York: Macmillan. *Join Harold and Bunnicula in a continuation of the Bunnicula story.*

Marshall, James. **GEORGE & MARTHA ENCORE**. (1977). Boston: Houghton Mifflin Company. *In five brief episodes two hippotamuses reinforce their friendship.*

Parish, Peggy. **AMELIA BEDELIA HELPS OUT**. (1981). Illustrated by Lynn Sweat. New York: Avon Books. *Amelia Bedelia shows her neice Effie Lou how to follow instructions to the letter as they dust the potato bugs and sew seeds.*

Sharmat, Marjorie W. **NATE THE GREAT & THE LOST LIST**. (1981). Illustrated by Marc Simont. New York: Putnam. *Nate the Great—the pancake-loving detective—is at it again. And Sludge, Nate's dog, is his new assistant.*

Sobol, Donald J. and Sobol, Rose. **ENCYCLOPEDIA BROWN LENDS A HAND**. (1993). New York: Bantam Books. *Match wits with the ten-year-old sleuth in ten more crime cases.*

BASIC ART DOUGH

the best and easiest uncooked dough

MATERIALS:
4 cups flour
1 cup iodized salt
1¾ cups warm water
bowl

PROCESS:
1. mix all ingredients in bowl
2. knead 10 minutes
3. model as with any clay
4. bake 300° until hard
5. or air dry for a few days

Steps in Binding a Book

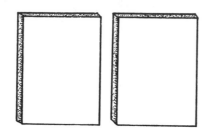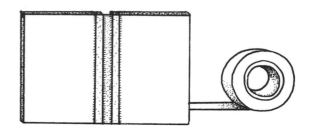

1. Cut two pieces of heavy cardboard slightly larger than the pages of the book.

2. With wide masking tape, tape the two pieces of cardboard together with ½-inch space between.

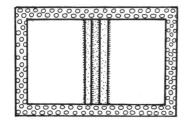

3. Cut outside cover 1½ inches larger than the cardboard and stick to cardboard (use thinned white glue if cover material is not self-adhesive.)

4. Fold corners over first, then the sides.

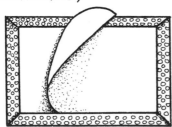

5. Measure and cut inside cover material and apply as shown.

6. Place stapled pages of the book in the center of the cover. Secure with two strips of inside cover material, one at the front of the book and the other at the back.

242

Sample Rebus Chart

Directions for Making Muffins

1. Preheat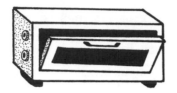

2. Place in

3. Empty into

4. Add 1 ⬭ and ½ 🥛 water

5. Stir

6. Pour into

7. Bake in

8. Serve and

243

CONSTRUCTING WORD-FINDS FOR POEM TITLES

Step One: Select titles of poems, preferably short titles.
Write the titles of the poems horizontally, vertically and diagonally.

```
B  O  A  C  O  N  S  T  R  I  C  T  O  R
W     L  F              I
H     I     O                 C
O     C           R                 K
      E              S  P  A  G  H  E  T  T  I
                     A
                     L
                     E
```

Step Two: Add letters to fill out the puzzle.

```
B  O  A  C  O  N  S  T  R  I  C  T  O  R  T
W  B  L  F  Z  M  K  I  X  A  Z  P  L  C  K
H  P  I  V  O  L  T  W  C  Y  K  S  C  R  J
O  R  C  D  L  R  O  B  R  K  H  Z  O  K  V
M  F  E  C  U  M  S  P  A  G  H  E  T  T  I
P  I  F  R  L  B  K  A  F  F  S  Y  J  U  B
W  T  C  K  V  F  U  I  L  G  B  U  Q  Z  K
A  B  V  Z  I  D  Q  N  D  E  M  A  H  L  T
```

244

INDEX

Titles

This * indicates books used as the foundation for the STORY S-T-R-E-T-C-H-E-R-S. If only one name is listed, the author is also the illustrator.

Centers or Activities

Art

Block Building

Classroom Library

Terms